Pilgrim Spirituality

Pilgrim Spirituality

Defining Pilgrimage Again for the First Time

RODNEY AIST

CASCADE *Books* · Eugene, Oregon

Cascade Books
An Imprint of Wipf and Stock Publishers
199 W. 8th Ave., Suite 3
Eugene, OR 97401

www.wipfandstock.com

PAPERBACK ISBN: 978-1-6667-0943-8
HARDCOVER ISBN: 978-1-6667-0944-5
EBOOK ISBN: 978-1-6667-0945-2

Cataloguing-in-Publication data:

Names: Aist, Rodney [author].

Title: Pilgrim spirituality : defining pilgrimage again for the first time / Rodney Aist.

Description: Eugene, OR: Cascade Books, 2022 | Includes bibliographical references and
index.

Identifiers: ISBN 978-1-6667-0943-8 (paperback) | ISBN 978-1-6667-0944-5 (hardcover)
| ISBN 978-1-6667-0945-2 (ebook)

Subjects: LCSH: Christian pilgrims and pilgrimages | Pilgrims and pilgrimages | Sacred
space

Classification: BX2323 A37 2022 (paperback) | BX2323 (ebook)

VERSION NUMBER 040822

To Janet and Sister Giovanna Negrotto

Contents

Preface | ix
Abbreviations | xi

  1 Introduction | 1

PART 1: DEFINING PILGRIMAGE | 13

  2 First-Person Stories | 15
  3 Defining Pilgrimage | 31
  4 Characterizing Pilgrimage | 51
  5 The Component Parts of Pilgrimage | 81

PART 2: BIBLICAL EXPRESSIONS OF PILGRIMAGE | 89

  6 The Metatemplate | 91
  7 Biblical Expressions | 95

PART 3: THE OBJECTIVE OF PILGRIMAGE | 109

  8 God | 111
  9 Self | 115
10 The Other | 119
11 The Union of God, Self, and the Other | 122

PART 4: THE DIMENSIONS OF PILGRIMAGE | 127

12 Time | 129
13 Place | 138
14 Journey | 150
15 People | 161

PART 5: THE PILGRIM EXPERIENCE | 165

16 Pilgrim Motives | 167

17 The Pilgrim Experience | 175

18 Pilgrim Practices | 187

PART 6: APPLICATIONS OF PILGRIM SPIRITUALITY | 199

19 Principles of Application | 201

20 Religious Travel | 205

21 Everyday Christianity | 207

22 The Social Applications of Pilgrimage | 210

23 Congregational Formation | 220

PART 7: MOVING FORWARD | 225

24 The Theological Contributions of Pilgrimage | 227

25 The Challenges of Pilgrim Spirituality | 233

26 Towards a Pilgrim-Themed Spirituality | 239

Bibliography | 247

Subject Index | 257

Author Index | 263

Scripture Index | 265

Preface

PILGRIM SPIRITUALITY EXPLORES HOW we think about Christian pilgrimage. Thought nurtures practice, ideas create possibilities, and intentionality strengthens experience. Presenting a framework for Christian formation, the book offers a pilgrim-themed spirituality for everyday Christianity, congregational life, social outreach, and religious travel. Sharpening the theological tools of pilgrimage, *Pilgrim Spirituality* equips Christians to explore lived experience, engage the Other, and embody the presence of God in richer, more meaningful ways.

I have engaged the thought and practice of pilgrimage for nearly thirty years, including an around-the-world journey as a young clergy and a PhD in Christian pilgrimage to Jerusalem. The book, in a way, is my personal compendium on pilgrimage, and I'm grateful for friends, family, and colleagues who have mentored, guided, and accompanied me along the way.

While consolidating decades of experience, the book is the fruit of more recent study. The Romans speaks of the spirit of a place, and as a book on pilgrimage, it seems appropriate to recognize the primary places where the book was written: Orkney, Colorado, and Milan. As I wrote, personal memories of meaningful places and journeys have provided both muse and distraction.

In the midst of writing the book, I began directing a doctor of ministry program in pilgrimage and spirituality for Drew Theological School. The opportunity to teach courses on pilgrimage, place, and memory, to be in conversation with Christian leaders about pilgrimage, and to have access to the library services of the university have inspired, challenged, and crystallized various ideas in the book. I want to thank the faculty of Drew, in particular, Javier, Melanie, Meredith, and Jesse, and especially the pilgrimage students Adalí, Asa, David, Donna, Ellen, Jenn, Matthew, Mike, and Stephen; Bonnie, James, John, Saffet, and Sherry.

The book is dedicated to my wife, Janet. It is also a tribute to my pilgrim mentor, Sister Giovanna Negrotto, whom I met in Assisi in December 1996, an encounter of pilgrims arranged by Bob Bronkema, who is mentioned in the opening chapter. My conversations with Sister Giovanna are testament to the impact that brief encounters can have on our spiritual life. We exchanged a few postcards in the aftermath of my two-day visit to Assisi, and after losing touch for a number of years, we reconnected in the spring of 2021. The blessings of pilgrimage are the people we meet along the way.

Abbreviations

BIBLICAL TEXTS

Gen	Genesis
Exod	Exodus
Deut	Deuteronomy
Josh	Joshua
2 Chr	2 Chronicles
Ps	Psalms
Isa	Isaiah
Ezek	Ezekiel
Matt	Matthew
Rom	Romans
1 Cor	1 Corinthians
Eph	Ephesians
Phil	Philippians
Col	Colossians
1 Thess	1 Thessalonians
1 Tim	1 Timothy
2 Tim	2 Timothy
Heb	Hebrews
1 Pet	1 Peter
Rev	Revelation

1

Introduction

I WAS ON MY way with Bob and Stacy to meet a group of Protestant–Catholic couples to discuss issues affecting their relationships when Stacy asked me, "How does pilgrimage relate to people living stationary lives?" In the midst of an around-the-world pilgrimage, I was staying for a week at Casa Materna, a Methodist children's home outside Naples, Italy, where Bob and Stacy, American missionaries, served as chaplains and pastored a nearby Waldensian congregation. As we talked about religious travel, Stacy wondered about the applications of pilgrimage for everyday Christianity. How does peripatetic experience inform the Christian life? *Pilgrim Spirituality* seeks to answer Stacy's question.

As a young pastor, I took a one-year, around-the-world journey, visiting local congregations, ecumenical communities, and institutional ministries. The journey ended with a forty-day wilderness experience in the Ozark Mountains. Throughout the year, I visited traditional pilgrim sites, met people of faith, and observed local Christianity in a variety of cultural and theological contexts. I spent time in prayer and worship, reading and writing, engaging Christians in conversation, exploring images of the pilgrim life.[1]

The trip came about in a curious way. As I neared the end of a three-year pastorate of two Methodist congregations in northern Arkansas, I was planning to go to graduate school when I received a call to go on pilgrimage instead. God gave me "permission" to go on an around-the-world journey, which God qualified by saying "but it has to be a pilgrimage." Except for

---

1. See Aist, *Voices in the Wind*; Aist, *Journey of Faith*.

an undergraduate course on medieval pilgrimage nearly a decade before, I knew little about the practice, and the call seemed to come out of the blue.[2] Happy to oblige, I began drafting sample itineraries. Focusing on personal interactions with global Christians, I would explore prayer, worship, and spirituality, participate in ecumenical communities, and visit local churches and related ministries around the world. In short, my embrace of the pilgrim life has been a personal, vocational calling, and the relational approach of my around-the-world journey remains central to my understanding of pilgrimage today.

So, how does pilgrimage relate to everyday Christianity, congregational formation, and the social mandates of the Christian faith? How can we enhance religious travel, and what are the undeveloped themes of the pilgrim life? What, in a word, is pilgrimage? I have spent most of my ministry years exploring these questions. My academic focus is Christian pilgrimage to Jerusalem before the Crusades.[3] I have studied pilgrimage in the Celtic context, walked over 750 miles of the Camino de Santiago, and have pastored in Rome. I have led and hosted mission trips, taught cultural immersion courses, and have directed family camps and retreats. As the course director at St George's College, Jerusalem, I have taught and guided pilgrim courses in the Holy Land. Working with clergy and laity from around the world, my time in Jerusalem has led me to view Holy Land travel—and pilgrimage more generally—as an exercise in Christian formation.

While holy sites, historical pathways, and short-term Christian community contribute to my understanding of pilgrimage, for me, engaging the Other epitomizes the pilgrim life. Pilgrimage is about being a stranger and encountering the unknown. To be a pilgrim is to cross boundaries, building life-affirming relationships with those "on the other side." From alienation to reconciliation, pilgrimage is the embodied celebration of human diversity. It's the gathering of nations as the people of God. My approach to the pilgrim life draws upon ministry experience in both indigenous and international contexts from the Navajo Nation to Novara, Italy, working with people rooted to the land as well as global migrants living far from home.

PILGRIMAGE TODAY

Pilgrim Spirituality embraces the contemporary revival of pilgrimage. People are rediscovering the ancient practice as a means of spiritual renewal, social

---

2. While I was generally unfamiliar with pilgrimage, I knew of gap years and around-the-world tickets from previous international experience.

3. See Aist, *Christian Topography*; Aist, *Topography to Text*.

engagement, and personal transformation. Pilgrimage is expanding spiritual horizons, enriching life experience, and reshaping our understanding of God, self, and the Other. People are adopting a pilgrim identity, speaking its language, and sharing impassioned testimonies of its transformational power. Pilgrimage is changing lives.

People are responding to the call to pilgrimage in various, creative ways. From long-distance walking to short-term mission trips, Christians are embracing religious travel like never before. They are participating in embodied forms of prayer, and Celtic Christianity, with its emphasis on place and journey, excites the religious imagination.[4]

Certain themes consistently appear in contemporary writings. First of all, there is a growing emphasis on embodied experience and God's preference for the particular, which is grounded in the Christian experience of the incarnation.[5] Second, a renewed emphasis on God's blessing of creation is displacing traditional dichotomies of the sacred–secular and the sacred–profane that have limited our perceptions of the contextual possibilities of spiritual experience. Third, there is a growing appeal to the perceptual dimensions of pilgrimage—to be a pilgrim is to see the world differently. Pilgrim spirituality focuses on our perception and awareness of God, self, and the Other. Fourth, there is interest in the theory of liminality, which applies to personal, institutional, and societal experience.

Despite the attention, pilgrimage remains a peripheral practice. We have yet to capture its comprehensive breadth or tap its capacity for Christian formation. Our explorations of the pilgrim life have only scanned the horizon, and we are merely at the start of where pilgrimage can take us. To move pilgrimage forward, the book precedes with the following premises:

- Pilgrimage is a prominent image of the Christian faith.

- The Bible embraces the image and practice of pilgrimage.

- Pilgrim spirituality has natural affinities with Protestant theology.

- Integrating personal and social holiness, pilgrimage is a comprehensive expression of the Christian life.

- Pilgrimage has transformative applications for religious travel, everyday Christianity, social outreach, and congregational life.

---

4. On pilgrimage themes in Celtic Christianity, see Aist, "Pilgrim Traditions"; Bradley, *Following*, 125–33; Sheldrake, *Living Between Worlds*.

5. The point redresses the division of the body and the spirit that has characterized Protestant thought.

- Despite its contemporary resurgence, pilgrimage as Christian formation remains largely untapped.

- Notwithstanding our familiarity of biblical, historical, and traditional images, we need to redefine pilgrimage. How we *think* about pilgrimage determines the way we approach it. Definitions matter, thought creates possibilities, and intentionality enhances experience. For pilgrim spirituality to realize its transformative potential, it needs a definitional framework.

AN INTENTIONAL ROADMAP

Notwithstanding the freedom of the road, pilgrimage involves plans, directions, and roadmaps, a sense of where we are going before we begin. A good method, or methodology, helps us get where we want to go. Our goal is the union of God, self, and the Other. Our vehicle is the image and practice of pilgrimage.

People who have walked the Camino de Santiago or have visited the Holy Land have experienced the transformational power of pilgrimage. Change, progress, and personal growth are intrinsic qualities of the pilgrim life, and those who have been on pilgrimage know its life-changing power first-hand. Transformation occurs, one way or another, in natural, uncoerced ways, which raises the question: does intentionality impair experience? Does method thwart the spirit?

It depends on the approach. A method may employ prescriptive checklists, mandating practices and dictating experience. Or, presenting possibilities, a method may offer tools, resources, frames, and perspectives. Pilgrim spirituality favors roadmaps over checklists, multiple lenses over a single monocle. A roadmap lays out the terrain; it offers information, orientation, and possible routes. It helps us chart the journey, keeping track of where we are and where we're going. Map, however, is not experience. It serves as a guide, incorporating the collective wisdom of others, but the journey is the actuality of our lives, requiring choices and decisions removed from the map. Pilgrimage takes place *out there* in the real world, where life is unscripted. *Pilgrim Spirituality* resources rather than dictates. Agency remains with the pilgrim.

As a roadmap for the pilgrim life, the book invites readers on an unfinished journey. The point mirrors pilgrimage itself—the tension between journey and arrival, between the not-yet-finished and the destination. The unique, irreducible nature of each individual journey, the exploration of unknown pathways, the persistence of mystery, and the unfolding revelation of lived experience render the pilgrim life wonderfully incomplete.

To advance pilgrimage, we need to begin from the start. What is pilgrimage, and how do we define it? What are the terms, images, and concepts of pilgrimage, its virtues, practices, and applications? What are the theological tools and perceptual frames for exploring lived experience? Helping us think as pilgrims, the book invests readers with a transformative identity for the Christian journey. Yet, it does so without telling pilgrims where to place their feet. Shunning prescriptive steps, the book equips the practitioner with tools, resources, and insights, while espousing the pilgrim life as a Spirit-led practice of personal discernment. While presenting a comprehensive definition of pilgrimage, *Pilgrim Spirituality* employs a myriad of definitions, underscoring the importance of multiple perspectives and the different functions that definitions serve.

Our approach accounts for the realities of the earthly journey. Pilgrimage is not always a walk in the park. Pilgrim spirituality speaks to the difficulties, disappointments, and emotions of life. Pilgrimage may be rewarding, transformational, and life-changing, but it is not a quick-fix spirituality. The pilgrim life is a long and laborious adventure. It takes us through lands of turmoil, chaos, and crisis, through times of sickness, suffering, and death. Pilgrimage is an arduous journey that ends, where it started, in the presence of God.

A PILGRIM-THEMED SPIRITUALITY

While the book explores religious travel, it is ultimately interested in a *pilgrim-themed spirituality*, or the application of pilgrim concepts to any and all areas of our lives. In doing so, the book takes a comprehensive approach to pilgrimage while likewise deconstructing it. What are the component parts of pilgrimage, including its images, themes, and theories?

There's a conceptual tension that stalks our task from the start: (1) pilgrimage is a circumscribed experience, a particular journey, a phase in our lives, a transition that comes and goes; (2) at the same time, it's the entirety of our earthly days, stretching from cradle to grave.[6] Although it's tempting to concede that the *everything* of pilgrimage renders it meaningless or effectively incoherent, theologically, we can either back off from the life-as-journey metaphor or engage the comprehensive nature of the pilgrim life. Life as journey is a conceptual metaphor, which is intrinsic to the way

6. Thus, a pilgrimage (religious travel) occurs within the context of a larger pilgrimage (the earthly life).

humans think and explore the world. Thus, we're compelled to expand it, not to restrict it, leaving us with the formable task of conceptualizing pilgrimage as *both* religious travel and everything else in a meaningful way. This begins by securing a comprehensive definition of pilgrimage and proceeding to break it down. In doing so, we'll view pilgrimage as the exploration of lived experience, which includes traditional forms of religious travel as well as everyday life. The resulting tools, terms, and theories form the basis of pilgrim spirituality.

This leads to additional points and observations that may seem contradictory on the surface. While asserting that all lived experience is pilgrim material (due to the life-as-journey metaphor), we are not suggesting that all journeys are pilgrimages.[7] However, since the life-as-journey metaphor is sourced from our knowledge of physical journeys, all journeys contribute to pilgrim spirituality. Both sacred and ordinary journeys provide perspectives, insights, and wisdom that apply to our earthly life.

All expressions of pilgrimage, whether physical or metaphorical, begin with or include a sense of journey. Yet, in certain instances, the element of movement is past, dormant, or less prominent than other dimensions, such as time and place. Abrahamic pilgrimage begins with a journey; place eventually takes over. Abraham is displaced, a stranger, far from home. If pilgrimage is a journey set aside for a meaningful purpose, it is time set aside as well. Pilgrimage as a stage or transition of life is grounded in the metaphor of journey, but its operative dimension is a period of time. While they are interconnected insomuch as motion is the change of position over time, there are expressions of pilgrimage in which the element of time or place is more important or has more meaning. *Pilgrim Spirituality* explores concepts of pilgrimage that focus on time, place, and people as well as journey (e.g., time-based, place-based, and people-based templates).

In defining pilgrimage, we must ask if it's somehow different from what we've assumed. Can a physical expression of pilgrimage, even if it began as a journey, be better explained in other terms? When does a metaphor, though rooted in movement, come to mean or be something else? When does the process of association render a new definitional frame? More creatively, how can we expand, transfer, and adapt related experience in theologically meaningful ways?

That said, our readjusted frame is rather straightforward: a focus on time, place, journey, and people, together with an emphasis on the stranger, or the Other. Pilgrimage, in turn, is a spirituality of journeys, stations, and

---

7. What makes a physical journey a pilgrimage is an important question. The book lets readers to decide for themselves.

status. While the phenomenon is incoherent without a prominent sense of journey, this effectively leaves it without a common denominator. What appears as a problem is resolved by the family resemblance theory, which states that a phenomenon may be held together by a series of overlapping similarities (see chapter 3).

In moving towards a pilgrim-themed spirituality, how we engage and adjust pilgrim language is important. We use the phrase, "on pilgrimage," to describe an actualized expression. However, pilgrim spirituality is much broader than that. To begin with, to be on pilgrimage is generally a rare experience. I've been around pilgrimage for years, its places, practices, and people, including leading and guiding others, but I only deem a handful of my life experiences as actual pilgrimages. We want to disseminate the call to go on pilgrimage and to enhance the practice of religious travel. Even so, being on pilgrimage is an exceptional experience. On the other hand, we engage pilgrimage concepts all the time. Our emphasis is on applying the themes of pilgrimage rather than being "on pilgrimage" per se.[8]

This raises the question of pilgrim identity, or who is a pilgrim. First of all, we do not need to be a pilgrim to participate in pilgrimage. Among its supporting roles, pilgrimage depends on guides, mentors, hosts, and companions, and providing hospitality to others is a primary act of pilgrimage. Secondly, pilgrim identity is self-determined. We want to offer transformative lenses to fellow travelers, not to determine who is or isn't a pilgrim.[9] We may debate whether time set aside for a particular purpose is a valid concept of pilgrimage, but one ultimately decides for herself. Finally, while a pilgrim identity transforms our faith, we do not have to use the words "pilgrim" or "pilgrimage" to engage in pilgrim spirituality.

PROTESTANT PATHWAYS

As a young Methodist minister, I received a call to go on an around-the-world journey, and pilgrimage has been fundamental to my life ever since. I view pilgrimage as a normative, Protestant-friendly expression of the Christian life, and the book assumes a positive rather than a reactive posture to the practice. Even in Protestant writings that embrace pilgrimage, there is often an underlying apologetic—a need to qualify the pilgrim life before the journey can begin. Associating pilgrimage with relics, indulgences, and

---

8. There are numerous types, or templates, of pilgrimage, such as embodied prayer and engaging the Other, that do not elicit the language of "being on pilgrimage."

9. This does not preclude us from talking about categories of pilgrims, such as forced or coerced pilgrims, pilgrims of the street, and strangers as pilgrims.

Marian theology, Protestants have generally viewed it as a matter of religious identity vis-à-vis Catholicism.[10] Sacred sites are contested by the doctrine of God's omnipresence, while the trappings of pilgrim piety, the emotionality of faith, the healing ("magical") propensities of material objects, associations of meritorious practice, and the moral incertitude of pilgrim behavior have raised further objections. Generally uneasy with physical expressions of the pilgrim life, Protestants have focused instead on the inward, spiritual journey.

The book's premise—that pilgrimage is a primary biblical image of the Christian faith with natural affinities with Protestant sensibilities—stands in sharp contrast to these critiques, while our assertion that pilgrimage is a comprehensive expression of the Christian life, including social practice, counters the Protestant rejoinder that pilgrimage is really about the inner life.

While the Bible is a touchstone of Protestant identity, we're not always as biblical as we think we are. As the Word made flesh, the incarnation conveys divine recognition of the material, the particular, and the importance of time and place. Protestantism, however, has championed the Western tendency to favor space over place, the universal over the particular, and to cleave the body from the soul. The Protestant division of the physical and the immaterial is at odds with the incarnational disposition of God. Whereas Protestantism has long criticized pilgrim practice, pilgrimage returns the favor, offering Protestantism a needful critique.

Pilgrimage, to be sure, is "enduringly contentious."[11] While Protestants have rightly rejected certain trappings of the pilgrim life, we owe it to ourselves to rethink pilgrimage, beginning with its biblical roots. Pilgrim theology engages tradition and honors the faith of our ancestors, finding riches in the historical witness of the church. Theology is an exercise in reexamining the past, tweaking, refining, and revising old ways of thinking, gleaning what we've previously overlooked. Pilgrim spirituality invites Protestants to engage aspects of the Christian life that they otherwise distrust, such as miracles, material objects, and sacred places. Even secular pilgrims on the Camino de Santiago speak of healing and wholeness, forgiveness and redemption, the miraculous and the inexplicable. Instead of throwing the baby out with the bath wash, to be a pilgrim is to look for Moses among the

10. Indulgences do not refer to the forgiveness of sin, which is obtained through confession, but the punishment of sin, which must still be exacted once the sin is forgiven. See Webb, *Medieval European Pilgrimage*, 20–30, 66–71. For a summary of common objections to pilgrimage, see Brown, *God*, 154–63 and Inge, *Christian Theology*, 98–101. Also see Wynn, *Faith and Place*, 139.

11. Wynn, *Faith and Place*, 138.

reeds (Exod 2:1–10). *Pilgrim Spirituality* invites Protestants to (re)discover their identity: reengaging the Bible, reencountering God, revitalizing Christian community, and recasting their place in the world.

The book reflects, in many ways, my Methodist heritage. Theologically engaged, it takes a practical, non-catechetical approach to the Christian faith. Grounded in Scripture, tradition, experience, and reason, pilgrim spirituality embraces personal and social holiness, acts of piety and acts of mercy, the individual journey and corporate experience, personal faith and sacramental grace. Just as John Wesley "plundered the Egyptians," adopting aspects of other traditions, pilgrim spirituality explores the riches of both Protestant and non-Protestant sources.[12]

Engaging inter-Christian, interfaith, and secular voices, what emerges is an ecumenical vision from a Protestant perspective. Pilgrimage is not a meritorious practice but a means of grace that heightens our perception of God's presence in the world. Not salvific in itself, pilgrimage creates pathways for redemption, healing, and reconciliation. As Protestants reexamine the biblical roots of pilgrimage, recognize its primacy among Christian images, and are transformed by its incarnational nature, the pilgrim life will increasingly define the Protestant experience.

INTENDED READERS

Pilgrim Spirituality is written for the religious traveler and the everyday Christian, for the seasoned pilgrim and the spiritual tenderfoot. It offers a spiritual framework for the Holy Land visitor, the Santiago pilgrim, the ecumenical retreatant, and the short-term missioner. It's a guide book for gap years, sabbaticals, and the transitions and interruptions of life. By embracing a pilgrim identity, the reader will engage lived experience in richer, more meaningful ways.

As a primer on pilgrimage, *Pilgrim Spirituality* is a textbook on the pilgrim life for denominational and congregational leadership. Equipping both the personal and corporate journey, the book resources pastors, chaplains, and spiritual directors. It accompanies those engaged in Christian worship, education, spirituality, and discipleship, camping and retreats, missional outreach, and social justice. Speaking to the broadest of Christian

---

12. The concept comes from Exod 12:35–36, which describes the Israelites receiving gifts from their former masters as they departed from Egypt. According to Outler, plundering the Egyptians is "a metaphor pointing to the freedom that Christians have (by divine allowance) to explore, appraise, and appropriate all the insights and resources of any and all secular culture." Outler, *Evangelism*, 77.

audiences, its inclusive approach and non-specialist language are conducive to ecumenical discourse.

The book has access points for non-Christian readers. Embodied experience, personal well-being, engaging the Other, peace and justice, and care of the planet have currency well beyond Christianity. Indeed, contemporary Christianity has been a latecomer to certain conversations. Pilgrimage offers a common parlance and a shared set of values for interfaith dialogue and secular engagement.

LANGUAGE AND TERMINOLOGY

While the book explores definitions, it's useful to clarify certain terms from the start, beginning with our understanding of *spirituality*. Although the word often denotes the opposite of worldly or bodily, our concept of spirituality is neither limited nor oppositional. Our usage follows the Greek word, *holos*, meaning the holy or the whole. Spirituality is not a specialization of the Christian life nor does it emphasize the inner life at the expense of exterior expressions of the Christian faith. Rather, spirituality is life as a whole, which complements our comprehensive approach to pilgrimage.[13] Spirituality encompasses prayer and worship, the quest for meaning, and the pursuit of God as well as social relations.[14]

Despite certain differences between *spirituality* and *theology*, the latter defined as the study of God and religious belief, *pilgrim spirituality* and *pilgrim theology* are used interchangeably. For the sake of brevity, cadence, and word flow, we will commonly use *pilgrim* instead of *pilgrimage* to modify phrases, such as pilgrim spirituality (instead of pilgrimage spirituality). References to the book, *Pilgrim Spirituality*, will be capitalized and italicized, distinguishing it from the thought and practice of pilgrim spirituality.

While the book employs numerous definitions, our comprehensive definition of *pilgrimage* is "the experience of God, self, and the Other through the dimensions of time, place, journey, and people and the thoughts, images, and reflections thereof." In turn, *pilgrim spirituality* is the application of pilgrimage themes to any and all aspects of our lives. Similarly, the *pilgrim life* is the lived experience of pilgrimage, which is synonymous with the *Christian life* and the *Christian journey.* While the *earthly life* denotes our time on earth, it does not differentiate between the *inner* and the *outer* journey.

---

13. On the definition of spirituality, see Sheldrake, *Spirituality*, 5.

14. The word, *spiritual*, will occasionally denote the immaterial.

Christian formation is the lifelong process of becoming like Christ. Encompassing *discipleship* and *faith development*, it includes personal, social, and missional aspects of the Christian faith. Christian formation—and faith development as a whole—*may* include but does not imply a structure, program, or formula. Rather, it's our absorption of the Christian life through various means and how well we live, or are formed, into that life. Although the distinction is not pronounced, for the most part, I use *transformative* to refer to the potential of transformation, while *transformational* implies an outcome.

References to *traditional* or *historical pilgrimage* refer to religious travel to a holy place. *Biblical pilgrimage*, a much broader concept, is discussed in chapters 6 and 7. The *Other*—which denotes other people, particularly strangers, God as mystery, and, more generally, the unknown—is capitalized, while *self*, evoking humility and introspection, is lowercased.

A couple of linguistic points are also in order. Although pilgrim spirituality is grounded in biblical and historical expressions, the book's focus is on Christian formation for the modern-day Christian. While our vision of the pilgrim life transcends language, we are working, of course, in the English language. The word *pilgrimage* is not as precise as its counterparts in other modern languages, and the English concept, which includes images of wandering as well as religious journey, is comparatively broad. German, for instance, has two words for pilgrimage, *Wallfahrt* and *Pilgerfahrt*, while the Dutch speak of *bedevaart* and *pelgrimage*. Likewise, modern Greek has various terms associated with travel and worship that can be translated into English as pilgrimage.[15] In short, we are exploring a concept that is shaped by the connotations and ambiguities of the English language.

Finally, while the book recognizes the function of language in shaping experience, as previously mentioned, pilgrim spirituality does not require the explicit use of the words, *pilgrim* and *pilgrimage*. Related idioms, such as journey, may have more resonance in certain contexts. Engaging the Other is pilgrimage by any other name, while short-term mission is a type of pilgrimage regardless of what else it may be. Not everything needs to be called pilgrimage to be one, and the scope of pilgrim spirituality is not limited by the explicit words that we use. That said, assuming a pilgrim identity profoundly shapes our Christian experience. *Pilgrim Spirituality* invites the reader not only to invoke pilgrim language but to see the world through pilgrim eyes.

---

15. The point also applies to other languages. See Margry, *Shrines*, 44; Reader, *Pilgrimage*, 20–22.

PART 1

Defining Pilgrimage

2

First-Person Stories

Pilgrimage is embodied, first-person experience. Consequently, our quest to define it begins with a series of autobiographical vignettes. The stories are steeped in emotion, full of serendipitous encounters, incomplete endings, and moments of resolution. They ask questions of life, explore the sacred, and engage the Other.[1]

The stories have been chosen, in part, because they have been remembered in the first place, which alone conveys their personal importance. They are not presented as inspirational narratives nor as pivotal flashpoints of my life. Their purpose is more prosaic: to introduce pilgrimage themes through first-person stories, which, for the most part, do not occur within the context of traditional pilgrimage.

The stories themselves are parabolic of pilgrimage. As lived experience is translated into text, flow is punctuated. Memory erodes and embellishes details. Narrative and interpretation intertwine. My lived experience has mostly vanished, while a swirl of fading memories, vague perceptions, and confused emotions reside just beyond the reach of words. Pilgrimage is a journey of constantly losing things along the way, including our memories. What we retain, we treasure and refine. Pilgrimage is experience and reflection, evaluation and redaction, things that happen, how they're remembered, and what they come to mean.

---

1. Using first-person experience as our starting point is not the same as conceptualizing pilgrimage as personal spirituality.

RUMMAGING THROUGH LOCKERS

The bell rang signaling the end of seventh period and, with it, the completion of my junior year of high school. I walked to my locker and stood staring aimlessly, oblivious to the whirlwind of movement around me, a cacophony of shouts and laughter echoing through the halls as fellow classmates left the school. I remained hesitantly in place with suppressed emotion and a lack of direction, aware of the importance of the passing moment but with little sense of what to do. I was lost in a familiar place.

I had known for three months that my family was moving. My father had taken a job in another state, and we would join him in a couple of weeks. My friends and classmates would reenter the school for their senior year without me.

I emptied my locker and walked slowly down the hall, looking for a friend—someone, anyone, to talk to. I was about to exit the building, when I met my best friend, Aaron, coming down the stairs with the same familiar look on his face that I had known since we were six: he was up to something. [2]He was carrying a slightly full sack in one hand and empty bags in the other. He handed me one and said, "Let's go!" as he opened a deserted locker and began pilfering through it. He found a couple of pencils and a used eraser and moved on to the neighboring locker. It was empty, but the next one yielded an Aerosmith t-shirt.

Aaron beamed. "C'mon," he said, "Help me!" And together we began rummaging through lockers, collecting pens and notebooks, discarded trinkets, and the odd piece of clothing. We found sandwiches and apples, squirt guns and bubble gum, art work and photos, broken watches, combs, and brushes. Fading flowers were taped inside a locker. Special moments never seem to last.

Over three and a half decades later, I still have one object from that ultimate afternoon with Aaron. A memento from those scurried moments continues to connect me with my past, to the finality of a passing childhood, full of friends and adventures, achievements, and lost promises, an object that reflects the changes in my life since I left that building years ago.

Inside one locker, I found a four-inch square mirror with a round sticker of a reclining Garfield in the lower right-hand corner with the words: "If I were any lazier I'd slip into a coma." I placed the mirror in my bag and took it home without thinking twice about it. But that summer and ever since, the mirror has traveled with me—or remained at home waiting patiently for my return. The mirror has reflected difficult moments and

---

2. Aaron Brown is currently a United Methodist pastor in Missouri.

positive changes in my life. It has reminded me of who I am, reflecting sadness and disappointment, joy and self-confidence. The mirror has become a personal relic, connecting my past with the present.[3]

Pilgrimage is much more than religious travel. It pertains to time, place, and memory, to our navigation of the unknown, and to the serendipitous moments of life. Pilgrimage is a physical, emotional, and spiritual journey. It occurs when we stand alone without direction, uncertain of our thoughts and feelings, and culminates in the union of God, self, and the Other. Pilgrimage is about location, past and present, and includes being lost and out of place. It speaks to where we have been and where we are going, to the here and the elsewhere. It is about movement, change, and transformation.

Pilgrimage is about our relationship with others: our desire for companionship, our love of God, and our encounter with friends and strangers. Pilgrimage is alienation—and the joy of being found.

To be on pilgrimage is to glimpse, like Paul, into a mirror dimly. It is rummaging for treasures, finding elixirs in the rubbish. The journey of faith is full paradox and surprise, immediate yet years in the making. Pilgrimage is an empty locker, a lazy cat, and leaving friends behind: lived experience, the search for meaning, and a God who is always by our side.

THE MERRY DANCERS

As the exploration of life's most important questions, pilgrimage pertains to life, death, and the afterlife, to the earthly and the ethereal, to the signs of sacramental encounter. Pilgrims seek places of divine irruption whence they glimpse beyond the veil.

I worked a one-week family camp in northern Minnesota for over twenty-five years. My first summer, I met Cathy. Thirty years my senior, Cathy loved camp: its activities, pranks, and practical jokes. She also loved Minnesota: its lakes, loons, and northern lights. Cathy was our favorite camper, and staff, like John, Jeff, Bill, and me, kept in touch with her throughout the year. For the ten years I knew her, Cathy struggled with reoccurring cancer, fending it off, miraculously at times, with strength and fortitude. She often told us: "I'll send you a sign when I get there." Knowing Cathy, we never disbelieved. She died in September, days after attending her final family camp. Cathy was cremated, and I was honored to eulogize her at her funeral in Cleveland.

---

3. The mirror is presently in a small wooden treasure box made for me by my father.

The following August, John, Jeff, Bill, and I returned to family camp. Cathy's daughter, Betsy, had originally planned to take her ashes to camp later in the fall, before deciding that family camp was the appropriate occasion for her mother's committal, even if she couldn't be there herself, and the next thing we knew, Cathy was in the post, packaged in a box, on her way to camp! We told Marty, the warehouse manager, to be on alert: "There's a special package coming. It's Cathy!" Cathy duly arrived; Marty signed for her, and she spent a couple of days in our cabin resting on a shelf.

Family camp came to an end. The families left, and staff was in camp for a final night. John, Jeff, Bill, and I gathered at the dock around dusk. With wildflowers in hand, we grabbed life jackets and headed to the pontoon boat. Tired from the week, I fought a rare headache as I anticipated what I had come to believe: something was about to happen. Throughout the week, I had stood on the dock, looking up at the stars. "Wait until Friday," I kept telling myself. Now that Friday was here, I was physically and emotionally exhausted.

Jeff steered us to the middle of the lake. He cut the motor, and we sat in the quiet stillness of the dying day. Stars emerged as the last traces of the sun were absorbed by the encroaching darkness. We shared stories about Cathy, her life, and her struggles. The night was calm and peaceful; time was suspended with meaning. We lingered in soft conversation until an awkward silence suggested that I should begin the brief solemnities: a short prayer, the scattering of the ashes, the laying of flowers on the water.

I sat with my back to the north, facing the others in the dark. As I opened my mouth to pray, John immediately straightened up. The whites of his eyes flashed in the darkness; his face was lit with joy. Tracing his gaze, I looked over my shoulder. The black night had given birth to rays of pulsating light. The northern lights, or merry dancers, were ensconced in the sky.

A year before, Cathy was a shadow, a crippled body refusing to die. Twelve months later, she was dancing above our heads to no one's surprise, having delivered the promised sign, leaving us speechless, tearful, shrouded in joy.

The northern lights only lasted a few minutes; both their timing and brevity verified the moment. We stood for ages, arm in arm, tears running down our cheeks. Cathy was doing just fine, safe in God's eternal arms.

Under the night's veil, I prayed, and we took turns committing her remains into the dark, primeval waters. Tossed flowers alighted upon the lake, buoyant with fragile beauty, superficial witnesses suspended between earth and sky.

We gently motored back to the dock, and back on land, we stared into the northern abyss, now black as coal but jeweled with stars. We felt the mysterious comfort of darkness. Light had appeared as a promise fulfilled, and we knew what it meant to be children of God.

Cathy's committal is layered with pilgrim themes. To be a pilgrim is to journey through illness, to dance in the darkness. Pilgrimage is our shared response to death: care for the body, gathering with others, loss and sadness, hope and promise, formal solemnities, and acts of memorialization. It encompasses objects and symbols, place and memory, the past and present, the here and hereafter. Pilgrimage is prayerful reflection upon our own mortality.

We are individually fated to "the undiscovered country from whose bourn no traveler returns," and pilgrimage is ultimately a one-way journey, crossing spiritual chasms through the darkest of nights.[4] Cathy in the sky speaks to the star-studded inheritance of Abraham's children. In the meantime, pilgrimage is being left behind as earthbound witnesses to ponder the signs, discerning between coincidence and correspondence. What lies beyond the borealis? Does the material hold meaning? Can we discern the transcendent in time and space? Pilgrimage confronts life's most important questions, none greater than life and death. What is the relationship between heaven and earth? Can we peer into the afterlife or receive signs from above? How porous is the veil? Pilgrimage is occasioned by surprises that fall from the sky, leaving us wide-eyed and gob-smacked as we ponder the mysteries of the world.

A VERY GOOD FRIDAY

It is not easy to celebrate a Good Friday birthday, as was the case one April while walking La Ruta de la Plata, or the Silver Road, of the Camino de Santiago, the pilgrim route of southern Spain. The route goes north from Seville, passing through Salamanca before joining the Camino's French Road, which crosses northern Spain, at Astorga, approximately 160 miles from Santiago. I began in Mérida, walking nearly three hundred miles in seventeen days.

The French Road, which I had previously done, is well-developed. Pilgrim amenities abound, and the road, especially in the summer, contains a constant stream of pilgrims. By contrast, I only saw seven pilgrims on the Silver Road and had more eye-to-eye contact with Spanish bulls in the Iberian countryside. The path crossed long sections of unpopulated land—plains, woods, and mountains—and more than once I had to walk until sunset before securing a place to sleep, often floor space offered by the local

4. Shakespeare, *Hamlet*, Act 3, Scene 1.

commune. The days were sunny but cold and windy. My feet were blistered. I was well alone. It was a great way—I unconvincingly assured myself—to spend Holy Week.

According to my guide book, the village where I would be spending Holy Thursday, Fuenterroble de Salvatierra, was a pilgrim "oasis of peace." Approaching the village with cautious anticipation, I soon found the parish house, which the priest had transformed into a pilgrim center. I was welcomed by a warm fire and spent the rest of the day enjoying parish hospitality overseen by a German volunteer. A couple of pilgrims arrived by bike, and members of the church dropped by throughout the evening. I enjoyed a common meal with others, and following a hot drink, I went blissfully to sleep under the covers of a warm bed.

I woke up to a Good Friday birthday, unsure whether to approach the day as one of celebration or reserved devotion. As the day revealed itself, divergent emotions became intertwined in unexpected ways. About a dozen members of the parish were commemorating the Stations of the Cross along a nine-mile section of the Camino in the direction I was heading. Their destination was Pico Dueñas, the highest point on the Silver Road, where they would erect a cross on the top of the mountain.

We set out from Fuenterroble in the cold morning air at a pace that was anything but slow, as one of us, a young man, shouldered a full-sized cross across the barren landscape. About every twenty minutes, we stopped to commemorate Jesus' journey to Calvary. Scriptures were cited; prayers were read, and the procession continued. I enjoyed the company, speaking broken Spanish with parish pilgrims. It was a joy to follow, not to worry about finding my way. After days of walking alone, it was nice to have an escort, a cohort, especially on my birthday.

During the steep, rocky ascent up Pico Dueñas, people took turns helping the one-to-be-Christ up the mountain by lifting the bottom of the cross off the ground. Near the top, we rested in gasping reflection. The final stations were duly marked; the real Christ was crucified, and the cross was erected. Below, a vast landscape stretched as far as we could see, while atop the mountain, wind whipped the barren ground, rattling the wooden cross, now securely wedged in the rock. Creation groaned in silence.

It was a Good Friday birthday that I will never forget. The image of the young man dragging the heavy cross, mile after mile, across the desolate landscape, sweat streaming down his brow. The friendly faces of my Good Friday companions, curious about my presence. Quiet conversations sprinkled amidst long moments of silence. Huddling together on a wind-swept hillside to commemorate Christ's final breath.

True of Good Friday pilgrims, we were a long way from home. I had another eight miles ahead of me, while the others needed to retrace their steps to Fuenterroble. We descended the far side of the mountain, and back on level ground, the home-bound parishioners sent me on my way with a pilgrim's blessing. I started down a tarmac road that stretched in an unbroken line towards the distant horizon, occasionally looking over my shoulder at the cross, silhouetted on the mountain top, conjoining heaven and earth. A day of friends and strangers journeying together to the cross, commemorating death, celebrating life, it was a Good Friday birthday full of undeserved gifts.

My Good Friday walk up Pico Dueñas exemplifies the layered texture of pilgrimage. Birthdays are signposts of our earthly life, while the Stations of the Cross is a kinetic commemoration recalling the passion of Christ. They occurred simultaneously during the course of a long-distance pedestrian journey.

Whereas I walked the Silver Road, a minor route, during the off-season month of April, I had traversed the French Road, the Camino's primary artery, during the summer height of a holy year. Walking the French Road was a long-anticipated experience, years in the making, and I was well-prepared for six weeks of intense, fluid community, measured days of walking, lush summer landscapes, architectural landmarks, churches and monasteries, and pilgrim-friendly amenities from designated lodgings to special menus in local restaurants. By contrast, walking the Silver Road, which offered an affordable spring break during graduate school in Britain, was a last-minute decision. Pilgrimage is a calling not an afterthought, and there's something to be said for proper preparation.

My Silver Road journey consisted of seemingly endless walks through empty landscapes, sunny days belied by a biting wind. Insufficiently provisioned for a cold Spanish spring, comfort was always a layer away. Dreams were the stuff of a proper sleeping bag. Even the joyful interlude of the Fuenterroble Friday quickly dissipated. Planning an Easter sojourn in Salamanca, I arrived to find no room in the inn, no place to lay my head, as the city was thronged for the Paschal feast. Discouraged, I shook the dust from my feet, walking well past the city before finding my place of resurrection at a roadside hotel.

Pilgrimage teaches us about God, self, and the Other. My Easter experience reminded me that Jesus died for those who have little choice but to be pilgrims: the poor and destitute, the lost and lonely. Many pilgrims miss the feast without the luxury of a roadside bed.

Often too tired to journal, the Silver Road largely vanished in the walking. Still, treasured takeaways remain in my memory: the hospitality of remote villages, the barmaid who looked like Cher, free drinks for a thirsty pilgrim, the key to a small room behind the school with a bunk bed for *per-egrinos*. "Welcome! Here's the key; make yourself at home." Pilgrims know succor when they see it.

While walking the Silver Road, I made another pilgrimage: the Stations of the Cross up Pico Dueñas, a corporate experience conjoining embodied prayer, physical movement, and narrative commemoration. Through the reenactment of sacred stories, including prayer walks, congregational worship, and children's plays, Christians participate locally in the biblical drama. In doing so, they translate the gospel far beyond the empty tomb. The passion comes to Pico Dueñas, and Easter is revivified in time and place around the world.

Finally, my Silver Road experience reminds us that pilgrimage is a sacrament of time as well as place. Seventeen days in April were set apart to walk an ancient pilgrim route, days that coincided with the annual celebration of Holy Week and the one-off occasion of a thirty-fifth birthday.

IT'S A SMALL WORLD

I decided to ride It's a Small World one last time. True freedom is being at Disneyland without your parents, though I spent the day revisiting memories from our family trip when I was five. The spinning teacups still made me sick, but this time Uncle Johnny did not turn into a ghost at the Haunted Mansion—I did. A form of homecoming that often occurs away from home, pilgrimage is repeat performance, the reiteration of past experience, walking in our own footsteps, reflecting upon change and continuity, personal identity, and our place within the world.

I was staying with friends two buses away. I got off at my connecting stop and began waiting in the dark for the bus that never came. Another man joined me. I am white; he was black. He liked to talk; I did not. I was not at ease. He told me that his car had broken down, that he was returning from a taekwondo class, that his wife was attending a professional basketball game. He was extremely friendly, and the more we talked, the more he gained my trust. He bought me some coffee. He let me use his phone. Encouraged by misinformed bus drivers who kept telling us that our bus was coming, we continue to wait. An hour passed, then another.

"Yesterday, my brother-in-law was sentenced to life in prison," he unloaded. "He hasn't committed any hard crimes, but 'three strikes you're out,'" he said, referring to California's limit of three convictions.[5] "He's thirty-two

---

5. California's Three Strikes sentencing law was originally enacted in 1994. My conversation with Brother Ben took place in April 1997.

and has already spent ten years behind bars." My newfound friend was Brother Ben, a local Baptist minister. "This has shaken up our church. He's the son of our senior pastor, my father-in-law."

We eventually decided to take a different bus—the *same* bus I had taken from Disneyland almost three hours before. As it turned out, the alternative route, bus to light rail, worked reasonably well for both of us. Brother Ben was the first to get off, and I watched my guardian angel slip off into the night, as I recalculated my anxiety based upon prejudiced judgments of the three remaining passengers. After reaching my station and a thirty-minute walk, I arrived at my friends' house well after midnight. It's a small world but a really big city.

A place of fantasies and fairy tales, personal adventures, and national narratives, Disney takes us to a special, manicured world beyond the realities of everyday life. My journey home likewise occurred outside my ordinary world but in a starkly different way. Was there cause to be concerned? Maybe. Maybe not. When we are out of place, we project our fears upon the stranger; we become afraid of the Other, and fear breeds from within. Pilgrimage is "the street," where we sense our vulnerabilities, confront our prejudices, listen to the voices of others, and receive the friendship of strangers. Pilgrims are guided by the angels of the night.

FIRST SNOWFALL

Full of arrivals and departures, beginnings and endings, my around-the-world journey was an undulating stream of emotions. I spent a week in November at the World Council of Churches graduate school in Bossey, Switzerland, where I quickly became friends with a diverse group of international Christians. On Sunday, my last full day, about a dozen of us went to Geneva to attend the English-speaking Lutheran church. We had a picnic in the park and returned to Bossey as the weather turned wet. Alighting at the local station, we walked down the lane to outbreaks of laughter. Enveloped by the warmth of a cold autumn's rain, I walked alone with everyone, recalling moments from the week, grateful for my newfound friends, aware of my pending departure. I smiled to myself as we walked through the mud.

The next morning, there was a tangible excitement at breakfast as the forecast called for the season's first snow. I said my good-byes and left Bossey, melancholic yet content, returning to Geneva, where I waited for my France-bound train. Soon, the sky began filling with large, fluffy snowflakes, and I was piqued to be missing the scene unfolding back at Bossey, where several students were experiencing snow for the first time in their lives.

The change of seasons excites emotions. The corn is felled; the earth laid bare. Snow blankets the ground. I was sad to have left, to miss the faces of friends marveling at the snow. Bossey was full of boisterous laughter, and I was onwards to France.

I was a bundle of autumn emotions, sentiments made poignant by the echoing softness of the snow: the transient nature of life, the discomfort of pleasant memories, the necessity of broken connections. Yet, far from diminishing the experience, my emotions saturated the morning with meaning. Emotions color our world, giving a patina to the surface of our lives. At times, what we see and feel merge as one: life is perceived through affective lenses, and the poignant moment . . . lingering . . . is an affirmation of life.

As heaven fell as snowflakes, the morning was a harbinger of blessing. Enveloped by feeling, I was reminded of my human limitations and my dependency upon God. In my laughter and my sadness, in times of strength and weakness, in or out of community, connected or alone, I knew that God was with me.

I boarded the train and found my seat. It was facing backwards, towards Bossey, in the direction of my heart's imagination. As the train pulled out of the station and Geneva slipped away, I stared into the snow-flaked sky, feeling the memories and emotions of the week. A few minutes later, now well into France, I stood up, turned around, and sat down in the opposite seat. With Bossey behind me, I dared to looked forward to where I was going.

Movement itself is transition. Physical travel conveys mental and emotional change, and a few hours later, I was on a local bus, traversing the darkness of the French countryside, heading towards the monastic community of Taizé. There were just three of us on the bus—myself, the driver, and another lone traveler, a down-under pilgrim named Paul, an Aussie I'm still in touch with after more than twenty-five years. The immediacy of Bossey had faded with the day, crystallizing as memory, cherished but past, overtaken by the arrival of a new location and the downstream movement of time.

Shaping our perception of events, emotions personalize the journey. They texturize experience; they color our world, especially during times of transition and change. Emotions accompany real-time events. They are affective reactions to the here and now, which generally dissipate as the journey continues, the scene shifts, and new settings emerge. Some emotions linger for longer periods, spilling over from scene to scene, while residual emotions affect our relational interactions with the world. Navigating the earthly journey includes the snowfalls of assorted emotions—sometimes, beautiful and delicate; at times, miserable and muddied—that variously stick, accumulate, and melt away.

SECOND-MILE STORIES

I met Jione Langi, a Methodist minister from Fiji, in a church car park in Auckland, New Zealand.[6] My host, Rushan, made a point of introducing us, since the next stop on my around-the-world journey was Fiji to visit Pacific Theological College (PTC) in Suva, 120 miles from the main airport in Nadi.[7] Jione was a graduate of PTC, had relatives in both Nadi and Suva, and offered to connect me with his family. A few days later, as I was leaving New Zealand, I phoned Jione from the Auckland airport.[8] He had hoped to have his brother pick me up at the airport, but Cyclone Gavin had hit the island. Phone lines were down, and Jione couldn't reach him. Disappointed by the news, I hung up to the announcement that my flight was delayed. I had no accommodations once I got there, which would now be after midnight. Anxious yet resigned, I began killing time in the airport.

I was reading *God of Surprises* when I saw Jione walking towards me.[9] Shocked, to say the least, I was extremely pleased to see him—he had driven out to the airport to find me! "I remembered my cousin, Samuela, who's also a Methodist pastor. He lives in the town north of Nadi. He'll be at the airport to pick you up. You'll spend the night with him and his wife, and they'll put you on a bus for Suva in the morning." The God of surprises was watching over me.

"When you get to Suva, my family will want to get together with you. . . . A lot of people would say this is all a coincidence, but I know that it's not. God has brought us together." After visiting for an hour, we said goodbye, and I watched Jione as he walked out of sight, grateful to have met such a

6. The Revd Dr Jione Langi (1941–2005) was born in Rotuma, an island located three hundred miles from the main Fijian islands. His ministry included working with Fijian congregations in Australia and New Zealand, helping his people to retain Christian community amid the individualism and materialism of modern society: "I am trying to bring back to life people who have gone astray, who have forsaken their Christian roots, and who feel lost or alienated from our culture and faith" (personal communication). Jione became president of the Methodist Church in Fiji and Rotuma.

7. Rushan Sinnaduray, a native of Sri Lanka, moved to Auckland with his family when he was a teenager. He was the youth director of a local Methodist church in Auckland when he hosted me in New Zealand. He is currently a United Church of Christ minister in my childhood state of Missouri.

8. The story takes place in 1997 without the benefit of cell phones and when non-passengers could still access airport gates.

9. Hughes, *God of Surprises*.

remarkable man, who, through his care and connections, had replaced my worries of a midnight arrival and no place to stay with a welcoming party of relational entry.

Samuela met me as scheduled, and engaged in collegial conversation, we drove along storm-strewn roads through the middle of the night to his house where more welcome awaited. After some short but satisfied hours of sleep, I awoke to an ample breakfast prepared by Samuela's wife. Following a relaxed conversation around the table, Samuela showed me his church, pointing out the damage caused by the cyclone, before putting me on a mini-bus headed for Suva.[10] Pilgrims are recipients of second-mile journeys made by people, like Jione and Samuela, who travel to us: to assist us, to befriend us, to give us what we need. The guardians of our journey help get us where we're going.

Stories of assistance generally occur closer to home, like the time in seminary, when my father drove through the night to rescue me when my car broke down in Tennessee on my way home for a visit. It came at the end of a summer internship in North Carolina, when two hours into an eight-hour journey, I found myself on the side of the road waiting for a tow truck. I phoned my parents in Arkansas from a rural garage, and my father immediately took off into the fading day to fetch me. Our rendezvous was an interstate rest area, where I took my pillow and camped out for the evening on the top of a concrete table. About one in the morning, a familiar voice woke me up: "Hey, Rod! Wake up!" We drove to the garage to retrieve the luggage from my car, then set off for home, six hours away, arriving well after sunrise.[11]

The story reminds us that the bulk of our lives concerns family and friends, hearth and home. Notwithstanding around-the-world journeys and interstate travel, life has a local address. The narrative also expresses the irreducible power of story. I could say that my father is generous and benevolent. Or, I could tell the story of a second-mile father who sets off into the night to find his son on the side of the road. Honoring others through words, our stories are offerings to those we can't otherwise repay. Whether in Auckland or Arkansas, we have been on pilgrimage when the actions of others become the stories of our lives.

---

10. During my week at Pacific Theological College, I visited Jione's family on multiple occasions. See Aist, *Voices in the Wind*, 210–15.

11. The story, which took place in 1991, was also without the aid of cell phones.

THE VOICES OF OTHERS

To be a pilgrim is to listen to the voices of others. The recipe of wisdom, we gain insights and compassion through other people's stories. We are inspired by seeing through another set of eyes.

My French Road experience of the Camino de Santiago was fundamentally shaped by the voices of others. On the approach into León, I began speaking with a Vietnamese woman who lived in Paris with her French husband. She was biking slowly, keeping pace with me as I walked. We spoke for less than ten minutes. "I am not a sports person," she said. "I've never done anything like this before. I'm amazed that I can just get on a bicycle and ride six hundred miles. Still, I'm very tired. Not just my body but all over.

"I am on the Camino with my father. We don't have a chance to see each other much. It has been a time of discovery for both of us. Unfortunately, what we have discovered about each other has not been good. Now, we are too tired to support one another.

"This is the first time in my married life that I've been away from my husband. It's been a time of rediscovery for us as well. In our daily lives, we take things for granted. But each day on the Camino, I realize that I love him more and more. He has many good qualities; he is a very good man. I need to tell him that." As the road began its descent into León, she waved good-bye and coasted out of sight.

～

"I feel so free on the Camino," said Eva, a Danish pastor walking on her own. She carried a wooden walking stick with the words, *I will always be with you*, carved by her husband. "I'm going to cry a lot on the Camino. I know that," she shared one rainy afternoon inside a café. "I lost a baby girl a year and a half ago. It has brought my husband and me closer together. For the first time in my life, I experienced resurrection. It wasn't all loss and destruction. The Camino gives me a way to express my sadness.

"I know a fourteen-year-old girl who purposely rode her bike into a car and died. I know another girl who is ill and in a wheelchair. One died; the other doesn't want to live. I see myself in these girls. I have always been afraid, unable to find life. Now, I have it. I feel life's freedom on the Camino. I want to help young women find life and be free. I am making this pilgrimage in the name of Saint George the Dragon Slayer. My dragon is fear."

～

Patrick, a fifty-year-old pilgrim from Ireland, told me: "God cannot be described. It's impossible. There are no predicates for God. Similarly, each pilgrimage journey is unique. Once we try to put words to the experience, our descriptions are false. They can't be explained. . . . I wanted to do the Camino when I was fifty to see if I was still alive. Fifty years does something to a person. What I wasn't prepared for was the constant pain. I would never do this again."

≈

I ate breakfast with Tobias, a theology student from Sweden. "I had my first religious experience last week on the Camino," he began. "It was storming, and I am very afraid of lightning. I began to shout at God. I told him that he could help me if he wanted. I felt that God heard me, that for the first time I had real communication with God. It was raining as I entered the village. I knocked on the door of the pilgrim house, and an old lady opened the door. 'Welcome!' she said, and she invited me in. There were twelve of us, including her. We sat around a table as she served us food. Our conversation was very intimate. After a while, she said something about one of our friends coming. We replied that none of us knew about another person. After a while, there was a knock on the door, and a thirteenth person came in from the rain. We felt as though Christ was in our midst."

≈

"For me, the Camino is like a jigsaw puzzle," said Paul, a pilgrim from Belgium, who began his journey by literally walking out of his house. He'd been on the Camino for over a hundred days. "I make many mistakes. But each day is a new day to learn."

At a restaurant one night, Paul asked me if I was ever lonely. "No," I said, slightly fibbing. "Can be. Can be," he replied. "At times on the Camino, I am very, very lonely."

Paul continued: "I was in a psychiatric hospital for four years," he said without any discernible emotion in his voice, though a tear ran down his cheek. "My wife divorced me while I was in the hospital. I haven't been able to see my three children for over six years. It's been a very difficult time for me. The hospital, though, was a very good experience. I was sick, very sick.

"Always remember to take a second look at people," he told me, citing how often he is labeled by others. We settled the bill, and on the way to the hostel, he commented: "The Camino is not about new things; it's about learning how to manage yourself."

$\sim$

Along with contextualized conversations, my Santiago journal contains a miscellany of quotes spoken by pilgrims I met along the way:

- "The Camino gives us time to examine our lives. This can be difficult, because we don't always like what we see. Life is full of mistakes."

- "Taking time to look at ourselves doesn't mean that we necessarily have to change but that we notice who we are."

- "Each time you reach a goal, it makes you stronger. You believe in yourself more; you gain more confidence."

- "I'm trying to find answers to what I believe and what I don't. Figuring out what makes sense to me. We think we have an answer for everything; yet, we don't actually believe anything."

- "I only know this and that," she told me, pointing her walking stick at what she could see in front of her. "I have no idea what is on the other side of that hill. I just put one foot to the ground, and I see what happens."

- "Problems come to the surface on the Camino, and some people can't handle them. Everyone has problems. I keep wondering when it will be my turn."

- "Life is constant preparation for the next transition."

- "We receive presents all along the way. You get what you need. You get what you ask for. Pilgrimage is being open to whatever happens."

The words of fellow pilgrims ostensibly take us beyond first-person stories. Yet, content, in whatever form, becomes the material of our lives.[12] The same holds true for books, films, news, entertainment, and advertisements. The material we encounter—big and small, meaningful or mundane—becomes the stuff of our lives and the substance of our stories.

12. We must be careful, however, not to possess the voices of others in ways that deny or diminish their experience.

SUMMARY

Our quest to define pilgrimage has begun with a series of autobiographical stories, some of which counter the traditional image of pilgrimage as
a place-centered journey to a holy site. Moving my senior year speaks to
the changes, transitions, and interruptions of life. Cathy's committal service
explores questions of death and resurrection. The Silver Road story depicts
the sacred drama of Jesus' passion on a pedestrian journey in a foreign land
while celebrating a Good Friday birthday. The LA bus stop saga is about
one-off encounters with strangers, feeling out of place, and addressing personal fears and prejudices. The Auckland and Nadi airports and the Tennessee rest stop are settings of second-mile journeys made by strangers, friends,
and family. The Bossey reflection reminds us that emotions permeate our
lived experience, while the Camino voices interpret the human condition.
Missing from these stories are more ordinary tales, accounts of depravity
and tragedy, and overarching narratives of life.

We end the chapter by noting similarities between pilgrims, artists,
and storytellers. Artists have been described as those who capture the nuance of experience, making pilgrims artists of the earthly life.[13] Pilgrims
gaze at the world with awe and wonder, sculpt meaning from experience,
and savor special memories. Pilgrimage is the art of lived experience, which
is conveyed to others through the sharing of first-person stories.

13. See Block, *Community*, 2; Hjalmarson, *No Home*, 38; Niebuhr, "Pilgrims," 12.

3

Defining Pilgrimage

Pilgrimage is the experience of God, self, and the Other through time, place, journey, and people and the thoughts, images, and reflections thereof.

—A COMPREHENSIVE DEFINITION

WHISKEY GALORE

FOR A NUMBER OF years, I maintained that Christian pilgrimage couldn't be defined or that no one definition adequately described it.[1] My view was based on both studies and personal experience. Pilgrimage is a broad and diverse phenomenon; it's no one thing but a category of Christian expressions. Our understanding of the pilgrim life is generally too narrow, and when we talk about pilgrimage, we inevitably leave things out. Pilgrimage, moreover, contradicts itself. Whatever we say about pilgrimage, the opposite often holds true. There are certain, recognizable themes, but what holds the pilgrim life together? I was stuck on the thought that it couldn't be defined. Apropos of pilgrimage, it was a stranger who urged me on.

I have spent a considerable amount of time on the Orkney island of Papa Westray (Papay) in northern Scotland, where, during the winter of 2018, I was writing *Jerusalem Bound*, a pilgrim spirituality for Holy Land travel. While I had plenty to say about how to be a pilgrim in the Holy Land,

---

1. See Aist, "Pilgrim Traditions," 4.

I was not planning to define pilgrimage itself. During a film night featuring the 2016 remake of *Whiskey Galore* (1949), I had a brief conversation with a hosteler, a young Scottish lass traveling between jobs, who was spending a week on Papay. As I explained what I was doing, she became interested in how pilgrimage pertained to her own situation, when her curiosity triggered the inevitable question: "So, how do you define pilgrimage?" I offered my usual reply: "Well, it's a very broad subject. It can't really be defined." I could hear the inadequacy of the answer. When we have yet to tackle a task, the push often comes from a one-off encounter. True of the pilgrim journey, innocent questions can change our lives or, at least, our thinking.

To allow ourselves to be questioned is to become the questioner, and in the ensuing days, I found myself in pursuit of a definition. I had queries for colleagues and reviewed my thoughts on walks by the sea. Concepts emerged; language began falling in place. A preliminary version appears in *Jerusalem Bound*. *Pilgrim Spirituality* develops the framework. The book surveys the landscape, identifies concepts, and envisions possibilities. Perhaps, that's the point. Defining pilgrimage is less about what it *is* and more about what it *can be*.

THE BREADTH OF PILGRIMAGE

Pilgrimage evokes images of biblical, medieval, and contemporary practice, expressed in art, hymns, and literature and informed by personal experience.[2] It conjures up thoughts of temples, relics, and sacred tombs, Jerusalem, Rome, and the Celtic fringe. It's marked by departures, arrivals, destinations, and journeys. Pilgrims are long-distance travelers and restless wanderers, vagabonds, sojourners, and second-place people. They are migrants, refugees, and labyrinth walkers, pioneers, explorers, and wayfaring strangers. Pilgrims attend feasts and festivals and flee religious persecution. They are pious and penitent, gullible and godly, saints and sinners. People like you and me.

Pilgrimage is a crowded tent, and while we may instinctively know what it is, when we move from image to definition, it becomes more difficult to capture. Pilgrimage is an elusive phenomenon, consisting of an array of diverse expressions. What does Abraham's call to leave his homeland have in common with the Magi's journey to Bethlehem? Is a pilgrim a religious traveler or simply a stranger? What do Dante and *Pilgrim's Progress* have in common, and what can we learn from *The Canterbury Tales*? How does the

2. On medieval pilgrimage, see Sumption, *Pilgrimage*; Webb, *Medieval European Pilgrimage*; Webb, *Pilgrims*. Also see Davies, *Pilgrimage*; Bradley, *Pilgrimage*.

Camino de Santiago mirror the earthly journey? Pilgrimage is physical and metaphorical. It includes round trips, one-way journeys, and never leaving home. Time and memory are as important as place and journey. How can pilgrimage be captured in a single sentence?

My understanding of pilgrimage is significantly influenced by the example of others. Sister Giovanna Negrotto of Assisi spent years walking the streets of Italy helping those in need. "By being a pilgrim," she told me, "my heart learns to hear the cries of those who have no choice but to be pilgrims."[3] Pilgrimage is a crossroads between the privileged and the poor, between desperation and compassion. Sister Giovanna challenges our notion of pilgrimage at the same time that she redefines it: pilgrims are the displaced and those who help others in need.[4] Pilgrimage as the "street" sees Christ in the face of the Other.

Called to leave home and go to the land that God would show him, Abraham is the biblical archetype of the pilgrim life. Abraham's pilgrim identity is less about the physical movements and faith challenges of his life, significant though they were, and more about his status as a stranger. Abraham's calling was to live out of place, to obey God in a foreign land, to seek the sacred far from home. Abrahamic pilgrimage is about traversing the unknown; it is related to location, social relations, and our sense of home.

The English word *pilgrim* is ultimately derived from the Latin, *peregrinus*, meaning foreigner or stranger, which aligns with the Abraham story. Pilgrimage is a journey between alienation and reconciliation, vulnerability and hospitality, loneliness and belonging. Just as foreignness is central to the Abrahamic narrative,[5] nothing can advance contemporary applications of pilgrimage more than recapturing its sense of the Other.

Pilgrimage is an expansive expression of the Christian life. It is a one-way trek into the unknown and a return journey to a familiar place, an iteration of religious travel as well as a metaphor for the earthly life. It includes the streets and alleyways of everyday life and times set aside for personal reasons. What, *in a phrase*, is pilgrimage?

3. My conversations with Sister Giovanna, which are referenced throughout the book, took place in Assisi in December 1996. For an autobiography of her life, see Cambiaso, *I Sentieri Inesplorati*.

4. The distinctions are not mutually exclusive.

5. See Gen 12:1; Gen 23; Heb 11:8–19.

THE NATURE OF DEFINITIONS

We consult dictionaries, thesauruses, and etymologies to understand words, terms, and concepts, generally accepting them as objective pronouncements. Something *is*, and a definition defines it. Occasionally, we are dissatisfied with existing frames of reference, and we redefine things for ourselves, formulating understandings based upon personal experience, knowledge, and opinion.

Either way, definitions are not the objective statements we think they are, and my search, from the start, has two stipulations. I'm looking, first of all, for a comprehensive definition, one that covers the breadth of pilgrim expressions. Setting broad parameters may permit things that we would not otherwise associate with pilgrimage. I am interested, however, in what pilgrimage is or can be, less so, in what it's not. Secondly, I'm seeking a definition that facilitates pilgrimage as a transformative practice of the Christian life. The question is not whether the definition is right or wrong but whether it is up to the task.

Definitions are dynamic tools for examining phenomena, and we are interested in the *types* and *functions* of definitions. While our comprehensive statement will set the table, we need other definitions to sample the fare. There is also a difference between creating and using definitions. *Creating a definition* synthesizes what we know, or want to know. *Using a definition* allows us, in turn, to engage the unknown. Our interest is less about explicating pilgrimage than it is in exploring lived experience.

SCHOLARLY DEFINITIONS

Our commitment to Christian formation places our definitional pursuit on a slightly different track from scholarly approaches. Pilgrims, however, are consummate gleaners, harvesting insights from others, and pilgrim spirituality engages academic definitions. A survey of scholarly definitions, mostly from the field of anthropology, affirms our observation of the complexity of pilgrimage and the challenge of defining it. This is telling since scholars, for the most part, limit their notion of pilgrimage to religious travel to holy places,[6] whereas we are interested in a broader range of expressions, including Abrahamic pilgrimage and pilgrimage as "the street."

According to Juan Eduardo Campo, pilgrimage is "a set of ritual actions involving specific human communities, institutions, and organized

---

6. See Greenia, "What Is Pilgrimage?"

travel to and from sacred places."[7] For Peter Jan Margry, pilgrimage refers to "a journey based on religious or spiritual inspiration, undertaken by individuals or groups, to a place that is regarded as more sacred or salutary than the environment of everyday life, to seek a transcendental encounter with a specific cult object for the purpose of acquiring spiritual, emotional or physical healing or benefit."[8]

Scholars are forthright about the elusive nature of pilgrimage. According to Barry Stephenson, the contemporary study of pilgrimage reveals a diversity of opinion, and a "straightforward, broadly accepted definition of pilgrimage is difficult to find."[9] John Eade and Michael Sallnow, who argue that pilgrimage is a contested phenomenon, state that "if one can no longer take for granted the meaning of a pilgrimage for its participants, one can no longer take for granted a uniform definition of the phenomenon of 'pilgrimage' either."[10] Margry has written that the definition of pilgrimage is once again in need of re-evaluation. Even though pilgrimage has been "regained, localized, re-invented, contested, deconstructed, explored, intersected, reframed, etc. from a variety of academic perspectives," these approaches have not led to a "fully crystallized academic picture of the pilgrimage phenomenon."[11]

One challenge, especially for anthropologists who have traditionally studied bonded communities, or circumscribed social fields, is the extended, fluid nature of pilgrimage. Victor and Edith Turner address the complexity of pilgrimage systems:

> Some will doubt the propriety of extending the notion of a pilgrimage system to embrace the entire complex of behavior focused on the sacred shrine. But we insist, as anthropologists, that we must regard the pilgrimage system, whenever the data permit us so to do, as comprising all the interactions and transactions, formal or informal, institutionalized or improvised, sacred or profane, orthodox or eccentric, which owe their existence to the pilgrimage itself. We are dealing with something analogous to an organism–environment field: here the "organism" comprises all the sacred aspects of the pilgrimage, its religious goals, personnel, relationships, rituals, values and value-orientations, rules and customs; while the "environment" is the network of mundane "servicing mechanism"—markets,

7. Campo, "American Pilgrimage," 41.

8. Margry, *Shrines*, 17.

9. Stephenson, *Ritual*, 98.

10. Eade and Sallnow, *Contesting*, 3.

11. Margry, *Shrines*, 13.

hospices, hospitals, military supports, legal devices (such as passports), systems of communication and transportation, and so on—as well as antagonistic agencies, such as official or unofficial representatives of hostile faiths, bandits, thieves, confidence men, and even backsliders within the pilgrim ranks.[12]

There is a primary tension, even among scholars, between whether pilgrimage more properly concerns *the journey* or *the destination:* "whether the essence of pilgrimage is located in travel to a sacred place or primarily in the actions engaged in when there."[13]

Ian Reader's summary captures the multidimensional nature of pilgrimage:

> The journey can have both real and symbolic meanings: movement to a physical place and metaphorical journeying to a spiritual destination. Pilgrimage thus can be universal in meanings as well as highly localized. Within this framework pilgrimage can provide the setting for expressions of individual development and self-awareness along with group-related senses of togetherness and belonging, and yet also provide potential for contest and conflict. In such ways pilgrimage encompasses a wide variety of themes and meanings, frequently dependent upon individual interpretations and volition, that are sometimes (for instance, in simultaneously offering pilgrims scope for a sense of communal harmony and a means of expressing difference) contradictory.[14]

The complexity of pilgrimage becomes even more apparent once its metaphorical nature is acknowledged, as Reader does above. Alan Morinis allows that pilgrimage "seeks out a place not located in the geographical sphere." Since pilgrimage may be a personal enterprise rather than a social affair, the "one who journeys to a place of importance to himself alone may also be a pilgrim."[15] Metaphorical journeys and individualized expressions expand the boundaries of pilgrimage.

12. Turner and Turner, *Image*, 22.
13. Reader, *Pilgrimage*, 23.
14. Reader, *Pilgrimage*, 41.
15. Morinis, *Sacred Journeys*, 4.

CHARACTERIZING PILGRIMAGE

Along with definitional statements, we characterize phenomena, and pilgrimage is no exception. Stephenson proposes four definitional criteria—destination, distance, magnitude, and motivation—concluding that pilgrimage is "a prolonged event, involving travel away from local territory, undertaken by many people, to a sacred place, as an act of devotion, informed by religious motivation."[16] Reader argues that pilgrimage incorporates three main elements: (1) travel and movement, (2) veneration in some form, and (3) a special place or places considered to have some deep significance that makes them stand out from the ordinary world. Pilgrims are "people who travel to and perform acts of meaningful significance such as praying and performing rituals at and on the route to such special places."[17]

Victor and Edith Turner identify four types of pilgrimage: (1) *prototypical* pilgrimages, which are established by the founder of a historical religion; (2) *archaic* pilgrimages, also referred to as *syncretic* pilgrimages, which retain traces of the beliefs and ideas of earlier religions; (3) *medieval* pilgrimages, which originated roughly between 500–1400; and (4) *modern*, or *post-medieval*, pilgrimages, often associated with apparitions, visions, and miracles, including numerous Marian shrines, which are actually anti-modern in their worldview, devotion, and piety.[18]

Eade and Sallnow suggest a triad of criteria—place-centered, person-centered, and text-centered sacredness—for differentiating the nature of sacred centers, while Campo applies a threefold typology to American domestic pilgrimage: (1) pilgrimages associated with organized religion in the United States; (2) those linked to the values, symbols, and practices of American civil religion; and (3) those connected with cultural religion, such as Graceland and Disney World.[19]

In short, we can characterize pilgrimage using various criteria, including its essential elements, its sequential stages, and its types, or variations. Offering a theological perspective, Leonard Hjalmarson states that learning, participation, seeing, and place are the elements of pilgrimage, while later identifying them as "[r]oots, a journey, and a future destination in a story authored by God."[20] For us, pilgrimage is personal, corporate, incarnational, metaphorical, and tensional (see chapter 4). The different types of

16. Stephenson, *Ritual*, 98.

17. Reader, *Pilgrimage*, 41.

18. Turner and Turner, *Image*, 17–20.

19. Eade and Sallnow, *Contesting*, 6–9; Campo, "American Pilgrimage," 43–52.

20. Hjalmason, *No Home*, 29, 176.

pilgrimage, which I call templates, are discussed in chapter 5, while the stages of pilgrimage, variously conceived, are addressed later in the book.[21]

PILGRIMAGE THEORIES

Beyond characterizations, definitions, and typologies, three theories have emerged from the fields of anthropology and religious studies that address the relationship between pilgrimage and society. The first, known as the correspondence theory, or the Durkheimian, or structural, approach, sees pilgrimage as promoting a collective identity that mirrors society (e.g., a national or regional consciousness). Pilgrimage is a means of disseminating religious orthodoxy, supporting hierarchical structures of church and society, and even legitimizing the social inequalities of the status quo.

Opposed to the structural approach is the consensus theory of Victor and Edith Turner, which has dominated pilgrimage studies since the late 1970s.[22] The Turners argue that instead of reinforcing social structures, pilgrimage partially or completely abrogates it. Opposing the structures, roles, and authority of society, pilgrimage is anti-structural. The consensus aspect of the theory speaks to the quality of intragroup relations (i.e., communitas) that is formed within the anti-structural context of liminoid experience (see chapters 4 and 17).

The Turnerian theory, which makes universal claims about the nature of Christian pilgrimage, has been challenged by a third view, represented by John Eade and Michael Sallnow, who note that the recurrent theme in a number of studies is the maintenance and reinforcement of social boundaries and distinctions.[23] They distance themselves from the other two approaches—that pilgrimage either supports or subverts the established social order. Instead, they view pilgrimage as a realm of divergent discourses. Pilgrimage consists of competing social, cultural, and religious elements and engenders or intensifies forces of conflict.[24] It is a competitive phenomenon rather than one of consensus. Although the position of Eade and Sallnow is now largely accepted, the Turners' theory continues to dominate the general discourse on pilgrimage and is often the only one cited. While their work

21. See chapters 14 and 17.

22. See Turner and Turner, *Image*.

23. See Eade and Sallnow, *Contesting*, published in 1991, which is the most important work on the anthropology of Christian pilgrimage since Turner and Turner, *Image*, which come out in 1978.

24. Summarized in Campo, "American Pilgrimage," 43.

is indispensable to pilgrimage studies, the Turnerian theory should be used with clarity and caution.

In sum, there are three primary theories of pilgrimage with respect to societal relations:

(1) The Durkheimian approach, or correspondence theory, views pilgrimage as supporting and maintaining societal norms, regional and national narratives, and institutional power.

(2) The Turnerian model sees pilgrimage as the abrogation of social structures, or an anti-structural phenomenon, characterized by consensus within the pilgrim community.

(3) The position of Eade and Sallnow maintains that pilgrimage is a realm of multiple competing discourses.[25]

SIDESTEPPING AUTHENTICITY

Academic definitions—and definitional approaches in general—designate, delineate, quantify, and qualify. In doing so, they determine standards of authenticity, the real from the false, or, in our case, the genuine pilgrim from the inauthentic one, either implied or explicit. When it comes to pilgrim identity, external criteria are problematic. Who is the pilgrim among us? While the academic may need to know, the Christian practitioner decides for herself. Scholarship has a lot to offer, but at a definitional level, we need to be careful. Sidestepping standards of authenticity, we want to cultivate pilgrim identity, not restrict it. Pilgrim spirituality is more interested in *who we want to be* than in what others say we are.

FAMILY RESEMBLANCE THEORY

Having surveyed the scholarly discourse, we renew our quest for a comprehensive definition that facilitates Christian formation. To our point concerning the breadth of pilgrimage, we return to our previous observation: pilgrimage lacks a common denominator. The phenomenon is clearly associated with journeys, transitions, and movement; yet, there are biblical, historical, and contemporary expressions of pilgrimage in which the dimension of journey is past, dormant, or less pronounced than other dimensions. There are local sites, time-based expressions, and templates that focus on

---

25. See Eade and Sallnow, *Contesting*, 1–5, which outlines the theories.

the Other. Despite its ties with the pilgrim life, journey is not always it's most prominent feature.

If pilgrimage lacks a common denominator, how can we conceptualize it, let alone, hold it together? We do so through the use of the family resemblance theory, made popular by Ludwig Wittgenstein, which argues that "things which could be thought to be connected by one essential common feature may in fact be connected by a series of overlapping similarities, where no one feature is common to all of the things."[26] The theory is based on the example of biological families, whose members physically resemble each other without any one feature necessarily being held in common. Siblings may share a physical likeness despite lacking the same hair color, eye color, or facial characteristics. Although no one attribute is present in every person, they can still be identified as a related family.[27]

A common example is the concept of a sport, or a game, which refers to a wide range of activities from chess to football. Not all sports require excessive exertion or a high degree of athletic ability. There are significant differences between motor racing, fencing, weightlifting, and darts. Competition is not an element of every sport nor are all competitions sports. The resemblance theory has also been applied to the concept of jokes and the definition of art.[28]

The family resemblance theory works on the idea that a web of commonalities and overlapping patterns allows us to group things together. The theory has three notable points. First, despite the lack of a common denominator, there is a core set of common expressions and identifiable themes. Second, the phenomenon becomes frayed around the edges, where expressions may seem less connected to the family than those near the center. Third, the theory holds things together that belong to the same conversation. The theory is more interested in exploring relationships of commonality within a given phenomenon than it is in determining whether something is or is not a particular thing. Whereas strict definitions can stifle discourse, categorizing things by similarities and resemblances facilitates exploration while more aptly representing how we actually perceive the world.

26. The quote is a standard description of Wittgenstein's theory. See, for instance, Sussman, *Substance*, 29, 317. According to Wittgenstein, "we see a complicated network of similarities overlapping and criss-crossing." Wittgenstein, *Philosophical Investigations*, paragraph 66. Also see paragraphs 65–67.

27. Criticisms of the family resemblance theory include a false equivalency between kinship and resemblance, the subjective identification of similarities and differences, and its tendency to arbitrarily determine boundaries.

28. See Stephenson, *Ritual*, 73–74, who applies the theory to the definition of ritual.

The family resemblance theory facilitates our approach to the pilgrim life. First of all, it helps us *conceptualize* pilgrimage. Pilgrimage is not a single entity but a category of interrelated religious expressions. While there's a core set of themes and expressions, no one concept or feature defines it. Certain elements, such as journey, place, and stranger, are generally present, but they may be absent in a given expression.[29]

Second, the theory accounts for the *breadth and diversity* of pilgrimage. Identifying common patterns, similarities, and resemblances, it holds things together that relate to the pilgrim life, while recognizing that expressions on the edges may seem less pilgrimage-like than those near the center. Spiritual retreats, religious travel, and short-term missions have overlapping similarities. As time-based expressions of the pilgrim life, sabbaticals and periods of personal transition belong to the conversation. Coerced pilgrims are, nonetheless, pilgrims, and hospitality is a virtue of the pilgrim life.

Third, providing a dynamic yet flexible means of conceptualizing pilgrimage, the theory helps us, in turn, to *explore* the phenomenon. We are not seeking an authentic standard that determines what pilgrimage is or is not but a definitional lens for probing the pilgrim life.

A COMPREHENSIVE DEFINITION

We can now proceed towards a working definition employing the following criteria:

- Pilgrimage is a broad phenomenon requiring a comprehensive approach. We are not interested in a narrow definition that implicitly distinguishes between authentic and unauthentic forms of pilgrimage. We are after a broad statement that encompasses the pilgrim life.

- Casting a broad definition will inevitably capture things that we would not initially consider, yet belong to the conversation.

- While allowing room to critique certain expressions, the definition should implicitly appeal to biblical, historical, and contemporary images, thought, and practice.

- The definition should encompass both physical and metaphorical expressions.

---

29. Even if journey is considered a common denominator, the theory is a useful tool for conceptualizing pilgrimage.

- We are seeking a definition that facilitates Christian formation. While the definition may not appear, on the surface, to be overly inspiring, it should lay the ground for transformative Christian living.

In sum, we are seeking a definition that captures the breath of pilgrimage while retaining a sense of the familiar. It should be theologically robust in the simplest of terms with agency to interrogate the Christian life. Encompassing the spectrum of pilgrim expressions, the definition will appeal to central themes rather than a common denominator. Our working definition of pilgrimage is:

> **The experience of God, self, and the Other through time, place, journey, and people and the thoughts, images, and reflections thereof.**

The definition meets the aforementioned criteria: it is broad yet recognizable, conventional yet innovative. While taking biblical and historical expressions into account, it resources contemporary applications of the pilgrim life.

Our comprehensive definition is merely the beginning of our definitional framework. While additional definitions and characterizations will follow, we offer three initial comments. First, following the family resemblance theory, the definition should be read as the experience of God, self, *or* the Other through time, place, journey, *or* people. It is not necessary that *all* elements are present in a given expression. Secondly, the definition does not explicitly refer to the *sacred*; pilgrimage traverses both the sacred and the profane (see below). Third, while pilgrimage involves experience, thought, and reflection, its ultimate objective is the threefold union of God, self, and the Other.

TYPES OF DEFINITIONS

We turn, in more detail, to definitional types as they relate to our quest of the pilgrim life. One can take a *comprehensive* approach, as we've done so far, which tries to capture a phenomenon in a single statement. One could likewise *itemize* definitions, listing different meanings as separate entries, as we find in dictionaries. A simple itemization of pilgrimage could be construed as (1) physical travel with a religious purpose; (2) metaphorical journeys; and (3) the experience of being a stranger.[30]

30. As argued throughout the book, proper attention to the stranger, or the Other, transcends the traditional twofold approach to pilgrimage as physical journeys and metaphorical expressions.

A return journey to a holy place is commonly viewed as a core definition of pilgrimage. We consider it instead as a *type*, or *template*, of pilgrimage (see chapter 5). Pilgrimage templates include round-trip journeys to a holy site, one-way Abrahamic journeys, pilgrimage as the street, and forms of embodied prayer, to name but a few.

Definitions can be ostensibly *objective*, based upon external criteria, or *subjective*, reflecting someone's perspective or agenda. Either way, definitions should not impose standards of *authenticity* on the pilgrim life.

Results-oriented definitions focus on outcomes. The dilemma, of course, is that we do not know the results of an experience until it's over (and sometimes long after the fact). A key aspect of pilgrim spirituality is the *retrospective* application of definitions, or applying a pilgrimage lens to past experience, which may render newfound meaning to previous times in our lives.

While most of these figure in our framework, the essential supplement to our comprehensive statement are *aphoristic* definitions, which are quotable quotes construed from personal experience or borrowed from others. Expressions of pilgrim wisdom, aphorisms function, in turn, as interpretative frames of ensuing experience. Aphoristic definitions of pilgrimage are the focused, inspirational statements that pilgrims most commonly use.[31]

ADDITIONAL DEFINITIONS

Complementing our comprehensive approach, our framework employs an unrestricted number of additional definitions. The following statements, many of which are aphorisms, express the breadth, depth, and foci of pilgrimage:

- Pilgrimage is an intentional journey inspired by the s/Spirit.[32]

- Pilgrimage is a physical journey that is spiritually symbolic.

- Pilgrimage is an emotional journey with physical demands.

- Pilgrimage is traveling with purpose.

- Pilgrimage is wandering after God.[33]

- Pilgrimage is the conscious quest for spiritual attainment.

- The function of pilgrimage is to awaken the heart.

31. Aphorisms are properly introduced in chapter 5.

32. The word, s/Spirit, refers to both the human spirit and the divine Spirit.

33. Foster, *Sacred Journey*, xv.

- Pilgrimage is a journey from alienation to reconciliation, from emptiness to wholeness, from death to regeneration.

- Pilgrimage is a journey of religious imagination.
- It's the metaphorical exploration of the Christian life.
- Pilgrimage is the commemoration of sacred stories.
- It's the juncture of place and memory.
- Pilgrimage is extroverted mysticism.[34]
- Pilgrimage is embodied prayer.

- Pilgrimage is an open-eyed encounter, a dialogue of the senses.
- It's first-person embodied experience.
- To be a pilgrim is to see the world differently.

- Pilgrimage is seeking God in the particularity of place.
- It's experiencing God through the human Other.

- Pilgrimage is a special world journey.
- Pilgrimage takes us beyond ourselves into the unknown.
- Pilgrimage crosses thresholds, boundaries, and borders.

- Pilgrimage is participation in the unfolding mystery of life.
- Pilgrimage is an extended appointment with the extraordinary.
- Pilgrimage is creating openings in our lives for transformative
  experience.
- Pilgrimage is a sentence of surprise.

- Pilgrimage is time set aside for a particular purpose.
- To be a pilgrim is to engage life's most important questions; to be on
  pilgrimage is to await the answers.
- Between memory and hope, pilgrimage is what we do in the meantime.
- Pilgrims are accustomed to living in the meantime of an unfinished
  journey.

34. Turner and Turner, *Image*, 33.

- Pilgrimage is life intensified.

- Pilgrimage is a microcosm of life.

- Pilgrimage is an exercise in intentional decision-making.

- Pilgrimage is a study in self-management; it's the art of self-care.

- Pilgrims seek meaning beyond the mundane.

- They find God through the routines and practices of everyday life.

- Pilgrims are on the way, between and betwixt, neither here nor there.

- Pilgrimage is an exercise in perseverance, resilience, and internal fortitude.

- Pilgrimage is a physical manifestation of hope.

- Pilgrimage is the intentional practice of uncomfortable experience.

- It's the crossroads of vulnerability and resiliency.

- It's a spirituality of struggle; it's life on the margins.

- It's to journey with God through the valley of death.

- To be a pilgrim is to be out of place.

- Pilgrims are second-place people.

- Pilgrimage is the search for a place to belong.

- Pilgrimage is transformation through displacement.

- Pilgrimage is engaging the stranger.

- Pilgrimage is the imitation of Christ.

- Pilgrimage is a grace-filled journey in the rest of God.

While the World Council of Churches defines pilgrimage as "transformative journeys that are ultimately directed toward the reign of God," it's hard to do better than Richard R. Niebuhr, who describes pilgrims as "persons in motion passing through territories not their own, seeking something we might call completion, or perhaps the word clarity will do as well, a goal to which only the spirit's compass points the way."[35]

A number of *definitions* play upon perceived distinctions between pilgrims and tourists:

---

35. World Council of Churches, *Come and See*, 9; Niebuhr, "Pilgrims," 7.

- On vacation, one goes to get away from life; on pilgrimage, one confronts life's most important questions.

- Tourists change their environment; pilgrims let their environment change them.

- Tourists walk through the land, while pilgrims let the land walk through them.

- Pilgrimage has goals, risks, and challenges that we generally would not accept on holiday.

- Tourists escape life, pilgrims embrace it: "Tourists are trying to forget; pilgrims are trying to remember. . . . [Tourists] hate to be surprised. Pilgrims love to be surprised."[36]

These are half-truths at best, and we should be cautious about dualistic thinking.[37] Yet, as introspective frames, rather than definitions that we impose upon others, the pilgrim–tourist dichotomy can be particularly useful.[38]

While the tourist is disfavored, the artist is cherished. We've previously asserted that pilgrims are artists of lived experience. Niebuhr describes them as poets who create by taking journeys.[39] An expression of spiritual aesthetics, pilgrimage is the pursuit of truth, goodness, and beauty. To apply the metaphor of art to our method, our comprehensive definition is the palette of possibilities, while aphoristic statements color the canvas.[40]

THE SACRED AND THE PROFANE

The Entirety of Our Lives

As previously mentioned, our comprehensive definition does not presume that the sacred is a requisite of pilgrimage. Rather, pilgrimage denotes *all* experience of God, self, and the Other, both unique and ordinary, positive, negative, and in-between. Pilgrimage is the entirety of our lives, including both good and bad moments, high and low places, wise and foolish deeds. It

36. Hjalmarson, *No Home*, 45.

37. According to Turner and Turner, "a tourist is half a pilgrim, if a pilgrim is half a tourist." Turner and Turner, *Image*, 20.

38. See Aist, *Jerusalem Bound*, 37–46. On academic distinctions between pilgrims and tourists, see, for example, Cohen, "Pilgrimage" and "Who Is a Tourist?"

39. Niebuhr, "Pilgrims," 12.

40. Theater likewise offers metaphors for exploring the earthly life, as Shakespeare does in his "All the World's a Stage" monologue in *As You Like It*, Act 1, Scene 7.

is a *journey*, so where we are, where we've been, and where we are going are all a part of the pilgrim life.

While our goal is the union of God, self, and the Other, pilgrimage takes into account the human condition. Pilgrims are sinners, lost and weary, down and out, confused, and bewildered. Temptation, harm, and danger lurk in the shadows. Just as Jesus encountered Satan in the wilderness, to be a pilgrim is to deal with the devil.

At the same time, God covers the surface of our lives. God is not a segment of the journey, only accessible from certain peaks and plateaus. Rather, God is an all-encompassing, accompanying presence who patrols the fields, streams, and byways of our lives. A word picture of divine pilgrimage, God as Good Shepherd searches for those who have gone astray. God's reach extends beyond what we presume to be holy.

The Sacred and The Secular

The assertion that pilgrimage is not limited to the sacred turns our attention to two related concepts: (1) the sacred and the secular and (2) the sacred and the profane. The sacred–secular approach, or Christ against culture, tends to divorce God from everyday experience, establishing a rigid partition between the church and the world, between what is considered godly and what is not explicitly holy.[41] What's religious is of God; what's secular is ungodly, evil, and worldly. The secular is irredeemable, while the sacred has eternal value. The sacred–secular perspective espouses a heightened sense of the holiness of God, while placing a hedge around sin. In effect, however, it diminishes the goodness of God's creation, the expanse of God's reign, the dynamic possibilities of change, and God's transformational work in the world. The position of Christ against culture is a reactive, often fear-based response to a Christian life that largely withdraws from the world.

The Sacred as Something Set Apart

While pilgrim spirituality distances itself from sacred–secular thinking, the sacred–profane dichotomy offers an effective theological frame. The profane is not a synonym for evil but refers to the ordinary. At worse, it speaks to primordial chaos, which contains the emergent possibilities of life. The classic Durkheimian definition defines the sacred as something set apart.

41. See Niebuhr, *Christ*, 45–82.

What is not set apart—i.e., the profane—is everything else.[42] We set things apart when we dedicate something or consecrate someone. A layperson is ordained to the priesthood. Holy days and holidays are set aside from ordinary time. A sacred place is set apart from ordinary space. A pilgrimage becomes sacred by virtue of breaking away from everyday life. As the opposite of things set apart, the profane is the ordinary, the commonplace, the mundane.

Building upon Durkheim's understanding of the sacred, Mircea Eliade describes the profane as absolute non-being. The profane is limitless chaos; the sacred is cosmos. For Eliade, only the sacred has meaning.[43] The profane is penetrated in places by hierophanies, or manifestations of the sacred, creating sacred centers, which are subsequently regarded as meeting places between heaven and earth. While pilgrims share Eliade's interest in sacred centers, they are cognizant of God's presence in the chaos, that the profane is part and parcel of our lives, having meaning before and after the irruptive acts of God.

Notions of the sacred also include Rudolf Otto's concept of the numinous, which he describes as a fearful and fascinating mystery (*mysterium tremendum et fascinans*).[44] The sacred is the wholly Other, evoking terror and power as well mercy, grace, and potential charm. The numinous is the pilgrim's experience of the sacred chamber, the holy mountain, and the inexplicable encounter with God. While it's nice to have some numinous, pilgrimage is largely a non-numinous journey.

The Sacred and the Profane

The sacred and the profane, or the ordinary and the set apart, provide a useful lens for engaging the Christian life. The concept is exemplified by our weekday experience of God. We can agree that Tuesday mornings hold possibilities for transformational encounters. The question is how do we frame it. While a weekday event may be sacred—I was married on a Tuesday morning—does it make the context holy? It is, in other words, still Tuesday. To rephrase the question, is a divine encounter sacred by definition, or does the context of Tuesday morning, the epitome of ordinary time, allow us to speak in terms of a *profane* encounter with God? Can something be spiritual and profane at the same time? Does a spirituality of ordinary experience

---

42. In Durkheim, *Elementary Forms*, 51. Things set apart as sacred are not necessarily good. Rituals may have good or evil intentions. Places may be set aside to do harm.

43. See Eliade, *Sacred*, 62–65.

44. See Otto, *Idea*.

strive to make all things sacred, or does it seek to find God in the common-place moments of life? Both views are valid, and the essence of theological exploration is not about what's *correct* per se; rather, it concerns the multi-faceted use of language, concepts, tools, and lenses to probe, perceive, and enhance our life with God.

Far from limiting our experience of God, self, and the Other, the sa-cred and the profane provides a dynamic frame for perceiving the world. Pilgrims see spiritual opportunities in every situation. They approach all circumstances as a possible encounter with God. Just as God inhabits the fullness of time, God is found in all types of places—high and low, near and far. The pilgrim life becomes significantly richer when sacred places are only one means of relating spatially to God.

The profane doesn't denote the negation of spiritual encounters; rather, it speaks to the context in which they occur, namely, through time, places, and people that have not been set apart. The pilgrim life is more richly tex-tured when we envision God's presence in both the commonplace and the consecrated, in both the ordinary and the sacred. Pilgrimage is a theology of multiple perspectives.

The God of Mundane Moments

Pilgrimage may be an extended appointment with the extraordinary, but the mundane is seldom missing. The pilgrim life takes hold as we learn to hear music in the noise, foster mystery in the fog, and find surprise in the surplus of everyday life. Pilgrimage is the art of allowing the drab and the driech to be transformed into the contraband of religious experience. The secret of pilgrimage is the ability to find meaning in the ordinary and to elevate the everyday to realms of spiritual encounter.

Life, at times, is worse than ordinary, and the prosaic appears as para-dise. Pilgrimage speaks to the trials, hardships, and devastations of life. It's a spirituality of struggle. Yet, pilgrimage bears witness that God penetrates the darkness, rescuing and redeeming, turning defeat into victory, death into life. As it unfolds, we see rainbows through raindrops and experience resurrection through tears. Omitting the sacred as a requisite of pilgrim experience recognizes that our earthly journey covers all types of spiritual landscapes and that the potentiality of divine encounter is never limited by the circumstances of our lives.

The Liturgical Calendar

Regulated by daily, weekly, and annual cycles of sacred and ordinary time that commemorate the events of salvation, pilgrims find meaning in the ordering of the hours, in feasting and fasting, and in the religious seasons of the Christian Year. From advent to Pentecost, the liturgical calendar reflects the movements of a pilgrim God who is variously near and far, present and absent, with us yet on the way, ascended yet posed to return. Adding memory and meaning to our Christian journey, the calendar reminds us that we experience God in a variety of contexts, moods, and situations, both sacred and profane.

Sacred Cautions

There are cautions, however, to viewing the world through the prism of the sacred and the profane. While we experience the Holy Spirit in ordinary times, familiar places, and routine situations, God's presence is more immense than we ever can imagine. The pilgrim journey causes us to rethink our understandings of God, recognizing that much of what we have considered to be ordinary and indistinct has been sacred from the start. On the other hand, although we think we know what's sacred, God continually surprises us, showing us time and again that the divine is neither contained by our sanctuaries nor restrained by our sense of the holy. Even worse, we marginalize what God has honored, and we need spiritualities, such as pilgrimage, to perceive the world with different eyes. Striving towards union with God, self, and the Other, pilgrims seek meaningful experiences that fall outside the norms of what is conventionally considered to be holy. More generally, dualistic thinking depicts a world lacking nuance and complexity, and dichotomies, such as the sacred and the profane, should be used as frames of perception rather than assertions of the world itself. In sum, (1) pilgrimage includes *all* aspects of our earthly journey from departure to arrival; it is neither limited nor circumscribed by the sacred; (2) pilgrimage expands our sense of God's presence in the world, which extends to the ordinary, the commonplace, and the mundane; and (3) finally, pilgrimage helps us see what's been sacred all along.

4

Characterizing Pilgrimage

Complementing our definitional statement, we characterize pilgrimage as personal, corporate, incarnational, metaphorical, and tensional.

PILGRIMAGE IS PERSONAL

Pilgrimage is first-person experience, viewed through a first-person perspective. Pilgrimage is a spirituality of sensuous perceptions, visceral experience, cognitive awareness, emotions, thoughts, and reflections. We see with our own eyes, walk in our own shoes. We share scenes with others but filter the world through a personal lens. Pilgrimage happens when experience becomes our own, when book is embodied, when the otherwise becomes firsthand.

Our life stories differ is striking ways, shaped by events, incidents, and accidents, contexts, circumstances, choices, and obligations that are unique to each individual. We have our own passions and preferences, weaknesses and limitations, skills, gifts, and talents. Our earthly journey is conditioned by age, gender, health, personality, family, culture, and ethnicity.

Autobiography is our personal interpretation of passing through the world. While doctrinal approaches, hierarchical ecclesiologies, and biblical literalism are suspicious of individual authority, personal experience, and self-interpretation, pilgrim spirituality recognizes the interpretative agency of the individual. The point exemplifies the tensional nature of pilgrimage: each person is an individual expert of the pilgrim life; yet, Christianity, with its emphasis on tradition, community, and biblical authority, contests the idea of the autonomous individual.[1]

Pilgrimage explores the seas, but it's not without its moorings. Anchored by the Holy Spirit, pilgrims adhere to the wisdom of Scripture, give heed to tradition, and rely upon reason. They seek the influence of community, the presence of companionship, and the counsel of others.

While life assumes a first-person perspective, our journeys are seldom our own. Pilgrim spirituality does not begrudge "me and my Jesus" moments; rather, it steers them towards the common good. Pilgrims share their stories of faith. They translate experience into wisdom. They put their faith into action, attending to the needs of others. They mentor through example, offering hope and encouragement as imitators of Christ. Pilgrimage is an interpersonal journey.

PILGRIMAGE IS CORPORATE

The individual pilgrim is a lonely figure, progressing, perhaps, but ultimately incomplete. Christians are called on a collective journey, and church occurs when, called by grace, sinners gather in the name of God. Christians are a sacred people, committed to a corporate life with God, which is envisioned as the pilgrim church and the body of Christ and expressed through various forms of short and long-term community.

The Pilgrim Church

The metaphor of the pilgrim church is sourced from biblical images. As Noah's Ark, the church is the sanctuary of God's people afloat on turbulent waters, a depiction that tends to convey a separatist understanding of the church.[2] Wandering through the desert, crossing the Jordan River, and entering the land of milk and honey have become metaphorical, liturgical, and eschatological images of and about the church. Viewed through the lens of the Exodus narrative, the pilgrim church is a work in progress, on its way between Egypt and the promised land. The pilgrim church is also expressed as the people of God marching towards Zion, a word picture that culminates

---

1. According to Hastings, "The Christian concept of a human person is not that of an autonomous individual, and especially that of the Western Cartesian notion of the self . . . [but] the notion of a human as person-in-community." Hastings, *Missional God*, 98.

2. The features of an ark are expressed in church architecture. Nave, for instance, is Latin for ship (*navis*).

in the gathering of the nations in New Jerusalem. Augustine associates the movement of the church with the city of God.[3]

The Body of Christ

The root word of corporate (corpus) is body, and Christian pilgrims are members of the body of Christ:

> For just as the body is one and has many members, and all the members of the body, though many, are one body, so it is with Christ. . . . Indeed, the body does not consist of one member but of many. . . . [T]he members of the body that seem to be weaker are indispensable, and those members of the body that we think less honorable we clothe with the greater honor. . . . If one member suffers, all suffer together with it; if one member is honored, all rejoice together with it. Now you are the body of Christ and individually members of it. (1 Cor 12:12–14, 22–27)

The pilgrim life is corporate, reciprocal, and responsive. As members of Christ's body, we are diverse yet interconnected. We serve and receive as we need.

A Journey towards Interdependence

Pilgrimage is a journey towards interdependence; yet, for much of the way, pilgrims depend upon others. Our pathways are largely determined by what others have done, by those who have gone before us, the authors and founders of our faith. We rely upon the wisdom of our ancestors, upon family, elders, and mentors. The spiritual journey is a relay of faith, passed down and handed on, which is the meaning of tradition. Pilgrims also depend upon guides, hosts, and strangers.

A paradox of interdependence is that it is best achieved by independent people. According to Stephen Covey, interdependence is a higher value then independence, but interdependence is a choice that only independent people can make. Interdependence is also more difficult to achieve. Personal and spiritual maturity is a progressive continuum from (1) dependency to (2) responsible independence to (3) effective interdependence. Dependence is the paradigm of *you*, which focuses upon another person. I need *you* to take care of me, or, conversely, I blame you for what happened.

3. See Augustine, *City of God* and Wetzel, *Augustine's City*. On the pilgrim church as an emphasis of Vatican II, see Mannion, "Pilgrim Church," 115–35.

Independence is the paradigm of *I*, or the self. I can do it. I can choose. I am responsible and self-reliant. Interdependence is the paradigm of *we*. It is cooperation and collaboration, the act of combining our collective experience, skills, and insight to create or achieve something with others that we can't otherwise do on our own.

Since interdependence is frequently confused with dependence, independence is often assumed to be the desired goal, and our quest for independence—to act rather than be acted upon—is driven, especially in the West, by societal attitudes against dependency. Yet, as Covey points out, interdependence is a more advanced state of being. Interdependent people are able to share themselves more deeply and meaningfully with others, while having access to the presence, gifts, and resources of their colleagues and companions.[4]

Short-Term Pilgrimage

The corporate character of Christian pilgrimage is expressed through various forms of short-term community.

Communitas

The scholarly discourse concerning the interpersonal dynamics of traditional forms of pilgrimage has been dominated by Victor Turner's theory of communitas, which he defines as "a relational quality of full, unmediated communication, even communion, between people of definite and determinate identities, which arises spontaneously in all kinds of groups, situations, and circumstances."[5] Turner argues that communitas spontaneously occurs in the liminoid context of pilgrimage.

To understand Turner's concept of communitas, we begin with the work of Arnold van Gennep (1873–1957), a French ethnographer and folklorist, who observed that rites of passage in traditional societies follow a threefold process: separation, margins, and reintegration.[6] Employing the

---

4. See Covey, *7 Habits*, 56–59.

5. Turner and Turner, *Image*, 250. Victor Turner used the term *communitas* instead of community to distinguish the modality of social relationships from an area of common living. Since his work on communitas and liminality predates *Image*, co-authored with his wife, Edith Turner, we will attribute the theories to Victor Turner. See the bibliography, though, for works by Edith Turner.

6. Written in French, van Gennep's *The Rites of Passage* (1909) was first published in English in 1960.

metaphor of a threshold, or limen, van Gennep also refers to the stages as pre-liminal (separation), liminal (margins), and post-liminal (reintegration) transitions. Turner, who specialized in ritual studies, applied van Gennep's theory to pilgrimage, focusing on the middle stage—the margins—which lies between separation (departure) and reintegration (return). Located in time and space between the world one has left and the one yet to come, the margins are described by Turner as the "betwixt and between" and "the neither here nor there."[7] He uses the word, liminoid (liminal-like), instead of liminal, however, to describe the middle phrase of pilgrimage largely because rites of passage in traditional societies are compulsory and absolute, whereas Christian pilgrimage is a voluntary, open-ended experience.

Communitas, in a word, is what happens relationally in the margins. It's the intimate sense of sharing that develops between people during the liminoid stage of pilgrimage. The bonds of communitas are "undifferentiated, egalitarian, direct, extant, nonrational, existential, and 'I–Thou' (in Buber's sense)." Communitas is spontaneous, immediate, and concrete.[8]

Communitas strains toward consensus, homogeneity, universalism, and openness; "what is sought and what happens is unity, seamless unity."[9] The individual is liberated from the constraints of societal norms; she is shorn from her past identity, forming spontaneous bonds with fellow participants. Members of communitas experience "joy, healing, the gift of 'seeing,' mutual help, religious experience, the gift of knowledge, long-term ties with others, a humanistic conscience, and the human rights ideal."[10]

On pilgrimage:

> Friends are made and a sense of sacredness grows as the days of travel go by. The religion and the forward urging of the people, often in collective prayer, together produce an elated sense of sisterhood among all, something that draws pilgrims to come again year after year. While the pilgrimage situation does not eliminate structural divisions, it attenuates them and removes their sting. Moreover, pilgrimage liberates the individual from the obligatory everyday constraints of status and role, defines her as an integral human being with a capacity for free choice, and within the limits of her religious orthodoxy presents for her a living model of human sisterhood and brotherhood.[11]

7. See Turner, "Betwixt and Between."
8. Turner and Turner, *Image*, 250. Also see Edith Turner, "Communitas," 97.
9. Edith Turner, "Communitas," 99.
10. Edith Turner, "Communitas," 99.
11. Edith Turner, "Communitas," 99.

In sum, communitas (1) occurs within a liminal or liminoid context, (2) has an anti-structural quality (whereas society, or the ordinary world, represents structure), and (3) consists of relational expressions of consensus, equalitarianism, and unity that stand in contrast to the structures, divisions, and hierarchies of society.[12]

Turner's theory of pilgrimage as an anti-structural phenomenon that produces communities of consensus has been challenged by a number of scholars, most notably John Eade and Michael Sallnow, who contend that conflict is endemic to pilgrimage.[13] Whereas Turner argues that pilgrimage abrogates existing barriers, Eade and Sallnow, who underscore that Turner's theory is unsupported by subsequent research, view pilgrimage as a contested phenomenon. At best, communitas is an ideal that may occasionally occur.

The scholarly debate over communitas raises questions regarding the communal dynamics of corporate pilgrimage. What is the nature of intragroup relations? How does pilgrimage change or reenforce the way groups perceive themselves? To what extent do pilgrim groups engage or separate themselves from others? Does corporate pilgrimage reinforce stereotypes of the Other, or does it transform how Christians interact with the world?

Short-Term Christian Community

Those who have been on group pilgrimage or have experienced the flow of social relations on the Camino de Santiago often testify to the nature of pilgrim community in communitas-like terms, and for many, the quality of human relationships—spontaneous, intense, intimate, and equalitarian— is one of the primary appeals of pilgrimage. While pilgrim spirituality is sympathetic to communitas, the theory, as we've noted, is contested. We can hold communitas as an *ideal* that speaks to the quality of human interactions within a liminoid context, but it doesn't provide us with a general descriptor of pilgrim community.

Christians, in any case, should have their own understandings of the corporate nature of pilgrimage. We do so with the prosaically-named concept of short-term Christian community.[14] Common to group pilgrimage,

12. Turner and Turner, *Image*, 252–55 discusses the three types of communitas: (1) spontaneous, or existential communitas, (2) normative communitas, and (3) ideological communitas.

13. See Eade and Sallnow, *Contesting*.

14. While the discussion concerns the intentionality of short-term community, we refrain from using the term *intentional community* to describe the phenomenon. Intentional community speaks to the aspired quality of both short-term and long-term forms of Christian community.

short-term mission trips, summer camps, church retreats, and ecumenical communities, short-term Christian community is a temporary expression of communal life, generally one to two weeks in length, sometimes less or longer, that serves as both a means and locus for transformative Christian experience.

Gathered, Set Apart, and Dispersed

Short-term Christian community brings participants together and sets them apart for a common purpose, creating a sense of sacred time, place, and people with temporal limitations.[15] Short-term community is formed by the act of gathering; shared experience occurs through time spent together (e.g., through the program, cause, or common activity), and the community is permanently dissolved through dispersal or reintegration, which participants commonly grieve.

Short-term Christian community is especially dynamic when it consists of a culturally diverse group of people who are initially strangers, which is characteristic of open programs sponsored by retreat centers, ecumenical communities, travel operators, and host institutions. While such groups will inevitably consist of people who are attached to other participants (e.g., couples and colleagues), individual pilgrims are especially well-positioned to participate in the common life, making relational connections with others. Sacred bonds quickly develop, and by the end of the experience, goodbyes can be particularly difficult as newfound friends depart and short-term relations become long-distance connections. Indeed, the nature of gathered communities is that they ultimately *disperse*. This is advantageous to disseminating ideas, training, and perspectives; yet, it means that individual participants return home to remember and apply the experience on their own.

By contrast, programs that originate from home, such as congregational trips and retreats, generally consist of people who are already know each other or, at least, have common connections. Relationships are likewise forged and strengthened in transformational ways. The advantage of locally-formed groups is the continuation of interpersonal relations and the collective effect of the experience after the program is over. *Together*, the group takes the experience home, where it is remembered, relived, and

15. The degree to which short-term communities are set apart from the world varies. Regardless, additional people contribute to the group's experience, including speakers, tour guides, bus drivers, institutional staff, service providers, local residents, other pilgrims, tourists, and travelers.

incorporated into the common life of the larger body (e.g., the congregation), ideally benefitting the community as a whole.

FORMALIZED OR FLUID

Another distinction concerns the degree to which participation is formalized or fluid. Formalized, or bounded, communities are those in which
participants can be numbered, listed, or identified—e.g., those who have
registered or those on the bus. Some communities have more porous
boundaries than others. Taizé, for example, hosts thousands of pilgrims at a
time; small groups are formed but participation is fluid and voluntary.

While organized groups walk the Camino de Santiago, the journey
is best experienced as an unattached individual, a couple, or an informal
small group. Along the way, pilgrims form intense but tenuous communities that ebb and flow on a daily basis based upon various factors from
people's walking pace to the availability of overnight accommodations.
Walking the Camino on my own, I experienced sustained phases of group
cohesion. I also had stretches without identifiable companions, socializing
mostly through one-off encounters. The communal nature of the Camino,
especially at day's end, is one of its most endearing features, while its fluidity
renders the unexpected boon of reencountering friends previously made
along the way. Although the dynamics of short-term community accords
well with the Camino experience, which is often experienced in communitas-like terms, the open nature of its common life is different from more
bounded expressions, such as church retreats, short-term mission trips, and
Holy Land travel.

THREE DEGREES OF EXPERIENCE

Short-term Christian communities commonly integrate three concurrent
experiences: that of the large-group, the sub-group, and the individual. A
family camp that I worked with for over twenty-five years is a case in point.
Offering traditional activities in an intergenerational context, the camp focuses on the family unit (the sub-group), while emphasizing the experience
and achievements of the individual camper. It does this, for instance, by encouraging adults, who are regarded as campers, to participate in the activities along with their kids, from crafts and candles to high ropes and horses.
Yet, what distinguishes family camp from other vacations is the large-group
experience, which can only, or most effectively, occur within the context
of an intentional community. Participation in the large group provides a

quality of experience and a sense of belonging that transcends both the self and the family unit: evening campfires, skit nights, and mealtime singing, coin hunts, regulated pranks, and random acts of kindness, listening to loons and watching falling stars together with others on the dock.

The same dynamics pertain to group pilgrimage in the Holy Land, particularly with open courses, like those I've taught at St George's College which are comprised of a mixture of individuals, couples, and parish groups. Holy Land pilgrimage is a personal encounter with biblical places, a first-person experience of God, self, and the Other. The large group experience consists of shared meals, bus rides, and site visits, common prayer, lectures, debriefings, and worship that transcends the sum of its parts. Just as pre-existing sub-groups (couples, colleagues, and church groups) experience deepened interpersonal relations among themselves, newly-formed networks are created throughout the course. Groups linger together at a holy site, sit around the dinner table, and enjoy late night conversations. Although short-term communities are not immune from divisive cliques, sub-groups, which are responsible, in turn, to the larger group, are a sacred component of corporate pilgrimage.

Sharing and Caring

Short-term communities foster compassion, empathy, and reciprocal care. Members attend to the needs of fellow pilgrims, offering encouragement, helping out, giving others a hand. Facilitating connections, conversations, and friendships, the experience of short-term community is one of shared emotions and interpersonal relations.

Short-term community is marked by laughter. The intensity of common life creates intragroup experience that becomes the subject of humorous imitation and the fodder of organized skit nights. The joy of short-term community is expressed through parody, while the sadness of dispersal is felt through the realization that the shared jokes and jargon of the group, which develop over the life of a community, no longer have a context for expression.

A Transient Sacrament

Provisionally embodying the kingdom of God, each iteration of short-term community is a unique, one-off experience. If pilgrimage is a quest for permanence, one of the ironies of the spiritual life is that brevity heightens our sense of the sacred. Short-term community is a transient sacrament of the kingdom of God.

LEADING SHORT-TERM COMMUNITIES

Short-term community formation is fostered in both implicit and intentional ways, which may include discussions at the beginning of a program on the nature of short-term community, the challenges of common life, covenantal responsibilities, and the transformative identity of being a sacred people on pilgrimage. While establishing the tone, parameters, and expectations of a group is important, setting rules is a balancing act. How much time should be spent on rules, instructions, and safety information, and how should they be conveyed? How permissive or restrictive should they be? How will conflict be resolved? Some rules are established by leaders, institutions, and guest houses, while behavioral expectations, whether specified or not, are generally determined by the group.

Short-term community responds best to visible, accessible leadership whom participants feel at ease approaching with needs, questions, and concerns. While leadership teams can be effective, having a single, recognized leader is generally preferred. As the visible face of the group, leaders of short-term communities are not ceremonial figureheads but the ones with direct decision-making authority (e.g., the teacher, the leader, the guide). Behind the scenes, leading short-term community requires proficiency in the details and objectives of the program.

Pilgrimage leaders are entrusted with a formidable responsibility: the curation of people's experience, which, in terms of religious travel, is often accompanied with "once-in-a-lifetime" expectations. Vital to the task is the efficient execution of the program: determining times of departure, pacing the visitation of sites, balancing group and personal time, ensuring timely comfort breaks, beginning meals on time, and navigating busy days with a steady sense of calm. Whether the context is a retreat, a mission trip, or educational travel, leading short-time communities is about setting the tone, managing time, and making decisions. Leaders should be flexible but decisive, sensitive, patient, and compassionate, with an affirming sense of humor.

Leading short-term groups requires the timely sharing of clear and concise information—at meal times, on the bus, at the end of a session— that conveys the ongoing what, when, and where of the program. Retreats, camps, and travel programs proceed incrementally—the next session, the next site, the next day's activities—and participants rely upon timely, thorough, and updated information. What does one need to know and know *now*? Where does one need to be and *when*? What should one expect or be thinking about in the meantime?

Along with repeated updates, communications include reminding the group of big-picture objectives, addressing the ebbs and flows of the pilgrim experience, offering encouragement, acknowledging individual achievements and celebrations, and delivering difficult news. Handling intimations, celebrations, and empathetic moments, performing symbolic and ritual gestures, conveying big-pictures ideals and attending to behind-the-scenes details are not only leadership tasks, they are keys to community formation.

Creating short-term community should be intentional but not coerced. While participation in a group experience necessitates certain restrictions on individual freedom, community thrives when people are given personal, theological, and cultural space—a sense of sanctuary for personal comfort, room for individual expression, permission for solitary exploration. Valuing the active participation of everyone, transformative short-term communities allow individuals to freely engage—or disengage—in the small group and large group components of the program. This may obligate a participant's physical presence; yet, respecting personal, cultural, and theological space, giving time to the process, being comfortable in silence, and leaving people prayerfully alone are marks of a mature, if short-term, community.

In sum, short-term community is a transformative expression of the Christian life. Camps develop the social self. Retreats foster fellowship with God, and religious travel takes community out into the world. While common life is challenging, short-term Christian community is a corporate expression of the *already* in *not yet* times. Grounded in the values of the kingdom of God, it's a communal foretaste of heaven on earth.

REVISITING COMMUNITAS

As an intentional approach to group experience, short-term Christian community has been largely overlooked in both concept and name. While communitas remains a theoretical ideal, short-term Christianity community has tangible qualities, from its threefold levels of experience to its leadership requisites. Even so, short-term Christian community is sympathetic to the interpersonal qualities of communitas. Pilgrimage fosters quick, free-forming bonds between people. Structures of the ordinary world have been temporarily suspended, and social hierarchies have been somewhat flattened. Our personalities emerge, while being defined by our past, or who we are at home, recedes to the background. Community is based upon present conditions rather than past considerations, but there are limitations to the equalitarian ideals of communitas. A suspended sense of personal status or a flattened hierarchy may mean that we see leaders in blue jeans, have conversational access to ecclesiastical authorities, or share blistered feet with figureheads; however, roles, status, identities, and prejudices are never fully swept aside, and pilgrim community may reflect rather than erase home-grown inequalities. That said, short-term Christianity community offers both the means and settings of life-affirming interactions that can permanently change our lives.

Pilgrimage as Group Identity

Communitas aside, a common function of pilgrimage is the formation and reinforcement of group identity. The staff retreat, the annual meeting, and the family reunion respectively foster a sense of cohesion, shared values, and common purpose. Pilgrimage as group identity can be positive, negative, or relatively neutral depending upon the views and values of the group. Our particular interest is how groups define themselves vis-à-vis others. While some espouse universal values, other groups derive their identity over and against the Other, sometimes in explicitly divisive ways. The Orange walks in Ireland and Scotland, for instance, are public, inciteful, and often violent expressions of Protestant identity fueled by anti-Catholic bigotry. In short, how do corporate expressions of pilgrimage reinforce intragroup narratives, especially with respect to the Other? Is pilgrim identity shaped by who we are, or by who and what we're not?

Corporate pilgrimage can foster group identity in positive ways. Religious travel often focuses on heritage journeys, and "return to the roots" experiences are prevalent expressions of denominational pilgrimage. Methodists visit the sites of John Wesley; Anglicans tour the cathedrals of England; the Reformed follow in the footsteps of Calvin. With a goal of enhancing cohesion back home, pilgrimage as group identity functions as a supplementary expression of long-term community.

While parish travel may be benign, we must be attentive to the values they convey. Religious travel can reinforce group-held prejudices and shared stereotypes of the Other, especially when contested landscapes, like the Holy Land, are involved. Pilgrimage is an exercise in narrative formation, which often occurs at the expense of the religious, political, or cultural Other. How is pilgrimage used to dismantle—or reinforce—colonial practices, racial stereotypes, and sectarian attitudes? Pilgrims should continually critique the values and actions of the groups they are in, evaluating explicit behaviors, implicit messaging, paternalistic attitudes, and off-hand statements, recognizing that narratives often operate in subtle, unrecognized, and unintended ways.

Identity-based pilgrimage is sometimes open to outside participants, as is generally the case with sites of conscience, which use place and memory to recognize past injustices, promote human rights, and create a better tomorrow.[16] The Minidoka pilgrimage is an annual event held at a former WWII Japanese-American internment camp in Idaho. The purpose of the pilgrimage is to remember, honor, and educate. For Japanese-American participants, it is an exercise in remembrance and healing, personal history, and group identity, while its educational program promotes participatory dialogue with the general public. Pilgrimage offers a dynamic means of engaging the stranger, crossing boundaries, breaking down barriers, and listening to the stories of others, which is not to say that every expression needs to focus on extra-group concerns.

In short, pilgrimage is an effective means of fostering intragroup identity. While this can be done in positive ways, the messaging of group pilgrimage should be continually evaluated. Even in subtle ways, pilgrimage can "other" the Other (see chapter 10).

Long-term Christian Community

Besides the special occasions of short-term community, we are called to be a sacred people on a lifelong journey committed to a corporate experience of God. We return to the image of the pilgrim church. The Exodus narrative depicts God's people on a wilderness journey to the promised land. Sometimes, the pilgrim church finds itself in exile, desolate, and oppressed, longing for Jerusalem. At other times, it is on the move, marching towards Zion. Pilgrimage is a lifelong commitment to sharing with others the presence of God.

Boundaries

While committed to incorporating new members, long-term communities must wrestle with the need for boundaries, both porous and permanent, which are vital to a group's identity, character, and purpose.[17]

16. According to the International Coalition of Sites of Conscience, a site of conscience is "a place of memory . . . that prevents [the erasing of the past] from happening in order to ensure a more just and humane future." See www.sitesofconscience.org.

17. See Westerhoff, *Good Fences*.

Hermitage, Pilgrimage, Community

The transformative dynamics of Christian community are reflected in the three great moments of life—hermitage, pilgrimage, and community—described to me by Sister Giovanna: "During times of hermitage, one is completely alone with God. As a pilgrim, one goes out into the streets, learning about the world, hearing the cries of others, and helping those in need. In community, people come together to share their experiences of God and the world." Sister Giovanna envisions community as a sanctuary of intentional sharing, and Christian community is shaped by real-world stories of faith. My seminary formation emphasized the gathered church as the starting point: the body of Christ is formed through worship and *then* sent out to serve the world. While worship is essential to the process, here community is the consequence of *regathering* with fellow pilgrims to share our stories of the street. What cries have we heard, and how has the world been served? How have we seen God in the face of the Other? Nurtured by our testimonies of God and the Other, long-term community is the outcome of sharing our lives together.

Shared Memory

Conveyed through stories, symbols, and rituals, shared memory is an essential element of generational Christianity. From biblical events to contemporary experience, the church is sustained through its memory of the love and faithfulness of God.

Public memory is created, contested, and commemorated. Commemoration is the recognition of both past and current events, important people, and significant places by religious, civic, and secular groups through placenames, monuments, tombs, rituals, symbols, and festivals. Pilgrimage asks: how and what do we remember? Who deserves a monument? How and when do we forget, remove, or decommemorate the past? What do shared memory and memorialization tell us about power, authority, and the relationship between dominant and non-dominant groups? What are the ethics of memory?[18]

Today and Tomorrow

While memory plays a special role in the life of the church, long-term communities declare the manifest presence of God. God is immanent, and they

---

18. See Margalit, *Ethics of Memory*.

know it. Leaning into the future, pilgrim churches anticipate the promises of God.

Ulysses' Ship

If in the course of his voyage, Ulysses replaces every board in his ship, is it still the same ship? The question speaks to the issues of continuity, essence, and identity. In other words, does identity consist of the continuity of substance or essence? The conundrum of Ulysses' ship addresses the long-term character of Christian community, including the make-up of the members that comprise church groups over time. I reflected upon Ulysses' ship when, years later, I revisited my childhood congregation, which had sent me and many of my teenage peers into lay and professional ministry. Like Ulysses' ship, parts had been replaced—people had died; others had joined—but had their essence as a faithful congregation remained the same? I sat with the parents of a best friend; a former classmate was leading the children's choir. Otherwise, I recognized few names and even fewer faces. Yet, as I worshiped, I grew increasingly reassured that while their parts had changed their character was the same. The challenge of our corporate Christian journey is undergoing inevitable change, while retaining our essence in Christ, who is the same yesterday, today, and forever (Heb 13:8).

PILGRIMAGE IS INCARNATIONAL

Contemporary pilgrimage writers emphasize embodied experience. Pilgrimage is marked by the comingling of spirit and matter, which sparked creation and culminated in God's Word made flesh. The incarnation leaves us gazing into heaven with both feet on the ground, subject to the gravity of our human condition.

The incarnation is divine affirmation of our embodied existence and the physicality of our spiritual lives. Time and place are the how and where of God's interactions with the world. We encounter God at specific times in specific places. The incarnation, in other words, is God's commendation of the material *and* the particular. We do not experience God in the abstract. Rather, pilgrims seek God in the physical contexts of their daily lives. The universal is revealed through the particular; the abstract is manifest through concrete expressions, and as lived experience in time and place, pilgrimage is the reckoning of the facts in which we find ourselves.

The classic misnomer of pilgrimage is that it is "really about the inner journey," as if the physical dimension of our earthly lives can be somehow detached from our spiritual existence. We cannot separate the inner life from our embodied selves, and it is a distortion of sacred design to denigrate the outward journey. Matter matters. Embracing the physicality of spiritual experience, pilgrims mingle between the material and the immaterial.

In the Beginning

Pilgrimage takes its cues from divine narration, beginning with the story of a transcendent God who spoke creation into being. Spirit hovered over the abyss, and the immaterial took material form. Having created the earth and seas, God brought forth plants and trees, the creatures of the waters and the sky, and the beasts of the land, and God declared it was good. Then God formed humankind, male and female, in harmony with creation, and, again, it was all very good. Creation brimmed with divine approbation.

Sometime after the seventh day, Genesis narrates an act of disobedience that spawned sin into the world. Expelled from the garden, humanity roamed the earth, lost, alone, and alienated. What about the rest of creation? Was it fallen due to human sin, or was it still the work of God? How does a reckoning of sin and evil influence Christian perceptions of creation and the earthly life? Whatever we may say about original sin, creation was never a one-off project. God continues to call matter into being. Spirit still hovers over the waters, and divine breath animates life around us. Genesis launched the human experience as an embodied journey, fusing divine breath and earthly substance. Sin changed our relationship to God, but God's solution to human alienation was to double down on the divine predilection for embodied existence—this time, *God* become flesh. Humanity was saved through the incarnation, and God affirmed that it was indeed very good.

The Word Made Flesh

Christian pilgrimage is patterned upon the incarnation, which guides our way through the world. Salvation takes the form of a divine journey. Jesus departed the heavens, sojourned on earth, and journeyed to the cross before returning resurrected. Laying the road to salvation, the incarnation was God's assumption of the pilgrim life. Word became flesh and dwelt among us in time and place. Immanuel, God with us, took on human attributes, enjoyed the pleasantries of the physical world, and was subject to human limitations.[19] Jesus saw the world through a human lens, experienced human

---

19. Incarnational theologies have tended to be docetic, leaving little room for the human nature of Jesus, particular in terms of his personal growth and development.

longing, and imparted compassion to real people in actual places. He taught spiritual truths using material examples, expired upon a wooden cross, and was translated into a rock-cut tomb. Cosmic drama on an earthly stage.

God assumed flesh to save embodied people. The incarnation restores our at-one-ness with the world, and Christ's bodily resurrection resets the script. The material and immaterial co-exist as divine design. Our inner and outer journeys are intertwined. Jesus of Nazareth was divinity in corporal form, and the Christian life is patterned upon the Word-made-flesh of God's incarnational presence. Revealing God's preference for the particular, the incarnation is divine assertion that the physical world is the realm of God's redemption. Annunciation is the angelic pronouncement that incarnation is the way of God.

The Sensuous Side of Pilgrimage

As embodied creatures, spirituality is sensuous, experienced not merely as an inner feeling but physically through the senses. Salvation is soaked in blood, sweat, and tears and reenacted through bread and wine. Following suit, pilgrimage is full of sights, sounds, smells, tastes, and touches. The sensuous contemplation of God's creation evokes awe, praise, and wonder. We comprehend the empirical, perceive beauty, and explore the marvels of the world. Pilgrimage is a hands-on, open-eyed spirituality.[20]

Jerusalem travel exemplifies the sensuous nature of the pilgrim life, expressed by the adage to "see the Holy Land." According to Paulinus of Nola (d. 431), "No other sentiment draws people to Jerusalem than the desire to see and touch the places where Christ was physically present, and to be able to say from their very own experience, 'We have gone into his tabernacle, and have worshipped in the places where his feet have stood.'"[21] Pilgrims desire a physical connection with the Christian past, a tactile encounter with place and story. Sensuous experience elicits memory, while grounding us in the here and now.

The Facts in Which We Find Ourselves

The incarnational nature of pilgrimage extends beyond sensuous experience to our contextual circumstances, to the "who we are" in time and place, or

---

20. An emphasis on sensuous, empirical experience is not at odds with intellectual reflection.

21. Paulinus of Nola, *Letter*, 49.14.

the facts in which we find ourselves.[22] This includes age, mental and physical health, personality and preferences, physical characteristics, gender identity, sexual orientation, family situation, ethnicity and nationality, language and culture, education and livelihood, means and resources, vocation, location, and living conditions, which may be a cause for pride or struggle, opportunity or limitation, agency or dependency, power or oppression. The facts of our lives, which are largely unchosen, form the baseline of our earthly journey.

The facts also speak to the contextual flux of our lives, to our situational status, to meantime living through the passage of time. We are in the final year of school; we are celebrating a work anniversary; we have a mortgage; we are following a TV series; our daughter is in the school play; we go back to the doctor in three weeks; it's almost Christmas. Pilgrimage is the intentionality of transitional living.

The facts in which we find ourselves include the missteps, wrong turns, and dead ends of life. The incarnation was God's response to a less-than-ideal situation. It was a divine reply to a world of wayfaring strangers that were lost and without hope (Eph 2:12). God finds us on mistaken pathways, in the wilderness, on the side of the road. The parable of the lost sheep is an encore performance of God.[23]

According to the Jesuit writer, Gerard W. Hughes, God is in the *facts*.[24] God is neither theory nor supposition but a creative, life-giving force immanently present in real-time events and long-term situations. God dwells in the actualities of life—not in the ifs and buts, not in what could have or should have happened, but in the actual occurrence of lived experience. God is not in the sunny day that failed to materialize but the rainy day that actually occurred.

Whatever happens, God is there. This is not a comment on the will of God nor does it explain why bad things happen. God is in the facts is not a predestined approach to life nor a form of spiritual resignation. Human existence is steeped in sin. Evil remains at large. Tragedy appears with impunity. Yet, God is always present in the circumstances in which we find ourselves: weeping with us, encouraging us onward, sowing seeds of transformation. Given the resurrection of Christ, Hughes further asserts that the facts are kind.[25]

---

22. See Hughes, *Walk to Jerusalem*, 119.

23. See Luke 15:3–7; Matt 18:12–14.

24. Hughes, *God of Surprises*, x, 71; Hughes, *Walk to Jerusalem*, 119. Also see Hughes, *In Search of a Way*.

25. Hughes, *God of Surprises*, x, 8, 71.

God is in the facts is the prism through which pilgrims see spiritual possibilities in every situation. It's the rainy-day mantra of the pilgrim life. We get sick on pilgrimage; accidents occur. The journey turns out differently than we expected; things don't go our way. Daily life is no different. Pilgrim spirituality embraces human emotion, disappointment, frustration, and failure. Resurrection is glimpsed through tears. Pilgrim theology is not a set of suppositions. It does not advocate spiritual escapism nor ponder hypotheticals. Rather, pilgrims face the facts, knowing that God calls us through the actual situations in which we find ourselves. God is in the facts, and the facts are kind.

PILGRIMAGE IS METAPHORICAL

Metaphorical Theories

According to modern theories, a metaphor is not a comparison between two things; rather, it is a linguistic trope that *creates something new*, offering a new way of seeing the world. Known as incremental or interactive theories, they have replaced centuries-held notions of metaphors as fancy forms of redundant language.[26] A metaphor is neither decorative language nor linguistic window dressing. It is not ornamental language that can be replaced by the direct meaning it presumably stands for, which describes substitution and comparison theories. The core function of metaphor is neither to explain difficult concepts in simpler terms nor to tell us what we already know. A linguistic means of exploring reality, a metaphor produces *an irreducible insight* that cannot be said in any other way.

Although the word *comparison* still commonly appears in definitions, there are few, if any, defenders of substitution and comparison theories in academic circles. It's more difficult, however, to explain the inner workings of a metaphor without slipping into comparative language.

The classic Aristotelian definition takes a substitutionary approach: a metaphor gives a thing a name that belongs to something else.[27] Janice Soskice, an advocate of the incremental theory, tweaks the definition by referring to metaphors as "a figure of speech whereby we speak about one thing in terms which are seen to be suggestive of another."[28] Our interest is honing the exploratory function of metaphor as a theological tool.

26. Modern proponents include I. A. Richards and Max Black. See Richards, *Philosophy*, 89–138; Black, *Models*, 25–47.

27. Aristotle, *Rhetoric*, 251.

28. Soskice, *Metaphor*, 15.

Etymologically, metaphor comes from the Greek *meta* (a passing over or a going from one place to another) and *phorein* (to move or to carry). Metaphors carry us from one place to another. They enable us to cross boundaries that are otherwise closed to us, to behold phenomena that we cannot otherwise perceive.

Pretending that "this" is "that," a metaphor takes something we know (a source) to explore a less familiar target.[29] That, of course, is how we learn: using the familiar to explore the unknown, connecting something new to what we already know. Metaphor searches for links and patterns; it looks for similarities between dissimilar entities, which is basic to human thinking.

The standard example is Shakespeare's "Juliet is the sun." Juliet (target) is the "thing," and the sun (the source) is the "something else." Metaphorical meaning is created when something familiar is applied to a subject that is less understood. In this case, the sun has familiar qualities that inform Juliet's essence, and what we learn about Juliet is based upon our experience of the sun. Here is where the theories diverge. We are not merely comparing Juliet with the sun. Rather, the interaction of the two subjects reveals something about Juliet, specific to her pairing with the sun, that is unique and irreducible. We cannot replace the sun with another image without losing its particular meaning. To do so conveys something else about Juliet.

How, then, do we articulate the irreducible meaning of a metaphor? We can't, since the use of direct language changes its meaning. We can discuss the connotations of a metaphor, but its irreducible nature means that the best we can do is to use another metaphor.[30]

In short, metaphors are assertive statements that change the way we see the world. Yet, metaphorical assertions are not true in a full or conventional sense. Is Juliet the sun? Juliet is like the sun, but she is also unlike it. There is an "is" and "is not" quality to metaphors. They say both "yes" and "no." Metaphors are half-truth assertions that explore phenomena through the unresolved tension they generate between the source and the target. The tensional interaction between Juliet and the sun produces something new. While our focus is on Juliet (the target), the interactive nature of the metaphor affects our understanding of the source as well, even in subtle ways, causing us to see the sun in a different light.

Metaphors are not true or false in a conventional sense. Rather, we measure metaphors by aptness. Do they make sense? Do they stretch and challenge our thinking? Are they apt? Do they fit? Are they suitable? Are

29. Alternative terms include vehicle and tenor, denotation and connotation, and primary and secondary subject. See Soskice, *Metaphor*, 20, who argues that not all metaphors have two distinct subjects.

30. Soskice, *Metaphor*, 94.

they relevant, or effective? This applies to the metaphor itself as well as the context in which it is used. Would a different metaphor be better or more insightful? While a given metaphor is irreducible, since understanding the target is the goal, the more sources we use the better. Metaphors love company.

What we should consider when engaging or creating a metaphor? A simple summary of metaphorical theory includes the following questions:

- What is the target, and what is the source?
- What are the "yes" and "no" aspects of the metaphor?
- What is the metaphor's irreducible insight?
- Is the metaphor apt?
- What other sources could be applied to the target?

While metaphor uses the familiar to explore the less familiar, both the source and the target are often physical entities. The computer (target) as body (source) metaphor uses familiarity with the human body to explore the less familiar workings of a computer. Metaphors are usually unidirectional, but occasionally, the source and the target can be reversed. The body (target) as computer (source) metaphor assumes that we know more about computers than we do about the human body (as the case may be). In each instance, the source and the target are physical entities. The more abstract something is the more we rely upon metaphor. Love is a red, red rose. Love is blind. Love is a disease. Language instinctively resorts to metaphor to explore human experience and the abstract qualities of life.

Religious Language

Metaphorical theory applies to religious language and the inadequacy of talking about God. The transcendent nature of God is beyond our comprehension. God is not merely beyond the world in the sense that we can imagine, for instance, a personified deity enthroned in the heavens. Divine transcendence means that we are unable to imagine God at all. As voiced in Isaiah 55:8–9, God is beyond human experience:

> For my thoughts are not your thoughts, neither are your ways my ways, says the LORD. For as the heavens are higher than the earth, so are my ways higher than your ways and my thoughts than your thoughts.

According to Augustine, our only way to talk about God is to speak "in halt-ing, inadequate words or to remain silent,"[31] while Thomas Aquinas states: "Then alone do we know God truly, when we believe that [God] is far above all that [we] can possibly think of God."[32] God is the inexplicable Other, and the best we can do is to stay quiet, speak in terms of what God is not, or resort to metaphor.[33]

With respect to the otherness of God, there's a notable oddity in the Hebrew Bible. Despite its stance against graven images, its authors embrace an abundance of literary images, none of which are regarded as literal, let alone adequate.[34] In a word, almost all biblical language that refers to God is metaphor.[35]

Jesus himself was a metaphorical theologian.[36] Recognizing that no one image can capture God, Jesus employs a multitude of metaphorical sources, such as shepherd, vine, gate, bread, and water, to name but a few. When we recognize that metaphor is our primary way of talking about God, it encourages us, as the Bible does, to employ a broad spectrum of sources. Relational images, like father, shepherd, and mother hen, are favored. In-animate sources, such as mountains, wind, and shadow, convey the sublime and mysterious, balancing images that domesticate God.[37]

God is a shepherd; Jesus is a vine. Using one thing to describe another, biblical metaphor employs indirect thinking. Jesus is not literally a vine; God is not a shepherd, but metaphorical imagery allows us to explore the nature of God in effective ways. The fallacy of literalist thinking is equat-ing the metaphorical source with the transcendent target. While literalizing metaphors turns our language of God into idols (see below), metaphorical thinking helps us understand that language about God must not be literal in order to be true.

The Bible uses anthropomorphic images, such as the hands and eyes of God. While they are commonly viewed as naïve, the biblical writers un-derstand that God's transcendence cannot be grasped. Once we recognize

31. Cited in McFague, *Metaphorical Theology*, 1.

32. Aquinas, *Summa* (book 1, chapter 5), 10; quoted in Campbell, *Thou Art That*, 39.

33. On negative, or apophatic, theology, see Davies and Turner, *Silence*. Also see, Lane, *Solace*.

34. McFague, *Metaphorical Theology*, 42.

35. Caird, *Language and Imagery*, 18.

36. Bailey, *Jesus*, 279.

37. McFague, *Metaphorical Theology*, 43.

anthropomorphic language as a conscious appeal to metaphor, biblical theology suddenly becomes more sophisticated.[38]

In other words, metaphor is how the Bible thinks, and Scripture contains a metaphorical sensibility to religious truth. The assertion that the Bible speaks in metaphor is a comment about its original intent. John Dominic Crossan states the case rather bluntly: "My point, once again, is *not* that those ancient people told literal stories and we are now smart enough to take them symbolically, but that they told them symbolically and we are now dumb enough to take them literally."[39]

The primary caveat regarding metaphorical language is not to confuse the source for the target, which, theologically speaking, is idolatry. Idolatry is substituting God for the symbol, replacing God with a false image. Since metaphorical sources are indirect and incomplete, any one that dominates our understanding of God runs the risk of idolatry.[40] The prohibition against graven images is not meant to suppress spiritual pursuit. Rather, it is a warning against substituting literal concepts for transcendent mystery. The more sources involved, the less likely we are to fix upon a particular one.[41]

Biblical metaphors raise a couple of concerns for contemporary Christians. While a source must be familiar to be effective, a significant portion of biblical metaphors appeals to pastoral images, ancient warfare, and temple practices, knowledge that is either obsolete or lacking in today's technological world. The agricultural images are more accessible to some than others. However, Christian education, including sermons, Bible studies, and Sunday School lessons, must first ensure that unfamiliar metaphorical sources are understood in order to access the spiritual targets behind them. Jesus' parables require accurate background explanations before their messages can be fully ascertained.[42] In terms of *method*, the Bible teaches us to explore the spiritual life with what we have around us: using familiar, everyday sources to target the mysteries of God.

The second issue is the contested nature of certain metaphors. The image of lord is oppressive for victims of abuse, slavery, and human trafficking.[43] Father, while beloved for some, is problematic for others. The issue is augmented by the dominance of patriarchal images in Christian language. The image of God as father offers an instructive case study on the interactive

38. McFague, *Metaphorical Theology*, 20.

39. See Crossan and Watts, *Who Is Jesus?*, 79. The italics are in the original.

40. See McFague, *Models*, which addresses the dominance of patriarchal metaphors.

41. See McFague, *Metaphorical Theology*, 1–29.

42. See Levine, *Short Stories*.

43. Compare its connotations with the image of God as liberator.

theory of metaphor.[44] While recognizing its centrality to biblical, historical, and trinitarian language, we are interested in how metaphors work, the problem of religious language, the discernment of apt metaphors, and the use of multiple sources. First of all, the metaphor of God as father implies that we know more about human fatherhood (source) than we know about the nature of God (target).[45]

Second, there is a "yes" and "no" quality to the metaphor that reminds us that God *is* and *is not* like a father. While God *is* like a father, God is not *literally* a father. Third, the interactive theory states that the God-as-father metaphor creates something new. It produces an irreducible insight that no other metaphor can convey. While this is initially a semantic point, to dismiss the metaphor is to lose an insight into God that cannot otherwise be obtained.[46] We likewise lose out when we neglect or suppress other sources, such as God as mother, lover, and friend.[47]

Fourth, the question of aptness brings theological discernment to the forefront. God as father is not true or false in a conventional sense. The metaphor contains aspects of truth without being literally true, but the issue here is whether it's *effective*. Is the metaphor fresh: does it stretch, excite, and challenge our thinking, or has it become more or less literalized, a dead metaphor that has lost its spark? The question of aptness extends to the context in which the metaphor is used today, namely, Christian communities and the individuals that comprise them. How suitable is the metaphor? It is effective, relevant, painful, or offensive? The issue not only concern people's individual experience of fatherhood but the dominance of patriarchal metaphors that reflect the patriarchy traditionally associated with Christian societies. One may choose to reject or limit the use of patriarchal metaphors for God, opting for sources, such as creator, mother, parent, or friend. The incremental theory tells us that we have lost something in the process (we cannot substitute metaphors without losing meaning), but this is effectively weighed in discerning their aptness. If a metaphor is not apt or effective, then its unique insight is of limited value.

44. For a critique of the theological model of God as father, see McFague, *Metaphorical Theology*, 145–92.

45. Some theologians have pointed out that we should derive our concept of fatherhood *from* God rather than applying attributes of human fathers *to* God. Simply based on metaphorical theory (not the merits of the argument itself), the position effectively negates the God-as-father metaphor, since it's precisely human fatherhood (source) that is applied to God (target). Secondly, it implicitly reverses the metaphor to father as God.

46. The concept of irreducibility does not put a value on the insight itself. It merely asserts its uniqueness.

47. These examples are discussed in McFague, *Models*.

In the case of patriarchal metaphors, aptness is also a question of balance, which raises the fifth point: the importance of using multiple sources to explore transcendent targets. We can affirm qualities of the God-as-father metaphor while asserting the need to supplement our language with the use of additional metaphors. It is important to remember that, while metaphorical direction goes from source to target, their interactive tension changes our perception of the source as well. God as father sanctifies, in subtle ways, the image of the human father. While patriarchal metaphors have elevated the status of fatherhood, other sources, such as mothering images, have been neglected and suppressed. The point makes language about God an accomplice to religious inequality: *our metaphors of God convey the worth we confer on human roles and relationships.* In short, we should use a breadth of human sources as well as inanimate images in our metaphorical explorations of God. As a linguistic theory for exploring lived experience and abstract phenomena, metaphorical theory weighs heavily on the side of employing a plethora of sources rather than restricting them, although some are more apt than others. As pilgrims of both physical and metaphorical journeys, we also want to use an abundance of sources.[48]

Life Is a Journey

How do we talk about the abstract nature of life? Life as a journey is one such way. The metaphor asserts that we know more about journeys (source) than we do about life (target). While recognizing that there are ways in which life is *not* like a journey, the metaphor uses our experience of physical travel to explore the mysteries of our earthly existence. The metaphorical interaction between life and journey renders insights that we cannot otherwise obtain.

Our objective, once again, is to probe the target as much as we can. Since metaphor is indirect exploration, it renders but a partial perspective, akin to only seeing a part of an elephant. Metaphors encourage company, and our exploration of life utilizes a spectrum of sources. Life is like a box of chocolates; you never know what you're gonna get. All the world's a stage, and we are merely players. Life is a book with many chapters. Life is a team sport. Life is (not) a competition. Some metaphors are more dynamic than others—life as a journey is especially so—but they all contribute to the task.

---

48. The importance of multiple sources speaks to our exploration of phenomena and the need to ensure that a given source does not overly dominate. In terms of identity, focus, and branding, including a congregation's mission, vision, and value statements, the consistency of language is important.

While fueled by metaphors of movement, liminality, and transformation, pilgrim spirituality appropriates any metaphor that explores God, self, and the Other. Of particular relevance are organic metaphors, which convey unity, growth, and interdependence (e.g., Christ as the vine, the body of Christ). The prejudice against mixed metaphors refers to the consistency of presentation not to the investigation of phenomena. With metaphors, the more the merrier.

Conceptual Metaphors

While our exploration of life employs a multitude of sources, the journey metaphor is particularly expansive. According to George Lakoff and Mark Johnson, life as a journey is classic example of a conceptual metaphor.[49] They argue that conceptual metaphors, such as time is money and argument is war, are central to the way we think, which, in turn, is expressed through language. Understanding life is a journey as a conceptual metaphor has significant implications for pilgrim spirituality. First of all, the theory states that *thinking* about the earthly life in terms of a journey is inherent to the human experience. Themes of movement are natural to the way we think, which should encourage us to use the language of journey even more. Second, as an expansive metaphor, life as journey has an extensive number of metaphorical expressions, or mappings, between the source and the target. This is implicitly what we're doing throughout the book, teasing out connections between the concept of journey and the Christian life. Mappings are reflected, for example, in the language of travelers, guides, companions, destinations, provisions, pathways, crossroads, getting lost, turning around, and arrival. Third, conceptual metaphors—and dominant metaphors in general—lend themselves as theological models (e.g., God as father, God as friend, life as journey).[50]

49. See Lakoff and Johnson, *Philosophy*, 52–53, 61–62. Their book *Metaphors We Live By* (1980), which explores how metaphors affect our thinking, actions, and behavior, helped establish the field of metaphor studies as a branch of cognitive linguistics.

50. While the book focuses on definitional questions, mapping pilgrim spirituality as a theological model warrants a work of its own. On metaphors as theological models, see McFague, *Metaphorical Theology*, 103–44. Also see McFague, *Models of God*; McFague, *Speaking in Parables*.

Physical and Metaphorical Journeys

While metaphor is fundamentally opposed to literalism, metaphor is not the opposite of physical reality.[51] Metaphor illuminates the immaterial by employing images from the material world. Far from oppositional, incarnational and metaphorical theology are complementary approaches. The incarnational emphasis on embodied experience is a recognition of the co-existence of the material and the immaterial. Incarnation embodies the abstract; metaphor explores it.

We can now address the common claim that pilgrimage is "really about the inner journey."[52] The statement generally implies a rejection of traditional practices, like the visitation of religious shrines, but it also discounts the physicality of spiritual experience. The outward journey may animate the inner one, just as internal transformation may lead to social action, but the interior life does not exist in insolation, independent of our bodily context. Making the inner journey the target of pilgrimage distorts the pilgrim life: its emphasis on embodied experience, social action, and engaging the Other. Likewise, spiritualizing pilgrimage overlooks our reliance on metaphorical sources. Since metaphor is fueled by empirical knowledge, to effectively explore the Christian life, including the inner journey, we need to be fully engaged in the physical world.

In short, pilgrim spirituality emphasizes the physical nature of spiritual experience while exploring transcendent realities through metaphor. As for contemporary practice, *both* the incarnational and metaphorical expressions of pilgrimage are underdeveloped. With its tendency to denigrate embodied experience, Protestant pilgrimage has been scarcely incarnational. Although metaphorical interpretations of the pilgrim life are as old as the Bible—and have been bolstered by five centuries of Protestant experience—few understand the explorative function of metaphors. According to C. S. Lewis, "What the church needs is not better arguments, but better metaphors."[53] What we need, to begin with, is a better understanding of how metaphors work.

51. See Foster, *Sacred Journey*, 149, who posits that physical pilgrimage makes us more conscious of metaphor.

52. Spiritualizing the Christian life is not the same as taking a metaphorical approach, which appeals to both source and target.

53. Cited in Hjalmarson, *No Home*, 188–89.

PILGRIMAGE IS TENSIONAL

Pilgrimage is tensional. Tension is the act of being stretched or strained, which generally triggers anxiety or excitement. Tension results when things are in opposition. It stems from the unresolved status of a situation. It's the state of suspense, when something is unfinished or incomplete. While tension can enervate, being stretched, within limits, can be a catalyst of growth. Fire germinates, pressure transforms, and exigency moves us forward.

Pilgrimage is both tensional theology and tensional experience. Pilgrim spirituality embraces the paradoxical concepts of the Christian life. God is transcendent yet immanent. Christ is both human and divine. God is everywhere; there are sacred places. While the doctrine of God's universal presence seems on the surface to refute the idea that God is found in circumscribed places, theology profits from a little imagination. Pilgrims speculate alongside Julian of Norwich that God is a point fitting within the palm of our hand and yet is present everywhere.[54] Tensional theology examines how religious contradictions and antithetical notions can still be true.

There's a conceptual tension to pilgrimage that stalks the discussion from the start, which parts the seas while muddying the waters: (1) pilgrimage is a circumscribed experience, a particular journey, a phase in our lives, a transition that comes and goes; (2) at the same time, it's the entirety of our earthly days, stretching from cradle to grave. It's tempting to concede that the *everything* of pilgrimage makes it meaningless or effectively incoherent, and our inclination is to choose one thing over the other, to simplify suspended equations. Our theological task is to hold things together, to illuminate complexity, to create pathways for *both–and* approaches.

As tensional *experience*, the Christian life is a journey of suspense, anxiety, and anticipation. Pilgrims search the unknown, uncertain of what they will find. They journey between mystery and discovery, the familiar and the unfamiliar, the past and the future. Pilgrims seek answers but accumulate questions. Spiritual exploration is a tensional endeavor.

The liminoid nature of pilgrimage, or living in the *betwixt and between*, adds to the tension. Pilgrims are on an unfinished journey, between departure and arrival, between separation and return. To be on pilgrimage is to stare into a mirror dimly, to journey through the fog. Faith is an antidote to uncertainty, "the assurance of things hoped for, the conviction of things not seen" (Heb 11:1).

54. Crampton, *Shewings*, 77.

While liminality is the *neither/nor*, Christians live, in the meantime, in the *already and the not yet*. Pilgrims navigate between the here and the elsewhere, between the *is* and the *yet to be*. We live in the age of the Holy Spirit. Christ's resurrection is already; the culmination of heaven on earth has not yet occurred.

Pilgrim spirituality offers perspectives on the tensional nature of the Christian life. First of all, personal experience sometimes trumps our own beliefs. Pilgrimage is an experiential spirituality, which means that our theologies may be stretched and strained and, at times, laid aside. The goal of the pilgrim life is not adherence to doctrine but union with God, self, and the Other. Second, pilgrimage affirms the concurrent truth of mutually exclusive mysteries of faith. God is immanent *and* transcendent; Christ is human *and* divine. We journey with *and* to God. God is ubiquitous; there are sacred places. Third, pilgrim spirituality encourages us to take a second look. Is there a different way of seeing things, another way to approach an issue, something that we're missing: a different frame, a hidden layer, or an unasked question? Tensional theology invites us to explore.

Sometimes, what we think is tension is actually balance. Pilgrimage integrates personal faith and sacramental practice, acts of piety (prayer and worship) and acts of mercy (compassion and justice), community, hermitage, and the street. Pilgrimage emphasizes divine grace as well as human agency, interdependence and personal responsibility. The pilgrim life consists of the mundane and the miraculous, boredom and beatitudes, hardships and the holy, temptation and enlightenment. Balance is the tension we strive for.

ADDITIONAL CHARACTERISTICS

As we interrogate the pilgrim life, additional characteristics emerge. Pilgrimage, for instance, is *exploratory, experiential,* and *equalitarian.* Both physically and metaphorically, pilgrimage is explorative theology. Pilgrims seek tissue-thin places, looking for cracks in the cosmos and the irruptions of a transcendent God. True to the tensional nature of pilgrimage, destinations in a complete sense are never reached. New horizons are glimpsed, but Land's End is elusive. Approximations are achieved, similarities perceived, and perspectives gained, but the earthly pilgrim never quite arrives.

Pilgrimage is experiential. It emphasizes lived experience and Christian praxis, including prayer, worship, and Christian service. Transcending the dos and don'ts of dogmatic religion, pilgrimage is practical theology. While it matters what we think, pilgrim spirituality takes a non-catechetical approach to God. In the words of Pope Benedict XVI, "Christianity is not an intellectual system, a collection of dogmas, or a moralism. Christianity is an encounter, a love story: it is an event."[55]

Pilgrimage is an equalitarian spirituality, epitomized by the image of pilgrim companions and the communitas-like qualities of Christian community. Pilgrim theology uses ordinary language for everyday people: the word pictures of time, place, and journey, references to the self and the stranger, and metaphors of God. Its language is clear, concise, and inclusive. Embodying the embrace of Pentecost, pilgrim spirituality promotes spiritual discourse on the simplest of terms: God's love is conveyed in our own language; s/Spirit speaks in mother tongue. Connecting laity and clergy, saints and sinners, Christians and non-Christians alike, pilgrimage offers a lingua franca for ecumenical, interreligious, and secular discourse.

As an equalitarian, non-specialist theology, pilgrimage spirituality takes a non-hierarchical approach to the Christian life. Pilgrimage is not a do-it-yourself spirituality, nor is it necessarily antithetical to hierarchical expressions of Christianity. There is not, however, a professional class of pilgrims. Pilgrim authenticity is self-determined, and we have equal access to the spiritual life. Pilgrims seek the guidance of Scripture, the wisdom of tradition, and the counsel of others. They find accountability in community and tutelage under spiritual mentors, but pilgrimage cannot be cornered. It belongs to everyday Christians and commonplace people: to you, to me, and to others.

Pilgrimage is *contemplative* and *sacramental*. While the contemplative journey is one of prayer, meditation, and discernment, in resourcing contemplative approaches, pilgrim spirituality insists upon an integrative balance between the inward and outward journey, between the pensive and active dimensions of faith.

Pilgrimage weighs sacramental possibilities. Whereas metaphor sees one thing in terms of another, a sacramental view holds that an ordinary thing may be or become a visible sign of a hidden reality. Participating in what it points to, the sign *is*, in some way, what it stands for (the bread *is* the body of Christ). A sacramental way of seeing the world holds the particular and the universal in creative tension. Pilgrim spirituality leaves open the possibility that time, place, events, and objects may assume a sacramental dimension.[56]

---

55. Ratzinger, *Homily*.

56. See McFague, *Metaphorical Theology*, 1–29, who argues that, generally speaking, a sacramental perspective aligns with Catholic sensibilities while metaphor characterizes the Protestant view of the world.

5

The Component Parts of Pilgrimage

WE TURN NOW TO the component parts of pilgrimage. Breaking pilgrimage down into its respective parts provides terms for discussing the rubrics of pilgrimage, which, in turn, allows us to understand pilgrimage better. The parts, moreover, are the functional units of pilgrim spirituality. Pilgrim spirituality does not require the iteration of complete expressions of pilgrimage; rather, it's the application of its constituent parts to the content and context of our lives. The parts themselves are flexible and overlapping. The construct of journey, for instance, can be a concept, element, image, or theme. The point is not to pigeon-hole the parts but to apply them in relevant ways.

THEMES

Themes are unifying ideas, prominent motifs, and reoccurring subjects. Pilgrimage coalesces around two sets of primary themes: (1) time, place, and journey and (2) the stranger, the unknown, and the Other. Journey is a function of time, place, and movement, and subthemes, such as departure and arrival, beginnings and endings, separation and return, have both a temporal and spatial dimension. Time and place are subjects of their own. Time is ordinary and sacred; it is linear (past, present, and future) and cyclical (seasonal and reoccurring). Temporal aspects of pilgrimage include memory and commemoration (past), intentionality and self-awareness (present), and hope and anticipation (future). Place-related themes include sacred ground and ordinary spaces, centers, edges, and margins. Pilgrims are in place and out of place. They visit sacred destinations, seek sanctuary, and long for home.

The other set of primary themes concerns the stranger—the unknown, the foreign, and the Other—motifs going back to Abraham. The image of the stranger concerns our place in the world, including alienation and displacement, being in the world but not of it (John 17:1–19). Engaging the Other speaks to the interpersonal virtues of the pilgrim life: hospitality, generosity, compassion, and respect.

Adding to the overarching themes, each pilgrimage field has its own emphases. Holy Land travel focuses on biblical landscapes and narratives, history and archaeology, ecumenical and interfaith issues, and peace and reconciliation. Complementing the landscapes, architecture, and local cultures of the Camino de Santiago, themes include the rhythms and challenges of long-distance walking, personal management, self-reflection, and conversations with fellow pilgrims. Spiritual retreat centers and ecumenical communities, such as Taizé and the Iona Community, each have their own identity, influenced by their location, history, programs, and worship. Mission journeys focus on a particular people, place, or project, producing themes defined by the destinational Other.

Each iteration of pilgrimage consists of irreducible events, incidents and accidents, conditions and conversations, people and personalities, yielding themes and subjects that may be privately perceived or shared by the group.

On the individual level, themes can be deeply personal. A pilgrimage may focus upon mental, emotional, or physical health, relational or vocational issues, personal pain and sorrow, life transitions, or a pending decision. A pilgrimage may be a time of intercessory prayer or a journey made in honor or memory of someone else. Personal themes may be the primary impetus for taking a pilgrimage in the first place or may surface once an experience has begun.

EXPRESSIONS

In thinking about pilgrimage, we need to differentiate between (1) specific sites, fields, and forms, which we will refer to as "expressions" (e.g., the phenomenon of Holy Land pilgrimage), (2) an iteration or experience of a pilgrimage expression (e.g., participation in a Holy Land pilgrimage), and (3) the grouping of pilgrimage expressions into types or patterns (e.g., Holy Land pilgrimage as a roundtrip journey to a holy place), which we refer to as templates (see below). Expressions, iterations, and templates have both physical and metaphorical dimensions.

TEMPLATES

Depicting the earthly life as a journey to God, Christian pilgrimage is based upon a *biblical prototype*, or metatemplate, which serves as the pattern of patterns of Christian pilgrimage (see chapter 6). While the Bible provides the prototype, pilgrimage consists of innumerable templates (i.e., sub-templates of the prototype), which are the types and varieties of pilgrimage, or the various groupings of similar expressions. Pilgrim templates are neither fixed nor finite but are logically and flexibly construed.

The most recognized template is a *return journey to a sacred place*, which we can break down into more specialized types, such as biblical sites, saints' tombs, and Marian shrines. The specificity of a template depends upon the criteria used, and a family of templates may include related subsets. For instance, the template of *religious travel* (as opposed, for instance, to the embodied prayer) consists of visits to *holy sites, ecumenical communities*, and *mission trips*. The template can be narrowed to *return journeys to holy sites*. More specifically, we could refer to a template of *Marian shrines* or even *Marian shrines in North America*.

Just as templates share elements in common, a given expression may be associated with multiple templates. While Holy Land travel is commonly driven by the religious sites, programs also focus on *peace and reconciliation, interfaith dialogue*, and *ecumenical Christianity*, thus, employing *a mixed, or hybrid*, model. Even Holy Land travel reminds us that the focus of pilgrimage is not always a sacred place. Pilgrimage includes *difficult places, or sites of conscience*, which use place and memory to commemorate loss, to tell alternative stories, and to promote human rights through education and dialogue. Similarly, a number of templates focus on *people* rather than places. Engaging the Other is a type of pilgrimage, while templates of compassion, service, and social justice—e.g., *pilgrimage as "the street"* and *short-term work trips*—address real-world needs. People-centered templates include *spiritual retreats, monastic stays*, and *ecumenical communities*.

Time-based templates cover gap years, sabbaticals, and periods of transition, discernment, convalescence, and bereavement, and we can construct templates around *objectives, motives, and motivation*. Pilgrimage types include times set aside for *personal reasons, solitary ventures*, and *individual adventures* as well as *group-focused experiences*. Some templates lack an operative sense of travel (e.g., local pilgrimages), while others embrace *the metaphorical nature* of the pilgrim life.

The contemporary imagination of pilgrimage has been especially captured by the template of *long-distance walking*, epitomized by the Camino de Santiago, the Via Francigena, and a growing number of regional walks in Europe and around the world (see chapter 26).[1] Walking templates also include one-day experiences focused on religious, historical, and natural destinations as well as forms of kinetic prayer, like the labyrinth and the Stations of the Cross. *Parades and liturgical processions, marches and protests* embody pedestrian elements of pilgrimage, while *forced marches and mass migrations*, such as the Trail of Tears and the Navajo Long Walk, express a darker form of pilgrimage.

Keeping in mind that they are flexible constructs, attention to templates enhances our understanding of pilgrimage. First of all, traditional definitions of pilgrimage have often focused upon a limited set of templates. A return journey to a holy site is a *template* of pilgrimage; it does not define the phenomenon *as a whole*. Secondly, the modern resurgence of pilgrimage has likewise emphasized certain templates, such as long-distance walking and embodied prayer. Surveying templates helps us identify overlooked and undeveloped aspects of pilgrimage, such as templates of social justice (see chapter 22).

Third, we can enhance the pilgrim experience by applying concepts from one template to another. Viewing foreign travels, like Holy Land pilgrimage, through the lens of Abraham—being a stranger in a strange land—adds perspective, humility, and self-awareness to one's experience. The contemporary witness of sites of conscience can frame religious travel as a dialogue in human rights, while Christian concepts of commemoration help us engage secular forms of pilgrimage (and vice versa), including public discussions on memorialization.

Finally, a survey of templates underscores the accessibility of the pilgrim life, which does not oblige us to travel far from home. Even if we cannot participate in certain templates, such as international travel, other forms of pilgrimage are knocking on our door.

---

1. Examples include the St Magnus Way (Orkney), St Cuthbert's Way (Scotland–England), the Pilgrims' Way (England), the Penrhys Pilgrimage Way (Wales), St Olav's Way (Norway), and the Abraham Trail (the Middle East), to name but a few.

RELATED DOMAINS

Pilgrimage-related domains are fields of interest and related subjects that belong to the conversation of pilgrim spirituality, whether or not they are otherwise recognized in pilgrimage terms. The family resemblance theory speaks of overlapping similarities, while noting that things become frayed on the edges. A domain-friendly approach to pilgrim spirituality allows us to transcend strict definitional questions, while reminding us that our objective is to enhance the Christian life.

Pilgrimage has overlapping similarities with a number of Christian practices. Are camps, spiritual retreats, and ecumenical programs forms of pilgrimage? Are short-term mission trips a template of pilgrimage or a related domain? The distinctions collapse, since they belong, either way, to the discourse. Is "coerced pilgrims" a valid concept? While the case that refugees are pilgrims is easy to make, a domain-based approach ensures their place at the table.

Scouring secular fields—gleaning them for language, images, and concepts that apply to the pilgrim life—yields valuable tools and resources. Developmental theories, such as Maslow's hierarchy of needs and Erikson's theory of psychosocial development, offer insights from the world of psychology.[2] The fields of narrative therapy, life review, and autoethnography as well as public history and memory studies are important related domains. Books such as *The Hero with a Thousand Faces*, *The Writer's Journey*, and *The 7 Habits of Highly Effective People* contain content, theories, and schematic material that inform the pilgrim experience, while inspirational content can be gleaned from travel writings, like *Blue Highways* by William Least Heat-Moon, and fictional works, such as those by Paolo Coehlo.[3] Since Christian pilgrimage is ultimately patterned upon a biblical prototype, it has the latitude to explore secular and interfaith sources.

ELEMENTS

Elements are the individual pieces of pilgrimage. They are the things, images, and concepts, big and small, that collectively comprise a pilgrim expression, a pilgrim experience, or a template pattern. Taking the template of a round-trip journey to a holy place, we can list its sequential elements—the call and decision to go, pre-trip preparations, departure, the outbound journey,

2. Additional theories include those by Jean Piaget, Jerome Bruner, Lawrence Kohlberg, and Lev Vygotsky.

3. See, for instance, Coehlo, *Alchemist* and *Pilgrimage*.

arrival, time at the destination, the inbound journey, the return home, and the aftermath—each of which can be broken down into smaller units. Attention to place yields elements, such as home, the holy site, and the stops and stations in-between. Holy sites render elements of commemoration, ritual, prayer, and worship. The interpersonal aspects of the journey include fellow pilgrims, local residents, and incidental strangers. The pilgrim experience contains elements of challenge, temptation, discernment, and fatigue as well as mystery, surprise, and discovery. Pilgrimage consists of material elements, many of which have a spiritual dimension, such as baggage, supplies, souvenirs, and mementos, while logistical elements include meals, lodging, and transportation.

Pilgrims learn as they go, and they do so by reflecting upon elements of the journey. What is involved in visiting a holy site? What decisions, temptations, and distractions might one face along the way? How does food, lodging, and transport affect the journey? When elements are emphasized, they turn into themes.

As with themes and templates, attention to elements allows us to practice pilgrimage in more intentional ways. We may symbolically mark the sequential stages of a journey, enhancing awareness, meaning, and memory. Reflecting upon the element of baggage, pilgrims distinguish between needs and desires, between useful supplies and needless distractions. They ponder the importance of mementos as physical reminders of spiritual experiences. Pilgrims are grateful for those who make pilgrimage possible: their hosts, guides, and support staff, including bus drivers and housekeepers, their back-home support group, and those who have shaped their journey of faith over the years, namely, mentors, teachers, family, and friends. By considering the elements of pilgrimage, we engage the experience in deeper, more meaningful ways.

Pilgrim spirituality does not necessitate going on pilgrimage; rather, it advocates the application of pilgrim-related elements to our everyday Christian life. To take the elements of departure, journey, and arrival, life is a continuous exercise of new beginnings. We begin, progress, and see things through. We struggle, persevere, and sometimes quit. We complete projects, reach goals, and achieve results. Life is full of transitions: doors open and close; the old ends, and the new begins. It's a series of transformations, sudden, pronounced, gradual, and subtle. The elements of life form the compound of faith.

IMAGES

An image is a word picture, a mental representation, or a physical likeness made visible. More generally, an image may refer to virtually any aspect of pilgrimage. In this respect, images are the same as elements with one imposed distinction—whereas an element is a part of a larger whole, a pilgrim image may exist independently of any actual expressions. An image may contain, in other words, standalone substance of the pilgrim life.

While such material abounds in our daily lives, of particular interest are Christological images that manifest pilgrimage themes. Jesus is the way, the gate, and the light of the world, the bread from heaven, and the water of life. Jesus is the Good Shepherd, who, in the mantle of a pilgrim guide, protects, leads, and nourishes his sheep. The image of Jesus as the alpha and the omega speaks to the entirety of our lives: Christ is our departure, journey, and destination, our life, death, and resurrection. Christological images sustain our journey of faith.

CONCEPTS

While images are word pictures, concepts are abstract notions. Pilgrimage is a conceptual spirituality, grounded in abstract tenets, like personal management, intentional decision-making, and short-term Christian community. The sacred and the profane are conceptual ideas. So, too, are virtues, such as hospitality, hope, and perseverance, as well as generalized elements, like departure and arrival. Concepts are embodied through concrete expressions. The Other is a concept until it has a face. The stranger is particularized as an actual person. Space becomes place when it's attached to a memory.

PILGRIM CONTENT: LIVED EXPERIENCE

The content of pilgrimage is lived experience or the actualized journey. Pilgrimage is embodied, first-person experience; it's our autobiographical reckoning of the world (see chapter 17).

PILGRIM WISDOM: APHORISMS

Briefly introduced in chapter 3, aphorisms are quotable quotes and shareable sayings that emerge throughout a pilgrimage.[4] Forged from personal

---

4. On aphorisms, see Geary, *World*. The pilgrim life is full of short, quotable sayings

experience or borrowed from others, they are short interpretative phrases of accumulated wisdom that express the lessons of the road: the journey is more important than the destination; life is a journey of constantly losing things along the way; the journey is never over. They are the mantras and mottos that emerge from lived experience, which function, in turn, as frames of perspective for interpreting past events, probing present situations, and readjusting our thoughts and behavior. Aphorisms are rules to live by, reminding us of who we are and what to do.

While conveying wisdom, aphorisms do not make universal truth claims; neither are they right or wrong. Rather, aphorisms are half-truth assertions that offer seasoned insights from a particular point of view that may not pertain to every situation. The "journey is more important than the destination" offers a valuable perspective; yet, surely, the goal is (also) to arrive. They also work by challenging our assumptions and shocking our sensibilities: "It is our light, not our darkness that most frightens us."[5] Invaluable to the interpretation and exploration of lived experience, understanding the function of proverbial wisdom is a much-neglected theological tool.

VIRTUES AND VALUES

Virtues are the principles that guide pilgrim behavior. They are the "what" that pilgrims always do, or, at least, when they're at their best. Seeking the fruits of the Spirit, pilgrims are associated with particular virtues, such as patience, hope, and perseverance, hospitality, compassion, and personal responsibility.[6] Pilgrim spirituality espouses a number of secondary, or relative, values that are not operative in every situation. Pilgrims navigate between intentionality and spontaneity, vulnerability and resiliency, persistence and adaptability, resolve and flexibility, austerity and extravagance, confidence and humility, courage and caution, which underscores the importance of situational discernment.

---

that go by a number of names, including axioms, adages, aphorisms, bromides, dictums, epigrams, maxims, mottoes, parables, platitudes, precepts, proverbs, quips, quotations, slogans, truisms, and witticisms (the list is courtesy of Geary, *World*, 7). While the meaning of the terms differs slightly—and not all pilgrim quotes shock or surprise—we will refer to the concise sayings of pilgrim wisdom as aphorisms.

5. Williamson, *Return to Love*, 190–91.

6. See Gal 5:22–23; Col 3:12; 1 Tim 6:11.

PART 2

Biblical Expressions
of Pilgrimage

DEPICTING THE CHRISTIAN LIFE as a journey to God, the Bible casts a prototype, or metatemplate, that governs the image and practice of Christian pilgrimage.

6

The Metatemplate

PILGRIMAGE IN THE BIBLE

NO ONE WORD IN biblical Greek or Hebrew equates to the English concept of pilgrimage. Various terms have been inconsistently rendered as pilgrimage, while the word appears sparingly in English translations of the Bible. The King James Version has three references;[1] the New International Version has two;[2] the New Jerusalem Bible contains five,[3] and the New Revised Standard edition has none.

Even so, translators employ a broad understanding of pilgrimage, reflecting the breadth of the English concept. *Magurim*, the plural form of *magor*, which appears in Gen 47:9, Exod 6:4, and Ps 119:54, means sojourn. *Mesillah*, better translated as highway (see Isa 40:3), occurs in Ps 84:5. *Derek*, used in Amos 8:14, is the common word for road. *Hag*, which denotes a festival, is used in Isa 30:29. Acts 8:27 refers to Jerusalem worship, while Gen 47:9 describes the earthly sojourn.

Since our discussion concerns English connotations of pilgrimage, our approach focuses on meaning, content, and substance rather than the translation of specific biblical words. That said, from narratives of alienation, exile, and return to metaphors of the earthly journey, from the Jewish pilgrimage festivals to the parable of the prodigal son, pilgrimage is a dominant image of the Bible.

---

1. Gen 47:9; Exod 6:4; Ps 119:54.

2. Gen 47:9; Ps 84:5.

3. Ps 84:5; Isa 30:29; Amos 8:14; Acts 8:27; 24:11.

THE BIBLICAL METATEMPLATE

Moreover, Christian pilgrimage is implicitly governed by a biblical prototype, or metatemplate, that envisions *the earthly life as a journey to (and with) God, culminating at the gates of New Jerusalem.* The prototype is an amalgamation of biblical images, concepts, stories, and teachings that depicts our relationship with God as a movement from sin to salvation, or, in pilgrim terms, from being lost to being found, from being out of place to spiritual arrival, from alienation to union with God. The prototype presents the human race as being lost, depicts a pathway to God full of provisions, choices, and challenges, and conveys destinational images of banqueting tables, New Jerusalem, and the kingdom of God, which may be partially experienced in the here and now. The prototype gives purpose, direction, and structure to the pilgrim life, providing the pattern of patterns upon which all other expressions of pilgrimage are based.

While the metatemplate projects the pilgrim's union with God, self, and the Other, it accounts for the human condition: life contains dead ends, false pathways, and failed journeys. To repent is to change direction, to make a U-turn, to find the right path. Grace is the strength to venture forth in the first place and includes times of being carried. The biblical prototype is not a set of precepts nor an outline of prescribed steps along a pre-marked route but a scriptural roadmap that gives agency to individual pilgrims who must interpret personal experience and situational context as they navigate their spiritual journey.

While the prototype contains indelible images, it is open to interpretation as evidenced by the spectrum of Christian traditions. What exactly does the prototype consist of, and what are its principal elements? Even when texts are agreed upon, interpretations vary. What is the relationship between grace and works, between divine providence and human initiative? Does the template speak to the many or the few? Who is on course, and who is off the map?

Even so, the prototype fundamentally shapes our understanding of the pilgrim life. First of all, the Bible depicts the Christian faith as a journey to God. Paul describes it as a race.[4] Secondly, Christian pilgrimage, whether physical or metaphorical, is not *any* or *every* journey but only those that adhere in some form to the metatemplate, which distinguishes *Christian* pilgrimage from non-Christian expressions.[5] Third, the characteristics (i.e., personal, corporate, incarnational, metaphorical, and tensional) and virtues

4. See 1 Cor 9:24; Heb 12:1; Phil 3:14; 2 Tim 4:7.

5. We are more interested in discerning the Christian character of pilgrimage than in asserting how it differs from non-Christian expressions.

(e.g., patience and perseverance) of pilgrimage are derived from the proto-type.[6] Finally, the template casts pilgrimage as a comprehensive model of the Christian life.

In short, the Bible gives the life-as-journey metaphor a Christian imprint. The template is no one text but a collection of complementary and occasionally contested Scriptures. The prototype is not a concrete blueprint of the Christian life; rather, it governs as an interactive roadmap. Charting pathways to God, the prototype is neither a cookie-cutter of uniformity nor an oracle of personal destiny. Each person's journey is unique.

THE IMITATION OF CHRIST

Along with narrative patterns, like the Israelite wilderness experience, concepts supplement the prototype. Pilgrimage is the emulation of others, namely, the imitation of Christ: "For to this you have been called, because Christ also suffered for you, leaving you an example, so that you should follow in his steps" (1 Pet 2:21). Pilgrimage is discipleship. To be a Christian pilgrim is to follow Jesus, sharing the mind of Christ, who "did not regard equality with God as something to be exploited, but emptied himself, taking the form of a slave."[7] The imitation of Christ—e.g., humility, service, and sacrifice—gives conceptual pattern to Christian pilgrimage.[8]

ADDITIONAL DYNAMICS

Some additional points are worth noting. First of all, the biblical prototype cannot be conveyed in pure form. This relates to its character as an amalgamation of biblical images. It likewise pertains to the nature of texts. We can quote texts, but once we begin to interpret them, our relationship to the material becomes indirect. Sermons and religious treatises as well as art, drama, and literature, such as *Pilgrim's Progress*, may explicate the prototype; however, any depiction will invariably contain extrabiblical details and the author's interpretation.[9]

Secondly, there is an implicit tension between the "straight and narrow" path to God and the exploratory nature of pilgrimage, which goes

6. See Gal 5:22–23; Col 3:12; 1 Tim 6:11.

7. Phil 2:5–7; also see 1 Cor 2:16.

8. See Thomas à Kempis, *Imitation of Christ*.

9. See Bunyan, *Pilgrim's Progress* (1678). Also see Edwards, "Christian Pilgrim," a sermon delivered in 1733, which can easily be found on the internet.

wherever the journey may lead. This is different from false paths and missteps or taking "the broad path that leads to destruction" (Matt 7:13). Pilgrimage explores the mysteries of the world; it's the spiritual practice of the road less traveled. Life extends in multiple directions, and the A-to-B journey is not always the one we should take. Pilgrimage honors the sentiment of going somewhere simply because we've not been there before, that the unknown is worth a look. Pilgrims live life by intentional detour, which makes for a longer, more interesting journey.

Third, although we often speak in terms of the Christian pathway to God, envisioned as a linear journey to a celestial destination (e.g., the city of God), the Bible contains other eschatological patterns, namely, (1) returning home (e.g., the Jerusalem return of the Babylonian exiles) and (2) God's journey to us (e.g., the parable of the good shepherd). The prodigal son is a parable of homecoming where salvation is experienced at the place of prior departure. Similarly, Christ as the second Adam appeals to a soteriology of restoration, or a return to the garden of Eden.[10] God's journey *to us* is embodied in the incarnation and is also present in the image of New Jerusalem, which Rev 21:2 describes as descending to earth.

Fourth, and likewise pertaining to the eschatology of pilgrimage, the biblical template contains an internal tension between the earthly journey and the heavenly destination. In other words, does the template leave us too heavenly minded to be of any earthly good? Christianity has too often been a "pie in the sky" religion, and the pilgrim sentiment of being aliens in the world is largely to blame.[11] Pilgrimage has a destinational focus, but our goal is union with God, self, and Other, not heaven per se. To treat the world as fly-over country on the way to heaven is to show contempt for God's creation and the gift of earthly life. What, in a word, is the relationship between heaven and earth? The incarnational nature of pilgrimage stresses the here and now in time and space, including interpersonal relations and our care for the planet. But what is the culminating vision of the Christian life? Heaven and earth are conjoined but where and in what direction? We should take better notice of the Revelator's vision, in which our earthly journey is not, after all, about going to heaven. Rather, New Jerusalem descends to earth, where the kingdom of God is among us.[12]

---

10. Rom 5:12–21; 1 Cor 15:21–29.

11. See John 17:1–19; 1 Pet 2:11; Heb 11:13.

12. See Rev 21:2, 10; Luke 17:21.

7

Biblical Expressions

HAVING CAST THE PROTOTYPE, we turn to a more detailed look at the biblical material. Scripture is a collection of narrative journeys from Adam and Abraham to Paul and the Ethiopian eunuch. The Israelite's wilderness experience and the Babylonian captivity are central motifs of the Old Testament, while Jesus' journey to Jerusalem gives structural climax to the Gospels. Additional journeys include the Magi's visit to Bethlehem, the prodigal son, and the road to Emmaus. From nativity to ascension, the arc of Scripture depicts the peripatetic footsteps of an incarnate God.

While the chapter focuses on representative narratives, the Bible speaks to all life experience in profoundly personal ways. Scripture provisions our spiritual journey, shines light on darkened pathways, and deals with matters, both marvelous and mundane, that concern our everyday lives. Just as the life-as-journey metaphor turns the entirety of life into a pilgrimage, Scripture provides a comprehensive roadmap that guides the pilgrim's journey.

Interpreting our experience of God, self, and the Other through time, place, journey, and people, the Bible is a pilgrimage text. The Bible engages the Other from Ruth to the good Samaritan. It is a testament to ritualized memory from the Jewish festivals to Jesus' institution of the Last Supper. Set upon a religious topography of boundaries, centers, and margins, the Bible describes personal pathways, corporate encounters, physical journeys, and allegorical destinations. Pilgrim themes pervade the text.

OLD TESTAMENT IMAGES

The Alienation of Adam

Epitomized by Adam's expulsion from the garden, pilgrimage is both a companion and counterpoint to alienation. Adamic pilgrims are those who have lost paradise, who wander without hope, estranged from God and at odds with others. Human alienation is transformed by Christ, who, as the second Adam, rewrites the story, restoring our relationship with God.

Noah Afloat

The church has interpreted Noah and the flood as a pilgrimage story, generally viewed through a dualistic prism. The world is evil and precarious. The ark is safe and protective. As Noah's ark, the church is adrift upon turbulent waters, focused on its own survival, waiting for the rainbows of a better world.[1] The interpretation reminds us that we read Scripture through layered traditions. Noah's Ark is a pilgrim narrative; how so is a different story.

Remembering Abraham

Abraham is commonly regarded as the Bible's quintessential pilgrim, and our understanding of pilgrimage leans heavily upon the Abrahamic narrative. God called Abraham to a land that God would show him (Gen 12:1). Abraham obeyed God, left home, and was led to the land of Canaan. Abraham's faith was frequently tested, most notably by the divine command to sacrifice his son, Isaac. Persevering through earthly trials, a popular understanding of pilgrimage, is exemplified in the patriarch's life.

What makes Abraham the archetypal pilgrim, however, is his foreign identity, and being a *stranger* is fundamental to the story. Abraham, moreover, never returned home; his was a one-way journey. The Bible describes Abraham and his descendants as aliens.[2] Upon the death of Sarah, Abraham declared to the Hittites: "I am a stranger and an alien residing among you" (Gen 23:4), and Abraham's descendants would remain "resident aliens in a country belonging to others" (Acts 7:6). Abraham's foreign status is underscored in Hebrews: "By faith Abraham obeyed when he was called to set out for a place that he was to receive as an inheritance; and he set out, not

---

1. The account casts the spiritual journey on water, which likewise occurs in the story of Jonah and whale.

2. Gen 15:13; 17:8; 21:23.

knowing where he was going. By faith he stayed for a time in the land he had been promised, as in a foreign land, living in tents" (Heb 11:8–9).

To be a pilgrim in the footsteps of Abraham is to experience God in foreign places. Called beyond the familiarity of home, pilgrims encounter foreign climes and cultures, placing their lives in the hands of strangers. Pilgrims feel the confusion, disorientation, and anxiety of being aliens in a strange land as well as the blessing of divine protection.

While it is often interpreted metaphorically, we lose important applications of the story when we fail to take Abraham's foreign status literally. Abraham was called to follow God to an unknown destination, living permanently out of place as a stranger in a foreign land. Abrahamic pilgrimage is not about journeying per se; it is about being away from home as a second-place person, whether by choice, calling, or coercion. Abraham's experience relates in special ways to missionaries, ex-pats, and international students. More poignantly, the story speaks to the experience of, and our response to, migrants, immigrants, and refugees. The twist in the story is that Abraham becomes the paradigm of hospitality. Pilgrimage as the imitation of Abraham calls us to entertain angels, offering succor to strangers, shelter to the vulnerable, and sanctuary to the weak and weary.

Ruth

Living life as a second-place person is a primary theme of the book of Ruth. Famine forces Naomi and her sons to move to the land of the Moabites, a sworn enemy of the Israelites. The sons marry; the sons die, and when conditions allow Naomi to return home to Bethlehem, her daughter-in-law, Ruth, insists on going along: "Where you go, I will go; where you lodge, I will lodge; your people shall be my people, and your God my God" (Ruth 1:16). Ruth left her native land, embracing the vulnerabilities and possibilities of a pilgrim. Gleaning, another pilgrimage image, is central to her subsequent story. Ruth's postscript is her role as a foreign matriarch of Christ (Matt 1:1–17).

Wilderness, River, Promised Land

Commingling confusion, longing, and resistance with divine guidance and protection, the Israelite wilderness experience is a journey from bondage and slavery to the brink of the promised land culminating in the crossing of the Jordan River. Wilderness is a place of fear and deprivation, despondency and the loss of faith, idols and golden calves. It is also a place of spiritual encounter, pillars of cloud and fire, and the sustenance of daily manna. River is both a physical and a symbolic boundary, a porous threshold from the old to the new, from journey to arrival, from promise to attainment. Crossing the river is an act of transformation: to cross is to change. Life is different on the other side.

As a destinational image, the promised land confronts us with questions. How does the desert shape us, and where, in the end, does wilderness lead us? What does destination require of us? Do we conquer the Other or join with the nations? What are the ethics of promised land living, and how do we ensure we belong?

Exile and Return

The first lesson of the Babylonian exile is that a life of milk and honey is not guaranteed. An expression of coerced pilgrimage, the existential threat of exile is that the loss of memory precipitates the loss of community and, with it, the loss of identity, meaning, and life itself. More positively, the Babylonian exile is a testament to remaining faithful through trying times. The exile speaks in profound ways to time and place, memory and dislocation, loss and longing, faith and perseverance. Its culminating theme, the Jerusalem homecoming, is about returning home as transformed people. As with the wilderness story, the Babylonian exile reminds us that pilgrimage is a transgenerational journey.

Erecting Memorials

The Old Testament records the practice of erecting monuments to remember important events. Abraham built an altar in Shechem after God pledged the land of Canaan to his offspring. Jacob set up a pillar at Bethel where he had dreamed about God's promise of descendants, land, and blessings, and the Israelites created a twelve-stone memorial in Gilgal upon crossing the Jordan River so their children would remember the benevolence of God.[3] Holy places are expressions of religious memory, markers of our spiritual past, that continue the centuries-old practice of the Gilgal stones.

---

3. Gen 12:6–7; 28:10–22; Josh 4:19–22.

The Burning Bush

Hierophanies, like the bushing bush, demand our attention (Exod 3). They cause us to look. They invoke us to advance without coming too close while insisting upon acts of respect. Aware of the inexplicable nature of the miracles of God, we're baffled nonetheless: "How can an immaterial light burn physically in a material object?"[4]

The Jewish Pilgrim Festivals

Appearing before God at a place of God's choosing, the Israelites were required to attend three annual festivals: the festival of Unleavened Bread (Passover), the festival of Weeks (Shavuot, or Pentecost), and the festival of Booths (Sukkot, or Tabernacles).[5] The Jewish pilgrim festivals have elements of divine calling, sacred time, sacred place, sacred people, and the reenactment of sacred stories.

A Sacred People Called by God

Jerusalem pilgrimage shaped Israelite identity as a sacred people formed by God. Although pilgrimage has never been a Christian mandate, God continually calls Christians on journeys, sometimes, individually, often, as a group. From iterations of religious travel to the long-term congregational journey, to be a sacred people on pilgrimage is to be committed to a corporate experience of God. Sacred communities live faithfully together through covenantal relationships that honor God, foster common life, and respect the individual, including personal and cultural differences.

The call to corporate holiness raises the question of what it means to be a Christian in today's world. What are the defining beliefs and behaviors of the Christian faith? Pilgrimage causes us to reexamine the assumptions of our Christian identity while recognizing our commonalities with the religious Other.

---

4. The question is asked in *The Voyage of Brendan*. See Davies, *Celtic Spirituality*, 189.

5. See Deut 16:16–17; Exod 23:14–17; Exod 34:18–23.

Sacred Time

Just as Scripture mandated the occasions of the Jewish festivals, Christian pilgrimage is a divinely appointed event. Pilgrims travel in God's time. To embark on a pilgrimage is to enter sacred time, leaving ordinary time behind. While the biblical festivals are seasonal, today religious travel occurs throughout the year. The individual pilgrim seldom decides the specific dates of group travel, but that is the nature of pilgrimage: its timing chooses us. The biblical festivals are linked to agricultural cycles, which evoke thanksgiving for God's providential care and material blessings. The festivals remind us that pilgrimage is a celebration of God's abundance.

Sacred Place

The Jewish festivals occurred at the place of God's choosing, a concept that likewise appears in the call of Abraham and the binding of Isaac.[6] A place is holy by virtue of the fact that we have been called by God to go there, summon to see something that God will reveal, an act that is simultaneously mysterious and intimate. Our local churches and volunteer centers as well as our homes, schools, and worksites are sacred places if we discern them as places revealed by God.

Ultimately disclosed as the place of God's choosing, the Temple site in Jerusalem was considered holy for additional reasons. Its holiness was enhanced by the idea that something significant had previously happened there, namely, the binding of Isaac.[7] Identified as Mount Moriah—the place where Abraham nearly sacrificed his son before the angel of the Lord intervened with a ram—the Temple location had Abrahamic associations. As the prototype of sacrificial worship, Mount Moriah imbued the site with additional sacredness. A place may be holy due to its association with past events.

Epitomized by Jesus' boyhood reference to "my father's house" (Luke 2:41–9), the Temple, notably the Holy of Holies, was recognized as the dwelling place of God.

Jewish thought, past and present, has viewed the site as a place that has *always* been holy.[8] The Temple site is the navel of the world, the cosmic

6. See Deut 16:16–17; Gen 12:1; 22:2.

7. Compare 2 Chr 3:1 with Gen 22:2.

8. In a muted sense, and never promulgated as official belief, Christians have occasionally cast a sacred cosmological status upon the places of salvation, shifting, for instance, the center of the world to the Holy Sepulchre. Overall, the Christian approach to sacred places has opted for history over cosmology. Calvary is sacred because of the *event* of crucifixion.

center that gives life to creation.[9] Emanating from the Temple are concentric circles of decreasing holiness: the holy of holies, the Temple precincts, the walled city of Jerusalem, and the land of Israel.[10]

In sum, the Jerusalem Temple evokes several concepts of sacred place:

- A place is holy because one has been called by God to go there; it is a place that God has revealed.

- A sacred place is where something significant has happened; it is a place of special memory.

- Set aside from ordinary space, a holy place is a venue of festival gathering, ritual worship, and sacrificial prayer.

- A sacred site is associated with the presence of God.

- Some places are considered intrinsically sacred; they were created holy.

While engaging these ideas to varying extents, Christian pilgrimage is not reliant upon a particular definition of a sacred place.[11]

Pilgrim Psalms

Pilgrims recited psalms as they approached the Temple: "Who shall ascend the hill of the LORD? And who shall stand in his holy place?" (Ps 24:3).[12] They proclaimed the sentiments of Psalm 84:

> How lovely is your dwelling place, O LORD of hosts! My soul longs, indeed it faints for the courts of the LORD. . . . Happy are those who live in your house, ever singing your praise. Happy are those whose strength is in you, in whose heart are the highways to Zion. . . . For a day in your courts is better than a thousand elsewhere. I would rather be a doorkeeper in the house of my God than live in the tents of wickedness.

The Psalms abound with references to steps, pathways, and walking: "Make me to know your ways, O LORD, teach me your paths" (Ps 25:4);

---

9. See Ezek 5:5 and 38:12.

10. Unlike Christianity, both Jewish and Islamic thought recognizes ontologically-distinct sacred places. Whereas Jewish tradition conceives the land of Israel as a series of concentric circles decreasing in holiness from the Temple outward, Islam believes in the elevated sanctity of three locations: the Great Mosque in Mecca, the Mosque of the Prophet in Medina, and the al-Aqsa Mosque in Jerusalem.

11. See chapter 13.

12. Pilgrim psalms include the Psalms of Ascent (Pss 120–34).

"For your steadfast love is before my eyes, and I walk in faithfulness to you" (Ps 26:3). God leads us down the true path, securing our steps as we go. Even though we walk through the darkest valley, God is with us; though we stumble, we will not fall.[13] God has "delivered me from death and my feet from stumbling, that I may walk before God in the light of life" (Ps 56:13).

Reenacting Sacred Stories

Commemorating elements of the Hebrews' exodus from Egypt, the Passover meal patterns an important aspect of Christian pilgrimage: the reenactment of sacred stories.[14] The Christian holy sites are stations of biblical storytelling, and Holy Land pilgrimage is a stational journey of remembering stories of faith: reading Scripture, observing the sites, performing story-related practices.[15] Commemorating the events of salvation likewise occurs in local settings. From Sunday worship to seasonal celebrations, such as Christmas plays and Easter cantatas, pilgrimage is the reenactment of sacred stories.

The Wisdom of Lived Experience

The meaning of life and the wisdom of lived experience are at the crosshairs of the pilgrim's journey. From chasing after wind to being swallowed by whales, Proverbs, Job, and Ecclesiastes and the prophetic misadventures of Jonah capture the sacred desperations of the accidental pilgrim.

Prophetic Voices

The prophets of the Hebrew Bible contest the status quo, speaking truth to power and bringing the mighty to account. They are pilgrims of justice, beacons of hope in a shadowed world, harbingers of a better way. Casting the pilgrim life in the simplest of terms, the prophets mandate mercy and compassion for the poor and vulnerable, the weak and the weary, widows and children: "what does the LORD require of you but to do justice, and to love kindness, and to walk humbly with your God?" (Mic 6:8).

---

13. Ps 23:3–4; 37:23, 24.
14. See Deut 16:3, 6; Exod 12:1–28.
15. See Aist, *Jerusalem Bound*, 30, 107–10.

THE NATIVITY NARRATIVES

The Annunciation

The annunciation, the Holy Spirit's confession of Mary's conception of Jesus, launches the incarnational focus of the New Testament. God is a pilgrim God, who descends to earth as Immanuel, God with us, in human form in time and place. The incarnation is central to pilgrim spirituality, and the annunciation is the lead story. God's promise becomes pregnant. Word gestates as flesh. Immateriality becomes material, and hope is on the way. As Mary welcomes God's descent, becoming host to the holy, annunciation announces that God is within us. Pilgrimage is participation in God's advance, nurturing God's word, carrying God's presence within us. Salvation springs from the inside out.

Mary's Sojourn

Mary spent the first three months of her pregnancy with her cousin, Elizabeth, who herself was pregnant with John the Baptist. Replete with pilgrimage themes, including hospitality, companionship, memory, hope, and anticipation, the visitation concludes with the Magnificat, or Mary's Song of Praise, one of the most beloved texts of the Bible.

Mary's visit required a physical journey of several days between Nazareth and Judea, but it's the time set aside at Elizabeth's house that drives the story. Mary's sojourn is a temporal expression of the pilgrim life. Pilgrimage is a state of *being* as well as a state of motion, a *status* as much as a journey. The visitation was a pilgrimage, not simply because she traveled, but as time set aside for a purpose.

Pilgrimage includes gap years, educational programs, and professional training, periods of unemployment, retirement, illness, convalescence, and bereavement as well as time set aside for healing, renewal, and discernment. It may also include pregnancy, which Mary celebrated by spending time with her cousin focusing on self-care and family relations.[16] Pilgrimage is the intentionality of temporal situations.

The Journey to Bethlehem

Mary and Joseph journeyed from Nazareth to Bethlehem to enroll in Caesar's census. It was a burdensome journey for a pregnant woman, and

16. On pregnancy as a pilgrimage, see Jansson and Freeman, *Fertile Ground*.

Christian tradition speaks of Mary resting along the way.[17] In Bethlehem, there was no room in the house, so Mary gave birth in a cave-cum-byre. The story contends that life happens on the road, that life's most intimate and vulnerable moments may occur in strange and unforeseen places. Despite being born in the city of David, the ancestral domicile of Joseph, Jesus' birth was out of place, beyond the norm, outside the lines, far from his Galilean home. Pilgrimage concerns our relationship to home and away, to welcoming and off-putting places, to crowded and all-alone spaces.

The Shepherds' Story

The shepherds lived simple, peripatetic lives, exposed to the elements, sheltering in caves. Showered with angelic solicitations, the shepherds were greeted by the good news of Christ's birth, and straight away they journeyed to see the gospel firsthand. Pilgrimage is the journey of commonplace people seeking space around the manger.

Jesus' Presentation in the Temple

Jesus' naming, circumcision, and presentation in the Temple underscore the role of place and ritual in the religious practice of the Holy Family as first-century Galilean Jews (Luke 2:21–38). Our lives are bound by time and place, cultural context, and religious identity. Pilgrimage continues the journey of past generations. Simeon and Anna represent the wisdom of elders, the personification of faith, and the embodiment of hope and anticipation.

The Journey of the Magi

The Magi are often regarded as the first Christian pilgrims.[18] Theirs is a round-trip journey to a holy destination, in this case, a person instead of a place. They left their country, traveled a long distance, worshipped the Christ Child, and returned home. Their story provides a model for Holy Land travelers, who likewise leave home on a long-distance journey to a foreign destination to see the people and places of Christ. More generally, the Magi's journey is an allegory of the Christian life. What does it mean to search for the Christ Child? What are the signs that stir us to action,

17. *Protoevangelium*, 17.

18. For instance, see Foster, *Sacred Journey*, 61.

that inspire our journey of faith? How are we guided along the way? What threatens to compromise our purpose, and what does it mean to bear gifts?

The Flight to Egypt

As the Magi returned home, Herod unleashed his jealous fury, killing the infant males in the region. Warned in a dream, the Holy Family took flight to Egypt. At risk in their own land, they sought safety through distance, seeking the succor of strangers. Pilgrimage, at times, is the result of desperate measures; the vulnerable become exiles, the unprotected refugees.

The Boy Jesus in the Temple

Luke concludes his nativity narratives with the boy Jesus in the Temple during the Passover festival (Luke 2:41–51). The account captures the communal nature of pilgrim travel with an added twist: the pilgrim journey is not merely about taking the right path but traveling with *the right people*. Who, in other words, is missing from our journey?

The scene of Jesus sitting with the elders of the Temple depicts the religious life as one of engaged debate. The boy Jesus probes with questions as he likewise did as a rabbi. His description of the Temple as his Father's house presents a classic understanding of a holy place as a place where God resides. Packed with pilgrim images, the nativity narratives provide a theological prelude to what follows in the Gospels.

NEW TESTAMENT IMAGES

Jesus as Jerusalem Pilgrim

Consistent with the nativity narratives, the Gospel of John depicts Jesus as a Jerusalem pilgrim who frequented the Temple festivals throughout his ministry.[19] Jesus was attending Passover when he overturned the tables of the money changers and discussed eternal life with Nicodemus. The healing of the paralytic at the pool of Bethesda occurred during an unnamed festival.[20] John 7–10 concerns conversations during the autumn gathering of Tabernacles, while John 10:22–39 records Jesus' presence at the feast of

19. See Freyne, "Jesus."
20. See John 2:13–25; 3:1–21; 5:1–18.

Dedication. All four Gospels set the final week of Jesus' life during the Passover festival in Jerusalem.

Jesus as Wayfaring Messiah

Jesus led a peripatetic life as an itinerant prophet with no place to lay his head.[21] His ministry was marked by the immediacy of the kingdom of God, and he never lingered long in the same location. He told a potential disciple who wanted to bury his father to "Let the dead bury their own dead; but as for you, go and proclaim the kingdom of God" (Luke 9:59–60). To another who wanted to say farewell to his family, Jesus replied, "No one who puts a hand to the plow and looks back is fit for the kingdom of God" (Luke 9:62). Following Jesus meant leaving the past behind, traveling without bodily comforts, and never staying long in the same place. He was a wayfaring messiah, constantly on the road, always on the go, at home in other people's houses. Pilgrims live in the urgency of the present moment, proclaiming the good news of God, called to locations where people have no place to lay their heads. Jesus' disciples are stewards of the streets, servants of the road, guests along the way.

The Ascetic Pilgrim

Related to the wayfaring image is the ascetic pilgrim: the one who lives simply, travels lightly, and practices acts of self-denial. Jesus sent the twelve disciples on a mission journey, telling them: "Take no gold, or silver, or copper in your belts, no bag for your journey, or two tunics, or sandals, or a staff" (Matt 10:9–10). Pilgrimage is the navigation of needs and desires. What should we always have with us, and what should be left behind?

To what degree is the Christian life one of self-denial? While Jesus made the ultimate sacrifice—and his harder words are extremely demanding—he was an ambivalent ascetic, especially in contrast to John the Baptist. Viewing his presence on earth in terms of a bridegroom, Jesus said: "The wedding guests cannot mourn as long as the bridegroom is with them [but] the days will come when the bridegroom is taken away from them, and then they will fast."[22] The question is not whether Christians should engage in ascetic practices, such as fasting and self-denial, but when and how often. Pilgrimage is what we do in the absence of the bridegroom.

---

21. See Matt 8:19–22; Luke 9:58–62.
22. See Matt 9:14–15; Mark 2:18–20; Luke 5:33–35.

Pilgrimage as Mission and Evangelism

In sending the disciples out into the world to proclaim the good news of God, Jesus gave them "authority over unclean spirits" and power to "cure every disease and every sickness" (Matt 10:1, 7–8). Pilgrims are missionaries, just as missionaries are pilgrims, serving the world, witnessing to the love and power of God. As heralds of the kingdom of God, pilgrims are instruments of healing, advocates of peace, arbiters of reconciliation.

Resident Aliens

The New Testament views the world, in places, as a foreign country. Christians are resident aliens who are "in the world but not of the world."[23] The heroes of faith "were strangers and foreigners on the earth . . . seeking a homeland . . . a better country, that is, a heavenly one" (Heb 11:13–19). Against these views, Jesus also asserts that the kingdom of God is among us (Luke 17:21).

Christological Images

As previously discussed, Christological images resource the pilgrim life. Jesus is the alpha and the omega, the A and the Z, the beginning *through* to the end. Christ, in other words, is a comprehensive presence: he is our departure, our destination, and every step in-between. Christ is with us in the meantime, in the liminality of time and space. He is our past, our present, and our never-ending future.

To journey well, we must see well. Jesus is the light of the world in a land full of darkness (John 8:12). Direction is everything; Jesus is the way (John 14:6).

Christ as shepherd is our guide and protector. Calling his sheep by name, the sheep follow him because they recognize his voice (John 10:2–4). The Johannine image builds upon the divine shepherd of Psalm 23, who leads his sheep to watered pastures. Jesus, the good shepherd, guides, comforts, protects, and provides.

The shepherd doubles as the gate. Jesus said, "I am the gate for the sheep. . . . Whoever enters by me will be saved, and will come in and go out and find pasture" (John 10:9). Life is a choice between the wide gate that leads to destruction and the narrow gate, which is Christ himself (Matt

---

23. John 17:14–15; also see Eph 2; Acts 7:6.

7:13). Warding off danger and harm, good gates create places of safety. The image reminds us that a holy place is a sanctuary of godly protection: "You are a hiding place for me; you preserve me from trouble; you surround me with glad cries of deliverance" (Ps 32:7).

Acts

From Jerusalem to the ends of the world, Acts depicts the pilgrim-like movements of the gospel itself. The rippling effects of the resurrection—the fury of Pentecost, the conversion of Jews and gentiles, and Paul's missionary journeys—fuel the centrifugal momentum of a pilgrim church, nascent but on the move.

Revelation

The paramount image of biblical pilgrimage is New Jerusalem, the city of God. New Jerusalem, a word picture of heaven, awaits at the end of our earthly journey. Pearly gates and streets of gold lead to the throne of Christ where we share the stage with the nations of the world. As previously noted, it's the city that *descends*. Our future home with God is heaven *on earth*.

PART 3

The Objective of Pilgrimage

WHILE PILGRIMAGE IS THE *experience* of God, self, and the Other (chapters 8–10), its ultimate objective is the *union* of the three (chapter 11), which we attain, not simply at the journey's end, but in profound, if incomplete, ways over the course of our lives.

8

God

WHICH GOD?

THE SPIRITUAL TENET THAT *God is in the facts* speaks to the question of God's location. Yet, in searching for God, the *what* proceeds the *where*. Life is full of false gods and spiritual mirages: golden calves, money, and mammon, pride, power, privilege, and possessions. *Which* god is the pilgrim after?

Christian pilgrimage constantly revisits Jesus' question at Caesarea Philippi: "Who do you say that I am?" (Matt 16:15). Caesarea Philippi was a cultic center full of Greek and Roman temples. An assemblage of religious pluralism, the place is a metaphor of multiple choice.

Life generates distorted notions of God. God is a tyrant. God is money. God is our own self-image, the face we see in the mirror. Pilgrimage is the process of stripping away false images of God.

Christians seek the God of Abraham through Scripture, history, and tradition. As Trinitarian mystery, incarnate in Christ, God is the one who creates, redeems, and sustains us. Patron of the pilgrim journey, God is the divide guide who calls, accompanies, and welcomes us with open arms. In pursuit of the God of virtue, pilgrims embrace faith, hope, and love, truth, goodness, and beauty.

GOD AS JOURNEY AND DESTINATION

God is both the journey and the destination, our actualized pathways and our promised arrival. God is the highway to Zion as well as the shadowed valley. At journey's end, God is a parental embrace.

> To know Thee is the end and the beginning.
> Thou carriest us and Thou dost go before,
> Thou art the journey and the journey's end.[1]

GOD AS THE TRANSCENDENT OTHER

God as the transcendent Other means that God is beyond the world. God views creation from a distance, only occasionally irrupting. An extension, or consequence, of transcendence is immanence, which is God's indwelling presence in the world, a role associated with the Holy Spirit.[2] The transcendent–immanent dichotomy expresses a dynamic tension: God is without and about and near and within, neither too distant nor overly familiar.

God is also beyond our comprehension in the sense that we are unable to imagine God at all. Returning to Aquinas: "Then alone do we know God truly, when we believe that [God] is far above all that [we] can possibly think of God."[3] God is the inexplicable Other, and the best we can do is to remain silent, use metaphor, or describe what God is not.[4]

CHRIST AS COUNTERPOINT

God confounds us, yet again, by partially negating the impasse: the God of inexplicable mystery doubles as a God of embodied revelation. Christ became human; mystery became tangible, and the incarnation bridges, in part, the Otherness of God. Christ revealed God through his teachings, virtues, and miracles, while God revealed Christ through the events of his life: baptism, resurrection, transfiguration, and ascension. The incarnation embodies the paradox: an unknown God can be known after all.

---

1. Attributed to Boethius (d. 542). Quoted in Appleton, *Oxford Book of Prayer*, 7.

2. The immanence of God is still fundamentally distinct from us.

3. Aquinas, *Summa* (book 1, chapter 5), 10; quoted in Campbell, *Thou Art That*, 39.

4. On negative, or apophatic, theology, see Davies and Turner, *Silence*. Also see Lane, *Solace*.

THE HOLY SPIRIT AS GUIDE AND COMPANION

God as Holy Spirit is our guide and companion, our counsel and comforter, our strength and shelter. The Holy Spirit nourishes and nudges, discerns and directs, reveals and unveils. Pilgrimage is a Spirit-filled journey towards destinations of completion.[5]

EXPERIENCING THE DIVINE

Pilgrims encounter God through actualized events, means of grace, and other people. Our experience of the divine is sustained through memories, thoughts, and reflections.

Lived Experience

Pilgrims encounter God in time and place through lived experience: through events, incidents, and accidents, one-off occasions and serendipitous surprises, everyday routines and long-term situations.

Means of Grace

Pilgrims experience God through means of grace, including personal prayer and corporate worship. From fasting and feasting to Holy Communion, pilgrims embrace spiritual disciplines, meaningful rituals, and sacramental encounters.

Through Others

Christ is in the gaze of others. Angels appear as strangers, and hospitality invokes the presence of God. Wherever two or more are gathered, Christ is with us, and the "least of these" is God in human form.[6]

---

5. Niebuhr, "Pilgrims," 7.
6. Matt 18:20; 25:40.

Through Memories and Reflections

The God of the journey is also the God of reflection. Our memories, thoughts, and interpretations are infused with the stirrings of the Holy Spirit.

9

Self

PILGRIMAGE IS THE PERSONAL self-reckoning of who we are. Each life is uniquely sacred, but sin has scarred God's image within us. The pilgrim life is a journey from self-alienation to personal transcendence, which involves emptying ourselves, submitting to God, and daring to find our place in the world.

ALIENATION

As spiritual heirs of Adam, we wander through life, closed off from the garden and cut-off from God. Aliens are estranged and separated, lost but aware, with no access to pathways of life. The alienated shouts in the wilderness: "What shall I do?"[1] Pilgrimage is God's grace-filled response to spiritual alienation.

SELF-DECEPTION

While the alienated are unhappy and they know it, the self-deceived are lost and unaware. Alienation is a reality check; self-deception is seeing ourselves through a distorted lens. Self-deception is the human tendency to think too highly of ourselves, to miscalculate—due to pride, overconfidence, or naiveté—who we are and where we are on our journey. Self-deception is living life by false pretenses, pursuing impermanent goals, following the

---

1. See Bunyan, *Pilgrim's Progress*, "In the Similitude of a Dream," opening lines.

wrong god. It is thinking we are *here* when we are actually *there*. Pilgrimage recalibrates our spiritual coordinates.

Pilgrim writers couch the spiritual journey as a struggle between our true and false self, in which transformation consists of shedding our distortions while nurturing the self God created us to be.[2] Pursuing God's wholeness within us is the antidote to self-deception.

ISOLATION

In *Brothers Karamazov*, Dostoevsky describes the destructive nature of individuality:

> For today everyone is still striving to keep his individuality as far apart as possible, everyone still wishes to experience the fullness of life in himself alone, and yet instead of achieving the fullness of life, all his efforts merely lead to the fullness of self-destruction, for instead of full self-realization they relapse into complete isolation. . . . For he is used to relying on himself alone and has separated himself as a self-contained unit from the whole. He has trained his mind not to believe in the help of other people.[3]

Pilgrimage is a journey from isolation to connectedness, from a false sense of self-sufficiency to the fullness of interdependence. The self is ultimately defined in relation to others.

SELF-ACCEPTANCE

Pilgrimage is a journey of self-acceptance in which we learn to love ourselves. The pilgrim life moves from self-forgiveness and acceptance to a life-giving faith that incorporates our passions, personalities, gifts, and talents. Pilgrimage is personal participation in the image of God shared in concert with others.

SELF-CARE AND PERSONAL MANAGEMENT

Pilgrimage redirects the Golden Rule, treating the self as one would treat others. Paul, a fellow pilgrim on the Camino de Santiago, approached the

2. See Heuertz, *Pilgrimage*; Granberg-Michaelson, *Without Oars*, 33–37, 50.

3. Dostoevsky, *Brothers Karamazov*, 357.

experience as an exercise in self-care: "The Camino is not about new things; it's about learning how to manage yourself." Acknowledging our limitations, weaknesses, and dependencies, self-care invokes help from a higher power. It also requires attention to preventive details. An Arab proverb attributed to Muhammad says: "Trust in God but tie your camel."

Self-care involves discipline, time management, and forward planning. For me, personal management on the Camino meant setting off early enough each morning to avoid the afternoon heat and, once I stopped for the day, attending to blisters, washing clothes in time to dry, taking afternoon siestas when the shops were closed, then finding an open market to buy food for the morning. Self-management for religious travelers includes taking medications, securing cash, charging phones and cameras, eating and resting well, and finding time to journal. The spiritual journey is propelled by practical tasks, and we pay the price when we neglect or forget them. Pilgrims take preventive measures, develop patterns of repetition, and attend to needs as they arrive. Transgressing self-care stops pilgrims in their tracks.

While self-care concerns personal matters of physical, emotional, and spiritual health, certain steps can be taken with others. Pilgrims share resources and provisions, offer counsel and guidance, and welcome suggestions and reminders. Bolstered by the support of others, pilgrimage is a concentrated exercise in personal management.

SELF-DISCOVERY

Personal enlightenment and finding our place in the world does not come by merely accepting what someone else has told us: each person has to discover it for him or herself. Stepping outside the roles and constraints that define us, pilgrimage takes us beyond ourselves, beyond the familiar, into the unknown. When we do so, we discover our passions and dependencies, our dreams and anxieties, our strengths and limitations. Engaging other cultures and traditions teaches us about ourselves.

PERSONAL QUEST

In the legend of the Holy Grail, each knight entered the forest at its darkest point, at a place where no path had previously been cut. To be a knight was to forge a new pathway, to go where no one had gone before.[4] Pilgrimage is a personal quest through uncharted terrain.

4. Campbell, *Romance*, 217.

This, in fact, is never quite the case. Pioneers become pilgrims when they recognize that the road less traveled has been traveled before. Surrounded by a cloud of witnesses, the most personal of journeys are guided by the wisdom, encouragement, and presence of others (Heb 12:1).

SELF-ACTUALIZATION

According to Abraham Maslow, self-actualization is achieving one's potential, which may pertain to a given area of life, for instance, as a mother, a father, a musician, or an athlete. Self-actualization is not a finalized level of attainment but a matter of degree. One is always, constantly improving.

TRANSCENDENCE

Maslow later acknowledged that self-actualization is not the apex of self-fulfillment. Recognizing that the ideal personal journey continues beyond the self, he revised his motivational hierarchy, topping it with transcendence needs that are fulfilled though religious faith, mystical experience, and service to others.[5] Pilgrimage is personal, first-hand experience, but it is not a self-centric journey. Defining the self in terms of one's responsibility to others is at the heart of the Christian life.

SELF-FOCUSED JOURNEYS

Pilgrim spirituality takes a holistic approach to the Christian life, but what does it say about self-focused journeys that have little, if any, engagement with others? We appeal, once again, to the family resemblance theory: any one element may not be present in a given expression of pilgrimage. We need, at times, to focus on the self, including being alone. As a personal journey of healing and wholeness, pilgrimage is an exercise in self-care, self-discovery, and self-actualization. Pilgrim spirituality recognizes the sanctity of self-focused journeys.

---

5. See McLeod, "Maslow's Hierarchy." Maslow also added cognitive and aesthetic needs, rendering a final hierarchy of (1) physiological, (2) safety, (3) belonging and love, (4) esteem, (5) cognitive, (6) aesthetic, (7) self-actualization, and (8) transcendence needs.

10

The Other

THE OTHER REFERS TO the general mysteries of God, the unknown quantities of life, and the wonders of the world in which we live. More specifically, it refers to *other people*. Pilgrimage places primacy on the human Other, welcoming strangers and foreigners, loving enemies and neighbors, and recognizing Christ in the "least of these."

AT HOME WITH THE OTHER

Hospitality, compassion, forgiveness, and reconciliation start with the proximate Other, with family, friends, and familiar foes. Home is our habitual journey, where our character is forged by everyday interactions.

LIKE A GOOD NEIGHBOR

Like the priest and the Levite in the parable of the good Samaritan, we often respond to others based upon calculations and stereotypes instead of the sanctity of human life (Luke 10:25–37). The parable depicts the religious, cultural, and ethnic Other as a person of compassion and mercy who possesses virtues that exceed our own: the good Samaritan is the consummate Other who is more like God than we are. The parable cautions us from treating the Other as the object of our own benevolence. Rather, it's the Other who bestows the blessing. Whereas the Samaritan acts as the ideal neighbor, the priest and the Levite become the Other to their own. Pilgrimage is the practice of compassionate self-giving to whomever is in need.

THE ENEMY OTHER

What's often misunderstood is that the Samaritan is not the *oppressed* Other so much as the *enemy* Other, resourceful rather than marginalized. Jesus said *love your enemies* (Luke 5:44), and pilgrims are not exempt. It is said that one cannot hate a person whose story is known, which frames enmity as a refusal to listen. Just as peacemaking is not possible as long as we demonize the Other, pilgrims promote peace by listening to stories.

THE DANGER OF A SINGLE STORY

When people are reduced to caricatures, we deny them the means to surprise us with behaviors that differ from our distorted expectations. Pilgrims recognize the danger of a single story.[1]

OTHERING OTHERS

Othering, as a verb, is excluding people, individuals, and groups that do not fit our personal, social, and religious norms; it places people in the margins, beyond the boundaries of our self-defined world. Othering others can be intentional, egregious, subtle, or unconscious. Othering is the denial of human dignity, the rejection of God's image in the Other, and has its own set of pronouns: they, them, and those. Othering is a sinful attempt to limit the love of God.

GOD IS IN THE OTHER

God is in the gaze of the Other. That's a relief—that God can be seen—as well as an indictment: when we refuse to meet their eyes.

THE DISTANT OTHER

Pilgrimage makes the world smaller by bridging distances, collapsing spatial buffers, and bringing the far away into view. Through religious travel, news and social media, and shared ministry initiatives, the distant Other assumes importance in our lives. Supporting fair trade, human rights, and economic justice, pilgrimage is a global journey with our distant neighbors.

---

1. See Adichie, "The Danger."

OTHERWORLD VIRTUES

Finally, pilgrims embody Otherworld virtues, beginning with empathy, mercy, and compassion. They are sensitive to the suffering of others. Pilgrimage penetrates barriers of division, dissolves the borders that divide us, and upholds the dignity of others. As expressed in the image of a common table, Otherworld virtues include respect, equality, collaboration, and companionship.

11

The Union of God, Self, and the Other

"The first law is that you and the other are one."

—JOSEPH CAMPBELL[1]

THE ULTIMATE OBJECTIVE OF pilgrimage is the union of God, self, and the Other. Spiritual union involves interpersonal relatedness, which belongs to the very nature of God.[2] This does not imply homogenization; rather, Christian unity preserves the participatory expression of our individualized selves. Our relatedness with God, which is characterized by asymmetrical reciprocity, is different from our relatedness with other people. While other words, such as mutuality, could be used to describe interhuman relations, we will retain the language of union.[3]

INCLUSIVE UNION

Jesus prays for the unity of all believers: "As you, Father, are in me and I am in you, may they also be in us. . . . I in them and you in me, that they may

---

1. Campbell, *Power of Myth*, 250, 281.

2. See Newbigin, *Open Secret*, 78.

3. The language of mutuality and asymmetrical reciprocity appears in Heuertz, *Pilgrimage*, 31–42.

become completely one" (John 17:20–26). The prayer refers to believers as opposed to those in "the world," which begs the question: does union with the Other refer to *everyone*? Who's left out, doesn't belong, or doesn't want to be included? Moreover, who decides? Certain biblical images suggest the exclusion of some, if not several. Other directives, like Jesus' command to love our enemies, establish the Other as everyone. While Jesus tells us to leave the sorting to God (Matt 13:24–42), the pilgrim's hope and objective is the union of all.

SPIRITUAL MARRIAGE

No biblical image expresses intimacy with God better than marriage. The relationship between Yahweh and the Israelite people is described as a wedlock (Hos 2:19). Jesus refers to himself as a bridegroom (Matt 9:15), while Paul writes, "I promised you in marriage . . . to Christ" (2 Cor 11.2). Initiated by God and sealed through a covenantal commitment, spiritual marriage conveys the intimacy of love, the union of wills, and the consummation of desire. While marriage is a person-to-person relationship, the biblical metaphor espouses a union between God and a people: in the Old Testament, the nation of Israel is the bride, while Jesus as the bridegroom becomes wedded to the church. As a metaphor of union between God and the self, the intimacy of spiritual marriage—the soul becoming one with God without losing its identity—has been favored by mystics.[4] Although spiritual marriage beautifully captures the union of God and the self—or God and a people—the weakness of the image is that the wedding party (i.e., everyone else) has a secondary relationship with the bride and the groom.

THE BODY OF CHRIST

Whereas spiritual marriage conjoins two entities, the body of Christ incorporates a host of diverse members.[5] The matrimonial image espouses commitment, love, and intimacy, while the corporate image projects a common purpose—the wellness of a body realized through the functional integration of its specialized parts. The image is one of organic unity between Christ, self, and others. Christ is the head. Each of us is a part. Rest of the body is everyone else. Much broader and inclusive than the metaphor of marriage,

4. Medieval writings on mystical marriage, also known as bridal theology, include the works of Catherine of Siena, Teresa of Ávila, Gregory the Great, and Bernard of Clairvaux. See Matter, "Mystical Marriage."

5. See Rom 12:4–5; 1 Cor 12:12–31.

the image of the body incorporates the primacy of Christ, the diversity of its individual members, and the imperative of interdependency: one for all and all for one. Still, the question of exclusion pertains: who does not belong to the body of Christ?

THE GATHERING OF THE NATIONS

Revelation casts a culminating vision of destinational union between God and God's people: the gathering of the nations surrounding the throne of God.[6] Whereas the promised land narrative is limited to the Israelite people, the city of God is inhabited by the nations of the world. Unity is choral, harmonious, and vocal. God lives among mortals. Saints and former sinners live in accord. Swords have been beaten into plowshares, and, together, the lamb and the lion have learned to lie down.[7]

Full of movement, anticipation, and confluence, the gathering of the nations is the consummate pilgrimage image. We are on a march, on the way, joining others as we go. Our journey begins in black and white and ends in color. Union is the illumination of God, and the hues of the nations are resplendent in the light of Christ. The union of God, self, and the Other has no shadows, restrictions, or qualifications. It prevails in a tearless embrace (Rev 21:4).

BUBER'S I-THOU RELATIONSHIPS

According to Martin Buber (1878–1965), we address each other in one of two ways, each represented by a word pairing: I–It and I–Thou.[8] I–It, which is the typical way we interact with each other, uses people as a means to an end. From practical necessities to personal desires, the I–It relationship manipulates others to get what we want. It is governed by what we know about the other person from past experience.

The I–Thou, which recognizes the full humanity of the Other, involves being completely present with another person. The I–Thou happens in the here and now, in the spontaneity of the present moment. For Buber, the I–Thou is the locus of all genuine spirituality, including transcendent moments. Human beings do not grow on their own in any significant way.

6. See Rev 7:9; Rev 21–22.

7. See Rev 5; Isa 2:4; 11:6, 65:25; Joel 3:10; Mic 4:3.

8. The archaic "thou" expresses the most familiar sense of "you." I–thou should be read as I–you.

Rather, personal growth requires I–Thou interactions that unfold between people rather than within the self. An I–Thou experience occurs when an external grace presents itself, which must be met by both parties with a willful response to enter into a relationship of reciprocal mutuality.

The I–It and the I–Thou also apply to our relationship with God, whom Buber refers to as the eternal Thou. Our prayers can objectify God (I-It), trying to manipulate God into giving us what we want and withholding bad things from our lives. Or, we may be fully present before God, acknowledging our human condition. Every I–Thou experience with another person is a participatory encounter with the eternal Thou. Attentive to I–Thou opportunities, pilgrims seek the eternal Thou of human relations.[9]

9. See Buber, *I and Thou*. The above summary is based on Dobson, "Buber."

PART 4

The Dimensions of Pilgrimage

HAVING DISCUSSED THE OBJECTIVE of pilgrimage—the union of God, self, and the Other—we turn to its means, or dimensions: time, place, journey, and people.

12

Time

"Where is it, this present? . . .
[It is] gone in the instant of becoming."
—WILLIAM JAMES[1]

TIME, WHAT IS IT? Among Augustine's confessions was his elusive understanding of time. If no one asked him, he knew what it was. If someone
asked, he couldn't explain it.[2] It surrounds us like water to a fish; yet, we
struggle to define it. Does time move toward us, or do *we* move through
time? How do Christians perceive and experience time, and what are the
temporal dimensions of pilgrimage?

Time is linear and circular, sacred and ordinary. Pilgrims commemorate the past, live faithfully in the present, and anticipate the future. They
repeat time and celebrate the seasons. Pilgrimage includes the bracketing
of time for a particular purpose. Comprised of temporal virtues, such as
perseverance, hope, and anticipation, the pilgrim life is our response to the
timing of God.

1. James, *Principles*, 608.
2. Augustine, *Confessions*, 11.14.

ON THE BANKS OF ROASTING EAR

At the end of my around-the-world journey, I spent forty days of solitude camping in the Ozark Mountains of northern Arkansas alongside a creek named Roasting Ear. Beside its waters I sat . . . and sat. Forty days is biblical for a really long time. The hermitage experience shifted back and forth between images of paradise and wilderness. Candle-lit evening prayer, nightly campfires, sunsets, starry nights, and the constant sound of spring-fed waters saturated my soul. Hours spent reading the Bible bestowed a treasure trove of peace.

At times, the contentment dissipated. I saw dozens of snakes, hundreds of ticks, and endured a severe storm that seriously damaged my tent. I was alone in a wilderness from which I needed God's protection.

While my hermitage experience was full of pilgrimage themes, what did it tell me about time and memory? Except for a Bible and a hymnal, I took no books, hobbies, or instruments—no extra things to fill my time. I read the Bible, prayed, journaled, and walked along the creek. I gathered wood and cooked over an open fire. Twice a week, I walked to an arranged drop-off point to collect food that my hosts, Bob and Kay, left in a bear-proof box.

I also choose not to take a watch. Journaling kept me abreast of the date, though I thought more in terms of the number of days I'd been there—and how many more I had left to go. Otherwise, time was marked by night and day. During daylight hours, I was largely aware of the position of the sun. Still, afternoon time was long and indistinct. I never knew how late I slept, what time I ate, or when I went to bed.

Sacred time was experienced through morning and evening prayer held in an open-air chapel that I "set aside" under some trees overlooking the creek. Outlined by a row of stones, the chapel was adorned with a small altar of unhewn rocks, candles, and two tree limbs lashed together to form a large cross. I celebrated Sundays with an additional time of prayer.

My experience was marked by event time rather than clock time.[3] Events, such as chapel prayer, journaling, and Bible reading, walks, collecting firewood, cooking, and meals, occurred when they happened, not at a specified time. With respect to the seasons—late April to the beginning of June—I sensed change through the warming of the days, the thickening of the foliage, and the growth of grass around my tent, which I kept at bay with a scythe. As the weather turned dry, the spring grew tired, and the creek began to fall.

3. On the distinctions between clock time and event time, see Levine, *Geography*, 51–99.

While I retain a slate of impressions, my memories of the experience are a modest montage of events that stands out from a timeless recollection of being. I remember the turkey hunter, wearing overalls and carrying a shotgun, whom I encountered near the creek. It seemed prudent to break my silence, my only spoken words for forty days. I remember the thunderstorm, the armadillo, and the snakes. For the most part, however, instead of true memories, I have mental images and emotional impressions—spring-fed waters, sunlit days, and evening campfires—because, in one sense, nothing happened.

It's been said that "monotony collapses time, novelty unfolds it."[4] I have countless stories from my previous nine months of global travel but limited memories from my time in the woods. Change, movement, and novelty—new surroundings and fresh events—expand our perception of time, while routine and the lack of distinctive events leave less detectable memories. Even so, experience transforms us independently of our recollections.

Memories aside, my sojourn on Roasting Ear Creek was a spiritual saturation in time. More accurately, it was a temporal saturation in God. The past and future converged in my prayers. Time was spent debriefing my around-the-world travels while reflecting on my ministry calling. The recent past was detailed with people, events, and stories. The future was open, opaque, and unknown. Bridging the past and the future was the real-time presence of God.

THE CHRISTIAN EXPERIENCE OF TIME

My sojourn speaks to our complex relationship to time—how we perceive, structure, and experience it. Time is not one thing but consists of a number of concepts, including duration, temporal order, tense, and the sense of nowness:

- Duration refers to the amount of time, or the interval, that elapses between two specific events.

- Temporal order is the sequence in which events occur.

- Tense has to do with the temporal distinction between the past, the present, and the future.

- Nowness is the subjective sense of the "right now," whatever that is.[5]

4. Foer, *Moonwalking*, 77.

5. See Burdick, *Why Time Flies*, 25–26. For books that discuss time, timing, and memory, see Burdick, *Why Time Flies*; Pink, *When*; Levine, *Geography*; Hammond, *Time Warped*; Foer, *Moonwalking*. For a novel using time as a leitmotif, see Mann,

Time also concerns timing and the optimum time to do certain tasks.[6] Deadlines determine when things should be done and when unfinished tasks must be set aside.[7] Life is stamped with sell-by dates, use-by dates, and times when things expire.

Ordinary Time

Unless it is set apart as sacred, time is ordinary, common, and profane. Ordinary time is the day-to-day passage of time. It consists of common events, mundane moments, and everyday routines. Ordinary time does not delimit our experience of God, self, and the Other; rather, it speaks to the context in which it occurs. Ordinary time is our experience of Tuesday morning; it's the non-special occasion. It's life off-camera; it's eating meals without a special place. While we could argue that an encounter with God makes the context sacred, our point is that ordinary time has meaning of its own, offering a different glimpse of God. God is great with special occasions—and excels on the Sabbath—but the divine does just fine as a weekday God.[8]

Sacred Time

While ordinary time is normal time, sacred time is time set apart. From the weekly Sabbath to seasonal festivals to the year of Jubilee, the Bible sanctions the sacredness of time. Christians follow suit, commemorating the events of salvation on a daily, weekly, and seasonal basis. While the liturgical calendar layers time with sacred meaning, every act of gathered prayer likewise invokes the presence of God. Personal demarcations of sacred time include special honors, achievements, and occasions, anniversaries of celebration and lament, and times set aside for a special purpose.

Magic Mountain.

6. See Pink, *When.*

7. Heschel, *Sabbath*, 3 describes unfinished tasks being left undone upon arrival of the Sabbath.

8. Liturgically, ordinary time occurs (1) between Christmastide and Lent and (2) between Eastertide and Advent. See sacred, cyclical, and worship time below.

Linear Time

As a historical religion, Christianity conceptualizes time as a linear continuum. Linear time moves in a line from beginning to end, consisting of the past, present, and future.

The Present

The present is the ongoing "now" of lived experience. It is life unveiled before our eyes. God's consolation is a real-time presence. Practicing the sacrament of the present moment, pilgrims savor the blessings of the here and now. Rarely, however, are we fully in the present; seldom is the present perceived in isolation. The present retains a sense that time has preceded it; at the same time, it anticipates the approaching dissolvement of the future.[9]

The Past

As the sequence of time that has preceded the present, the past may be arranged chronologically by dates or narratively according to events. Like links in a chain, narrative is a composition of successive events that leads up to and accounts for the present, which allows us, in turn, to view the present in the context of a story in progress. Without an organized sequence of remembered events, the past dissipates or lingers as unrelated episodes in our lives.[10]

How we live in the present—and look to the future—is shaped by our relationship to the past. Remembering God's acts of salvation, Christians revivify biblical memory through rituals, the reading of texts, and the reenactment of sacred stories. Moreover, as individuals, we are in search of a past that informs who we are, shapes our identity, and empowers the purpose of our lives. Pilgrimage is a foray into the past, and our personal histories matter.

More generally, remembrance, commemoration, and memorialization are fundamental pilgrim practices. We remember people, places, and events by marking locations, including tombs, monuments, and memorials.

9. Scientists speak of various types of present time, such as the perceived present, the specious present, and the dilated presence, which are discussed in Burdick, *Why Time Flies*.

10. On narrative theory, see Abbott, *Cambridge*; Bal, *Narratology*.

The Future

The distant future lies hidden beyond the horizon, while its nearness is constantly upon us. We try, at times, to keep the future at arm's length, to stick our finger in the dam of time. Sometimes, it can't arrive soon enough. We are all too ready to turn the page, to relegate the present to the past, or simply eager for what lies ahead. Hope and anticipation look forward to the future; worry and trepidation view it as a foe.

In the 2003 film *Seabiscuit*, racehorse owner Charles S. Howard, played by Jeff Bridges, distinguishes between initial success and ultimate goals: "This isn't the finish line. The future is the finish line." Destinations, goals, and objectives lie in the future, which is a temporal point that we haven't reached or has yet to arrive. For the Christian pilgrim, the union of God, self, and the Other is the finish line, which, from time to time, is partially expressed in the present. In the meantime, Christians journey towards the far side of the future. Scripture envisions an age when life with God becomes timeless. As linear time ends, the temporal gives way to the infinitude of God.

Time-Based Virtues

Virtues have a temporal component. Remembrance, commemoration, and walking in the footsteps of others are virtues that value the past. Perception, attentiveness, and discernment pertain to present situations. Hope and anticipation place faith in what is yet to come through patience and perseverance in the here and now.

Cyclical Time

While linear time is progressive, circular time is reoccurring, repetitive, and cyclical. Time doesn't advance; it repeats. Circular time is patterned upon natural, seasonal, and planetary rhythms. It is expressed in the seven-day week. The Bible sanctifies reoccurring time, namely, the weekly Sabbath, the seasonal festivals, and the Sabbath and Jubilee years.

The liturgical calendar inlays circular time with narratives of past events. By imbedding linear time into a cyclical template, events are commemorated at reoccurring intervals, such as Christmas and Easter, birthdays, and anniversaries. Linear and circular time are interdependent reckonings of temporal experience, which, together, create a spiral. While the liturgical calendar gives a cyclical character to linear time, each iteration of the Christian Year marks the advance of historical time. A similar pattern of repetitive progression pertains to our individual lives.

The Pilgrimage of the Day

Every day is a pilgrimage, marked liturgically by the canonical hours, also known as the divine, or daily, office, dividing the day into fixed times of prayer.[11] Prayer, work, and play comprise our pilgrimage through the day.

The Sabbath

Although sabbaticals are associated with renewal, the Sabbath wasn't created as a day of replenishment in order to commence another week. Rather, Sabbath occurs in the wake of something that has been realized or accomplished (i.e., the creation of the world). A day of restful ceasing, it is a spiritual celebration of what God has done. While the six days are *good*, the Sabbath is *holy*, containing what Abraham Heschel describes as "a spectral glimpse of eternity."[12]

Worship Time

We've introduced the concept that historical time is summoned through worship, that the past becomes present. Yet, the events of salvation are not commemorated at random. Everyday isn't Christmas; neither is Easter determined by human factors, but by the movements of the heavens. This, at least, was the view of medieval Christians, who believed that earthly worship should mirror the form, content, and cyclical patterns of the heavens, the source of true worship. The imperative of worship was to synchronize itself with the celestial choir of New Jerusalem by replicating the what and when of the city of God.

The idea of a heavenly liturgy reminds us that worship is not something we create; rather, its time set aside to participate in heavenly patterns of Christian prayer. As the imitation of heavenly virtues, worship invokes a real-time connection with God.

---

11. See Wiederkehr, *Sacred Pauses*. Also see the *Rule of Saint Benedict*. Various versions of the divine office are recognized by Catholic, Orthodox, and Protestant traditions.

12. Heschel, *Sabbath*, 36. Also see Wirzba, *Living the Sabbath*.

The synchronization of worship is a mark of Christian unity. Celebrating Easter on the same day expresses the oneness of the body of Christ, while liturgical disjunction conveys Christian disunity to the world.[13]

Chronos and Kairos

Christians take cues from the Greek concepts of *chronos* and *kairos*. Chronos is sequential time; it moves in a line. It can be measured and quantified by clocks and calendars. It's determined; it lacks freedom; it's the chronology of time. Kairos is the time of moments; it's quality time, the right time, numinous time, the ripeness of time. Full of joyful expression, kairos is festival time, dance time, feast time. Boundless, free, and uncontrolled, kairos is the time of dreams, visions, and fresh-baked pie.

Virtual Time

While worship time asserts that timing matters, the virtual world flexes time and space. A live event can be experienced simultaneously around the world; a recorded event can be viewed at a later time. As Christians explore how online communities can be created and sustained, virtual encounters will increasingly enrich the pilgrim life.

PILGRIMAGE AS TIME SET ASIDE

A central concept of pilgrimage is the bracketing of time for a particular purpose. One sets aside two weeks to visit the Holy Land or a month to walk a portion of the Camino de Santiago. In doing so, it becomes sacred time as well as a sacred journey. Pilgrimage is setting time aside to reflect upon our lives, such as vocational choices, relational issues, and life transitions. A gap year, or taking time out between work, family, or educational commitments, whether for adventure, growth, healing, or renewal, expresses the same idea. Similarly, retreats and sabbaticals, which may not require spatial movement, are temporal templates of pilgrimage.

---

13. It matters, therefore, when Christians use divergent calendars. One of the primary reasons for the Synod of Whitby (664) was that King Oswiu and Queen Eanflæd observed Easter on different days. While calendar discrepancies remain between the Western and Orthodox churches, today, as a sign of unity with neighboring Orthodox churches, Episcopal (Anglican) congregations in the Holy Land have begun celebrating Easter in accordance with the Orthodox calendar.

Pilgrimage includes difficult periods in our lives, such as illness, convalescence, bereavement, divorce, and unemployment. At the societal level, times of war, pandemic, and natural disaster may be conceived in pilgrimage terms.

A pilgrim experience may not be recognized at the time. Pilgrimage lends itself to retrospection, or the ascription of meaning to past experience. Reviewing life through the lens of pilgrimage allows us to perceive God's presence and purpose in ways that have been previously overlooked.

13

Place

"There is a day when the road neither comes nor goes and the way
is not a way but a place."

—WENDELL BERRY[1]

PILGRIMS TRAVERSE ALL TYPES of terrain. Our physical, social, and spiritual
landscapes consist of mountains, fields, and valleys, cities, and urban spaces,
and holy places are but one means of experiencing God spatially. Pilgrims
reflect upon the concept of sacred places, the distinction between space and
place, and the nature of differentiated places.

SACRED PLACES

Notwithstanding the proliferation of pilgrim shrines, the idea that certain
places are holier than others—that God is more present or accessible here
than there—has always troubled Christianity. The association of circumscribed places with the location of God runs counter to the sensibilities of
most Christians. Piety and place do not wear well, especially in Protestant
circles; yet, sacred places are nothing, if not, resilient, full of paradox and
personal exemptions. At issue is the doctrine of God's omnipresence—that
God is everywhere—which may imply that God's presence is also uniform.

---

1. Berry, *Timbered Choir*, 216.

Couched in these terms, "God is everywhere" and "there are sacred places" are mutually exclusive.

A common understanding of a sacred place is a place that God inhabits, whether in nature or in shrines. The view is epitomized by Jesus' reference to the Temple as "my father's house" (Luke 2:41–49). The notion of God dwelling in a place evokes the following questions: is God more present in some places than others? Is God somehow confined by human constructions? Pilgrim spirituality engages these questions. What we discover in the process is that appealing to God's omnipresence is insufficient grounds for dismissing holy places.

Pilgrim theology takes a nuanced approach to the sacred. Along with the question of God's location, the Bible conveys additional concepts:

- A sacred place is a place that God calls us to; it's a place that God reveals. It may be a place of discovery or self-disclosure.[2]

- A sacred place is where something of importance has occurred (e.g., an event, vision, or theophany), which is subsequently remembered or revivified through commemoration, ritual, and story.

- They are places where promises are made and kept.[3]

- A holy place is a place of prayer and worship, commonly of transgenerational use, that generally has an eschatological dimension.

Religious studies adds to the conversation. For Emile Durkheim, a sacred place is a space that has been set apart. Mircea Eliade conceptualizes a sacred center as a hierophanic irruption, where a physical manifestation of the sacred has penetrated the chaos of the world. Jonathan Z. Smith emphasizes the role of ancestors in the creation of sacred landscapes.[4] A place can also become holy due to individual or collective suffering, which testifies to the sacredness of human existence.[5] Pilgrim spirituality engages various notions of sacred places without being dependent upon a particular one.

While holy places are important to our faith, God may be encountered in any and all locations. Our theological task is to reflect upon our spatial experience of God, or *how* and *why* a place has meaning. Transcending a simple categorization of the sacred and the profane, pilgrim spirituality

2. The idea of sacred place as the disclosure of a new identity occurs in the story of Jacob wrestling with God at Peniel, where Jacob is given the name Israel. See Gen 32:22–32.

3. See Brueggemann, *Land*, 5; Inge, *Christian Theology*, 36.

4. See Durkheim, *Elementary Forms*, 51; Eliade, *Sacred*, 62–65; Smith, *To Take Place*, 11.

5. The point emerged from a class discussion on sites of conscience.

considers the question of *differentiated* places. We turn, however, to another dichotomy—the distinction of *space* and *place*—which is critical to a Christian theology of place.

Space and Place

According to Walter Brueggemann, "'Space' means an area of freedom, without coercion or accountability, free of pressures and void of authority. . . . Place is space that has historical meanings, where some things have happened that are now remembered and that provide continuity and identity across generations."[6] Space is undifferentiated and generally unbounded. Place is a differentiated location that has history, meaning, and value. Spaces, in turn, are the areas, gaps, and passageways between meaningful places. If we think of space as that which allows movement, then place is pause.[7] Space is the ability to move; place is the ability to dwell.[8]

We live in a world in which space and time dominate place.[9] While pilgrimage mirrors this in ways, seeking unbounded movement and the freedom of space, its contemporary resurgence should be viewed, in part, as a reaction to the subjugation of the local and the particular. Places matter, and the appeal of pilgrimage is the particularized nature of destinational locations. Pilgrims seek *places*, and, in doing, they oppose the homogenizing forces of globalization.

The concept of space and place provides frames for viewing the motives, templates, and ramifications of pilgrimage. While giving room to space-based expressions, Christian pilgrimage has a decided preference for place, which reflects its incarnational nature. Pilgrimage, for the most part, turn spaces into places.

DIFFERENTIATED PLACES

How else can we think of places? In discussing the sacred and the profane, as well as space and place, we've introduced the concept of *differentiated* places. While God may be the same, places are not uniform. Places differ

---

6. Brueggemann, *The Land*, 4.

7. Tuan, *Space and Place*, 6.

8. Tuan, *Space and Place*, 14.

9. On the demise of place in Western society since the Enlightenment, see Inge, *Christian Theology*, 1–12.

one from another, and our experiences of God are mediated by the spatial locations in which they occur.

John Inge defines place as the "seat of relations or the place of meeting and activity in the interaction between God and the world."[10] In stressing the interaction of God, place, and people, Inge focuses on what he calls sacramental events. While the meaning of a place may be ascribed to the events that occurred there, if places are otherwise the same, they are merely receptacles of the events they contain. If a place is not somehow distinctive, unique in and of itself, meditating the experience that occurs, then the meaning of an event would be the same if it happened someplace else.[11] *Where* I proposed to my wife, which was on the rooftop of the duomo of Milan, wouldn't matter. The concept of differentiated places asserts that places are not homogeneous containers; they are *different*, somehow, one from another.

In short, place mediates our relationship with God, and our encounters with others are irreducible from the locations in which they occur. If there is no differentiation of place, then pilgrimage itself is called into question, and the world in which we live becomes significantly less interesting. The concept of differentiated places, which still acknowledges the ubiquitous presence of God, allows us to explore our spatial relations with God, self, and the Other in more nuanced and meaningful ways.[12]

TOPOGRAPHICAL ELEMENTS

Topography refers to the detailed features of a landscape, which may be physical or metaphorical. Having personal, social, and religious meaning, landscapes contain elements that the observer perceives, navigates, and remembers.

Locational Points

A locational point is our position in space—where we are, here and now, in time and place. They are points of perspective from which we observe the world. The lost lack locational orientation; the self-deceived believe they are somewhere else.

10. Inge, *Christian Theology*, x, 52.

11. This is known as the container theory, which Inge is careful to avoid.

12. See Wynn, *Faith and Place*.

Horizons

Horizons are the limits of what we can see around us. Delineating earth and sky, they extend into the distance. Projecting hope and expectation, they beckon us to what lies beyond. Occasionally, the horizon appears in the foreground, collapsing our perspective. Or, it's obstructed altogether, displaying a wall of shadows instead of a projection of dawning light.

Pathways

Pathways are the lines along which a person customarily, occasionally, or potentially moves, such as streets, walkways, highways, and hallways. Pathways are generally the most predominant features of a person's mental map.[13]

Edges

Edges, which include borders, boundaries, and barriers, are linear elements that are not used or recognized as pathways. They are linear breaks in continuity, such as walls, fences, and shore lines, with various degrees of permeability. Edges close one area off from another; they delimit access and the movement of people. They are the railroad tracks separating sections of town. Edges may also be seams that join regions together.[14]

Landmarks

Landmarks are external points of reference that one sees but doesn't enter, such as a sign, a building, or a mountain. They stand out, for various reasons, among surrounding possibilities. A landmark may be particular to a person or shared in common with others. They may be widely recognized or restricted to local knowledge.

Districts

Districts are areas that have a common identifying character. They are spaces that one can enter into, belong to, or recognize from the outside,

13. On pathways, edges, nodes, districts, and landmarks, see Lynch, *Image*, 47.

14. Here, an edge refers to a linear feature that is not a pathway rather than an outer periphery per se. For edges as outer margins, see below.

such as parks, neighborhoods, and commercial centers. Districts may be areas of social integration or sections associated with privilege and exclusion, poverty and disempowerment, fear and prejudice.

Nodes and Centers

Nodes are concentrated areas, or spatial cores. They are junctions and intersections where pathways cross and converge. A node may be the spatial focus of a district, like a public square. Nodes are destinational points of travel and may be where people break or change their mode of transportation, such as an airport or a train station. While nodes are places of convergence, centers deserve mention of their own. Centers are associated with political, economic, and religious power, and the locational points of pilgrimage are commonly perceived in terms of their proximity (or distance) to a sacred center.[15]

Outer Margins

Although the margins may be places of alienation and neglect, God has a preference for the periphery.[16] The perimeter is a paradox. Outer edges excite. There's freedom on the verge that's missing in the middle, and balance is maximum on the edge of the precipice.[17] Straddling cosmos and chaos, pilgrimage is a journey to the margins, a spirituality of the fringes, where the divine is encountered on the rim of the world.

Mental Maps

The above features form the basic elements of our mental maps, which we instinctively construct and adjust to navigate the world. An examination of our personal maps reveals our relationship with the places and spaces in which we live. Our maps consist of the pathways we use, the locations we inhabit, and the landmarks that orient our world. They contain the meanings,

15. On sacred centers, see Eliade, *Sacred*, 62–65. Also see Smith, *To Take Place*, 41–46, who states that people in power see the world in terms of symmetry and reciprocity, while people in a state of subordination see the world in terms of hierarchy, centers, and margins.

16. See Foster, *Sacred Journey*, xiv, 64, 68, 150, who argues that God has a particular fascination with people on the edge.

17. Street graffiti, Milan, Italy: "È sull'orlo del precipizio che l'equilibrio è massimo."

memories, and emotions that we attach to places in our lives. Our mental maps also expose *terra incognita*, the unknown and uncharted parts of our world, as well as areas that we have bordered off and, consequently, ignore.

While mental maps teach us about ourselves, they are important tools for understanding social relations in proximate spaces. The proximate Other often takes different pathways, perceives edges in different ways, and finds some districts and centers of power more or less accessible than we do. Through attentive observation and intentional dialogue, we can use mental maps as a tool for better understanding one another, including those who differ from us by age, wealth, profession, gender, politics, culture, race, and religion, whether they share the same household with us or live on the other side of town. A comparison of mental maps can help us see and celebrate the diversity of local perspectives, while exposing issues of access, equity, and equality as well as bias, prejudice, and social injustice.

JUXTAPOSITIONS OF PLACE

Places are defined in relationship to other locations, the presence of other people, and the perceived presence of God. Paradise gives meaning to wilderness; the desert is defined by what it's not. Places are strange and familiar, recognizable, and unknown. Pilgrimage is informed by the juxtapositions of place.

The Particular and the Universal

The dichotomy of place and space relates to the particular (place) and the universal (space). Pilgrimage has a penchant for the particular. It prefers place over space.

Mediated and Unmediated Places

Space may be given, but places are social constructs. We attach meanings to places based upon personal experience, shared histories, and cultural perspectives. Since history and habitation give meaning to place, pure unmediated places don't exist. The meaning of a place, which is never impartial, differs from person to person and culture to culture.

Physical and Metaphorical Places

A place can be both physical and metaphorical. Biblical locations, like Jerusalem and the Jordan River, are metaphors of ordeal, death, hope, and salvation. Geographical metaphors also refer to life situations. We cross the Rubicon and take the road to Canossa.

The Ordinary and the Special World

Pilgrims traverse thresholds between the ordinary and the special world (see chapter 17).

Thick and Thin Places

In certain places, the threshold to the world beyond seems tissue thin. If permeable places do not allow us to cross over to the other side, they resound, at least, with the murmurings of God.[18]

Consecrated and Desecrated Places

Far from static, the status of sacred and profane places may change. Places are ordinary, then set aside; profane, then consecrated. They may be defamed, defiled, and desecrated, renewed and reconsecrated, destroyed and abandoned. Holy sites are built upon holy sites and replicated anew in virgin space.

Ancestral and Virgin Land

Ancestral grounds are places where generations before us have lived and died. Ancestral land contains the footsteps, place names, and memories of our ancestors, and, most sacred of all, their graves, tombs, and cemeteries. By contrast, virgin territory is unexplored, untouched, and untarnished. There is a numinous quality to pristine space.

18. See Foster, *Sacred Journey*, 125.

Empty and Inhabited Places

Whether rightly or wrongly perceived, places are empty or inhabited, and human history has often mistaken the difference. From the conquest of the promised land to the doctrine of discovery and manifest destiny, settler colonization has denied the humanity of indigenous people. The conquered, dispossessed, and exiled are the victims of crusader forms of pilgrimage.

Near and Far Places

Places are near and far away. The local is familiar and personal; yet, given its knack for routine, the local may be predictable, unimaginative, and stifling. While foreign places may feel strange and dangerous, the far away beckons adventure. Flipping the lens, pilgrims perceive the heterogenous at home while finding the familiar in faraway places.

Localized and Globalized Destinations

Pilgrims long to see the particularities of localized places. Globalization impose sameness upon the world.[19]

Old and New Places

The age of a place can be defined by chronological time (e.g., the year a building was built) or by our personal connection to it (e.g., when we first became aware of it). Our childhood house, our elementary school, and our grandparents' church are old places, while places that we have recently learned about or visited for the first time are new, despite their age. Pilgrims seek new places and revisit old ones.[20]

The Here and the Elsewhere

We think in terms of the here and the elsewhere, or the here and the some-place—anyplace—else. We have a penchant for being elsewhere than in the spaces where we are.[21]

19. For a critique of globalization in light of a Christian theology of pilgrimage, see Inge, *Christian Theology*, 14, 107–8, 111–12, 126–28.

20. See Mayes, *Old Places*; Page, *Preservation Matters*.

21. Hjalmarson states, "Human have an incredible ability to be elsewhere than the space they physically occupy." Hjalmarson, *No Home*, 148.

Home and Away

Home is a broad and subjective concept that evokes a sense of belonging: to be alienated or estranged implies a loss of home. Home may be where we are originally from or a place that we have moved to. It may be an actualized reality or an elusive condition that we continue to search for. Home, for many, is their everyday space, familiar and nurturing, while, for others, it is a specific location that they long for, grieve over, and may occasionally revisit. Home is in permanent tension with pilgrimage. Home is what we seek, but it is also something that we are called or forced to leave. Pilgrimage takes us away from home to far away destinations, and the homesick pilgrim longs for home. For others, home can only be found on the journey, where home and away converge as one.

In Place and Out of Place

Based upon our sense of where we ought, or want, to be, we are in place or out of place, located or displaced, lost or at home. Pilgrims experience both the despair and the grace of being out-of-place people.

First and Second-Place People

Called, forced, or impelled to leave home, pilgrims are second-place people. To be a pilgrim is to journey through territories that are not our own.[22]

ADDITIONAL CONCEPTS

Genius loci

In Roman religion, a *genius loci* was the presiding god or spirit of a place. Pilgrims sense the presence of place.

Storied Places

Place is a text, layered with meaning.[23] As social constructs, places are storied.

22. See Niebuhr, "Pilgrims," 7.
23. See Sheldrake, *Spaces*, 17; Hjalmarson, *No Home*, 137.

Stability

In the Benedictine tradition, stability, or staying put in a place, is a primary vow. By contrast, wandering monks are the worst of the lot.[24]

Topophilia: The Love of Place

Places elicit emotions. We long for places that we miss and experience separation anxiety over places we're attached to. We grieve for places and suffer with them. Topophilia, or the love of place, describes a strong affinity towards a physical location which may instill a sense of cultural identity. Negatively, topophilia can be a contributing factor to nationalism and social exclusion.[25]

Utopias

If topophilia is the love of actual places, utopia refers to ideal locations that don't exist. Utopian visions assume the temper we give them. They may be inspirational and virtuous or deceptive and nefarious.

Determinism

Tell me the landscape in which you live, and I will tell you who you are.[26] Does place make people, or do people make places?

Sites of Conscience

A site of conscience is a place of memory, generally with a difficult or contested history, that uses the past to create a contemporary dialogue for a more just and humane future.[27]

24. See *Rule of Saint Benedict*, chapters 1 and 58.
25. See Tuan, *Topophilia*.
26. Attributed to José Ortega y Gassett.
27. See www.sitesofconscience.org.

Placemaking

Placemaking brings people together to collectively reimagine and reinvent public spaces in local communities and neighborhoods. It's an intentional, collaborative process that pays special attention to the physical, cultural, and social dimensions that define a place.[28]

ABRAHAMIC PILGRIMAGE

Transcending sacred centers and ongoing physical movement, Abrahamic pilgrimage recasts our understanding of the pilgrim life. To be a pilgrim in the footsteps of Abraham is to be out of place, displaced, away from home; it's to sojourn in a strange land as a second-place person.[29] Abraham's example is cited in Irish and Anglo-Saxon sources, which depict the pilgrim life as leaving home and living for Christ on foreign soil.[30] Once the pilgrim has relocated—Anglo-Saxons permanently settled near the tomb of Peter in Rome—pilgrimage ceases to be a journey; rather, it's a status, a station, or a state of being in which physical movement no longer has an operative meaning, and pilgrim identity is based upon one's relationship to place. Abrahamic pilgrimage has implications for religious travelers who hear the call to follow God in a foreign land. It speaks to the experience of international students, missionaries, diplomats, and ex-pats. It applies, most fully, to those living outside their homeland on a permanent basis, including immigrants, migrants, and refugees.

28. See the resources of the Project for Public Spaces (www.pps.org).

29. For first-person stories of refugee writers see Nguyen, *Displaced*.

30. On Irish expressions of Abrahamic pilgrimage, see Aist, "Pilgrim Traditions." On Abraham and the social applications of pilgrimage, see chapter 22.

14

Journey

WE NOW TURN TO journey, the leitmotif of pilgrimage, which is a function of time and place: motion is the change in position over time. While we have identified expressions of pilgrimage in which the dimension of journey is dormant, the phenomenon is incoherent without the prevalence of itinerant expressions. Pilgrimage is a spirituality of movement and motion, steps and stations, change and transformation. Is every journey a pilgrimage? Presumably not, but any journey could be.

JOURNEY TYPES

Sacred and Profane Journeys

Journeys are sacred and profane, often intertwined. Pilgrims navigate between alienation and aspiration, sorrow and salvation. Sacred journeys are defined by purpose and motive, content and context, by who we are with as well as where we are going. Sacred journeys lead to places in the special world, to destinations of completion. The sacredness of a journey may be recognized at the time or acknowledged retrospectively.

If sacred journeys are exceptional, they are also the exception. The pilgrim life is the collective experience of ordinary journeys. Life is full of cul-de-sacs and alleyways, local streets, common pathways, and public thoroughfares. We experience God, self, and the Other during our daily commute, in shop aisles and check-out lanes, and on our way to church. We arrive to the sacred through ordinary means.

Physical Journeys

From religious travel to daily walks, pilgrimage consists of physical, embodied journeys. Pilgrims traverse earthen pathways and concrete locations, rural settings, and urban landscapes.

Metaphorical Journeys

Metaphorical journeys take us to places we've never been before, to destinations we could not otherwise reach. From the inner journey to life as journey, metaphorical possibilities are sourced from our knowledge of physical travels and actual places.

Interior Journeys

Interior journeys express a particular type of metaphorical movement that directs our quest to the center of our soul, which is explored in mystical writings, like *The Interior Castle*.[1] Pilgrimage is the lifelong discovery of God's indwelling presence in our lives.

Individual Journeys

Pilgrimage is a personal journey that seeks to make sense of our place in the world. While life is peopled with companions, guides, and mentors, we must ultimately walk alone. With God's help, we must find our own way.[2]

Corporate Journeys

At the same time, pilgrimage is a corporate journey. We are interdependent travelers walking together as the people of God.

One-Way Journeys

Life consists of one-way journeys that never return to the place of departure. Full of surprises, challenges, uncertainties, and rewards, one-way journeys

1. See Teresa of Avila, *Interior Castle*, first published in Spanish in 1588. Also see Ahlgren, *Entering*.

2. See Hughes, *God of Surprises*, 33.

are seldom straightforward. Some travelers look over their shoulder. Others never look back.[3]

Return Journeys

Having an outbound and inbound component, return journeys culminate at the place of departure. On a roundtrip journey, we go forth only to return, arriving back as different people. Returning home marks, to our surprise, the beginning of another journey.[4]

Direct Journeys

Direct journeys go from A to B with limited breaks or distractions. They focus on getting us there.

Slow Journeys

While pilgrimage, at times, intensifies life, we do well to slow things down. In the words of Vincent de Paul (1581–1660), the one "who is in a hurry delays the things of God."[5] To linger is a luxury that pilgrims long for.

Shortcuts

Shortcuts are alternative routes that take less time. They are accelerated pathways. Shortcuts may be taken as a means of protection or self-care; they allow us, for instance, to arrive before a storm. They may also shortchange an experience. A shortcut may be easier or more hazardous, recommended or discouraged, expediently wise, or inadvisably foolish.

3. One-way journeys and related theories include Abrahamic pilgrimage, the earthly life, rites of passage, and developmental theories, such as Maslow's hierarchy of needs and Erickson's theory of psychosocial development.

4. Patterns of return journeys include Campbell's theory of the hero's journey and the homecoming parable of the prodigal son. See Heuertz, *Pilgrimage*, 42, 49–50, 128, who argues that pilgrimage is never a round trip.

5. Quoted in Hjalmarson, *No Home*, 148.

Detours and Delays

Journeys get re-routed and delayed. Detours are made to avoid something or, conversely, to see something along the way. Detours take us out of the way to get us where we're going. They are directional changes that continue to chart the course. Sometimes, we take the long way out of a sense of adventure; at times, we are cautioned to go home by another way. Delays, by contrast, are temporal extensions that prolong the journey.

Wrong Ways

While detours are digressions that take us where we're going, wrong ways lead us in false directions. Travelers get lost. Hikers stray off the path. Pedestrians lose their bearings. Confusion and disorientation are the nemesis of travel. Wrong turns and false pathways lead to precarious adventures; being lost is a dangerous endeavor. Still, losing our way is a necessary step in discovering who we are. Purpose is found through trial and error, and the mistaken journey sometimes becomes a life-giving pathway.

Short Journeys

Local pilgrimage was, by far, the most common expression of medieval pilgrimage. It's a historical reminder that journeys don't always take us far from home, that we practice pilgrimage on local terrain. Pilgrimage includes journeys to proximate places for prayer and healing, walks through nearby landscapes, and visits to neighbors in need. One little journey is enough to renew ourselves and the world.[6]

Everyday Alterations

Journeys are a response to situational needs that arise throughout the day. Our child is sick at school. We're out of milk. We left something at the office. Pilgrimage is a spirituality of everyday alterations.

---

6. Translated from the saying attributed to Kurt Tucholsky: "Eine kleine Reise ist genug, um uns und die Welt zu erneuern."

Repeated Journeys

We repeat some journeys on a daily basis, out of necessity, routine, or habit. We replicate other journeys because we enjoyed the experience or didn't get it right the first time. Pilgrimage is the grace of *once again*, the practice of repeat performance. Trying, failing, and doing it again. Lessons, learning, memories, and meaning stick more the second time around.

Forced and Unplanned Journeys

Some journeys are the cause or effect of events that forever change our lives. War, political oppression, natural disasters, and economic necessities force people to move and migrate, often without planning or preparation, and returning home may not be possible.

Unfinished Journeys

Pilgrimage is the ongoing continuation of unfinished journeys that have started but are incomplete. Pilgrims are in progress and on the way.

Uncompleted Journeys

While some journeys are never over, others are abandoned. We fail to finish, frustrated by destinations that allude us and deadlines that come and go. We lack the time, opportunity, resources, or willpower—at times, the ability—to complete what we've started. Sometimes, an ending is imposed upon us, and continuing is not an option. Life is the reckoning of failed attempts, abandoned plans, and uncompleted journeys.

Anti-Journeys: Stopping the Treadmill

Pilgrimage is not always embarking on a journey; sometimes, it's applying the brakes. To be a pilgrim is to get off the treadmill, to abandon the rat race, to stop and smell the roses. When the pace of life is unrelenting, pilgrimage offers an antidote. It's taking the off-ramp and walking the road less traveled. Pilgrimage, at times, is an anti-journey, a countercultural rejection of worldly power and secular values. Pilgrimage is an in-the-world witness to a better way.

JUNCTURE POINTS

A pilgrim is always at some point on the journey. Juncture points, or locational positions, include departure, arrival, and the places in-between.

Pre-Departure

Pilgrimage begins before it's begun. It includes planning and preparation, longing, waiting, and anticipation.[7] Pilgrim spirituality reminds us that we are constantly on the brink of journeys that await to unfold, standing on the cusp of new experiences yet to be revealed. Many journeys are unplanned, unannounced, and even unnoticed, and only later do we look back to see who we were and what we were doing before they began.

Preparation ensures a safer, more meaningful journey, though, at some point, it must begin.[8] In many ways, the journey itself prepares us, and what is necessary is learned along the way. Preparation cannot be underestimated, but neither should it hold us back.

Departure

Denoting a new beginning while bringing the past to a close, departure is the act of separation from people, places, and temporal phases. Departure points are the platforms we take off from, the what and where of leaving places behind, pushing off, stepping way. Departure points set pilgrims in motion towards other people and places, towards new opportunities and unrealized possibilities. Embracing both joy and sorrow, we mark departure with symbols, gestures, rituals, and blessings.

Arrival

Arrival points draw journeys to a close. To arrive is to reach our destination, which signifies fulfillment, attainment, and completion. Arrival is the actualization of what we could not otherwise know, experience, or achieve. Just as departures are endings, arrival is a new beginning. Graduation is commencement. To arrive is to start again.

---

7. "By failing to prepare, we prepare to fail" is an adage of preparation.
8. On the preparations of pilgrimage, see Aist, *Jerusalem Bound*, 139–50.

In-Between Points

Between departure and arrival, a journey is the progression of locational position, a point-to-point continuum of the in-between, marked, at times, by landmarks, intersections, and benchmarks. If the destination and its distance are known, then we can identify where we are with respect to what's ahead. When the destination is unknown or unclear, we locate ourselves in terms of time and distance from our point of departure.

Forks in the Road

Forks in the road force choices of consequence. While the earthly life contains bifurcated pathways, or either/or journeys, it generally consists of multiple choices.

Stops and Stations

Journey points include rest stops and waystations, shelters, and sanctuaries. Pilgrims seek places of sojourn, posts for pausing, locations for rest. Journeys are broken up by travel hubs, transit centers, checkpoints, and border crossings.

PROVISIONS

Journeys require provisions, resources, supplies, and nutrition. What should we take with us, and what will the road supply? Pilgrims testify to provisions being miraculously provided along the way.

Nutrition

What are the nutritional needs of pilgrims? Emphasizing their dependency upon God, pilgrims espouse a daily bread spirituality grounded in the Lord's Prayer and the Israelite wilderness experience of daily manna. There is both a physical and spiritual aspect to the bread of life. The loaves and fish were multiplied for consumption; yet, one does not live by bread alone. Spirit, virtue, and community are the food of the soul.

Supplies

Supplies are the external provisions that equip the journey. Pilgrimage puts a premium on sturdy footwear, layered clothing, rucksacks, bedrolls, and walking sticks. The right supplies shelter us from the sun, wind, and cold. While pilgrims travel lightly, being sufficiently equipped offers options, solutions, safety, and protection. Having to carry our supplies encourages us to discern between luxuries and necessities, between what we want and what we need.

Supplies include tools that guide and direct us, such as maps and compasses. What do pilgrims need to carry with them to guide them along the journey, to keep them from getting lost, to ensure their safe arrival? In *Pilgrim's Progress*, the Bible is Christian's roadmap, while the armor of God provides spiritual protection.[9]

RUNNING THROUGH RIVERS

Beyond earthen pathways, pilgrims traverse rivers, seas, and oceans.[10] On a foot journey, the landscape remains static. We walk on our own accord or take vehicles to transport us, but the terrain is stationary. By contrast, water is a world in motion. The river is always moving. Standing in it, we feel its force against us. From the bank, we watch it come and go. Life is often more like a moving river than an inert pathway. Our surroundings are in motion, and we must reckon with the rapids. If we channel its energy, a river can take us to destinations with ease. If its force is too strong or if we lose control, we can be swept downstream. At other times, our lives move against the flow, and life is an upstream paddle. Even to stay in place requires a concerted effort; to advance is to overcome the current.

The pilgrim life is a littoral journey. Heading out to sea, life is tidal, tossed by the waves. We drift away from land, between anchor and harbor, between shipwreck and shelter. Jonah is the maritime prototype of the chastened pilgrim, but his is not the only pattern. Irish pilgrims explored the seas, looking for a desert in the ocean, seeking their place of resurrection.[11]

9. See Bunyan, *Pilgrim's Progress*.

10. Recent books that employ water metaphors include Granberg-Michaelson, *Without Oars* and Bolsinger, *Canoeing the Mountains*.

11. See Aist, "Pilgrim Traditions," 14–15; Adomnán, *Life*, 1.16.

METAPHORS OF MOVEMENT AND CHANGE

As a spirituality of movement, pilgrim spirituality embraces metaphors of change, transition, process, and progress, including sanctification and metamorphosis. Pilgrim writers characterize the stages of spiritual transformation in various ways. Walter Brueggemann speaks of the movement from orientation to disorientation to new orientation.[12] Charles Foster employs the traditional steps of invitation, start, journey, arrival, and return,[13] while Phileena Heuertz conceptualizes the spiritual journey as: (1) awakening, longing, darkness, death, transformation, intimacy, and union, (2) construction, deconstruction, and reconstruction, (3) shedding, detachment, and abandonment, and (4) incubation, gestation, and growth. She also speaks of purgation and illumination.[14]

Spiritual Inertia

According to the law of spiritual inertia, a body in motion tends to stay in motion. Fueled by grace, perseverance, and momentum, those moving towards God continue to get closer. A body at rest tends to stay at rest. Once we stop, we tend to get stuck.

Life as Change

Pilgrimage is the reckoning of constant change. Even during times of apparent stagnation, nothing remains the same. Transformation may be imperceptible in the moment, but change is always occurring. Pilgrimage is a journey of losing things along the way. Change hurts; we mourn the loss. Change also occurs because we gather as we go; we're altered by positive addition. Transformation is a twofold process of loss and gain. Life gives and takes. It prunes; we grow.

Journey as Process

The metaphor of journey speaks to the concept of process, or the sequence of how something happens. Used in both secular and religious contexts, the journey metaphor is a common (auto)biographical frame, such as a

12. See Brueggemann, *Message*.
13. See Foster, *Sacred Journey*, esp. 76.
14. Heuertz, *Pilgrimage*, 89, 91–93, 145, 189.

politician's pathway to public office, a musician's road to the main stage, or an archaeologist's journey to the Holy Land.[15] In a 1958 article, entitled "My Pilgrimage to Nonviolence," Martin Luther King Jr. describes his intellectual journey to nonviolence.[16] In 2019, the World Council of Churches published *Come and See: An Invitation to the Pilgrimage of Justice and Peace.* The document, which reflects upon the biblical tradition of pilgrimage, expresses a processual sense of journey.[17] As the latter two examples indicate, the journey-as-process metaphor may refer to (1) personal experience, such as an intellectual journey or a pilgrimage of enlightenment, or (2) a collective initiative couched as a corporate journey. The metaphor may describe a retroactive understanding of a process or a proposed step-by-step sequence.

The question of process metaphors is the degree to which they convey substance as well as form. While it may denote little more than a chronological narrative, a sequential explanation, or a person's personal story, pilgrimage as process generally conveys a sense of the arduous, the circuitous, and the lengthy or long-awaited. If aptly used there is an implied appeal to religious virtue. We would rightly take exception to a "pilgrimage to violence" or an "invitation to a journey of injustice."

Journey as Progress

When a process metaphor appeals to a sense of growth, development, or improvement, it expresses the more robust concept of progress. A process is simply how something happens; progress is movement towards a desired goal. It's really *not* about the journey, if the journey doesn't show signs of advancement. The pilgrimage metaphors respectively employed by King and the World Council of Churches espouse outcomes consistent with the highest virtues of the Christian faith: non-violence, justice, and peace. Christian formation is a journey of growing in love, developing into the likeness of Christ.

While pilgrims are a work *in progress*, the phrase has another meaning. "In progress" refers to concurrent activity, as when a television channel joins a program *already in progress*. Pilgrim spirituality raises the question: *what else is going on?* What is happening in other places? What are other people doing, and what are we missing? Pilgrims are mindful that things are happening elsewhere, that their perspectives are limited, and their experience

15. See Gitin, *Road Taken.*
16. See King, "My Pilgrimage."
17. See World Council of Churches, *Come and See.* Also see chapter 22.

is partial. Pilgrimage is the practice of joining things in progress while welcoming others to join what we doing.

Sanctification

Sanctification is the process of becoming more and more like God. Pilgrim people are always on the move, advancing closer and closer to God. The greatest two commandments are "Love the Lord your God with all your heart. . . . [And] Love your neighbor as yourself" (Matt 22:34–40). Pilgrims ask: "Do I love God more than I did yesterday, last week, and the year before?" Sanctification is a lifelong journey; it's a process not an event. Sometimes, we take a step forward, at times, two steps back; yet, pilgrims are committed to pathways of perfection in their love of neighbor, the Other, and God.[18]

Metamorphosis

Metamorphosis is a change in the form or substance of something into something completely different. Metamorphic change is dramatic, comprehensive, and complete. The classic example is the metamorphosis of caterpillars into butterflies. The baptism imagery of death and resurrection, becoming a new creation in Christ (2 Cor 5:17), expresses the metamorphic nature of the Christian life.

18. See Aist, *Journey of Faith*, 18–19, 30–32; Aist, *Voices in the Wind*, 117–18, 184–85.

15

People

WHILE THE UNION OF God, self, and the Other is the objective of pilgrimage, our emphasis here is on the roles people play along the way.

COMPANIONS

Companions, etymologically, are people with whom we share bread (Latin *com panis*), and the concept extends, by association, to those with whom we travel, share stories, and live out our lives. Companions are people we set off with as well as those we meet along the way. Companions share time, space, and resources, experience, stories, and values. A faithful companion is one of life's most precious gifts, and pilgrims prize soul friends, conversational partners, and walking with others in silence. To journey with someone is a sacred experience.

Companionship transcends the physical presence of those we know by name. Pilgrim spirituality challenges us to consider our global neighbors as fellow travelers, irrespective of culture or religion, finding common ground, shared purpose, and mutual goals with those beyond our immediate horizon.

MENTORS, GUIDES, AND SCOUTS

While companions are fellow travelers, others perform specialized roles in our journey of faith, such as mentors, guides, and scouts. Mentors teach, inspire, and encourage us. They give us gifts, wisdom, and resources. Mentors prepare us for the challenges of the journey, but they can only take us so far. We must ultimately complete the journey on our own.[1]

Whereas the mentor has a personal connection with the pilgrim, the guide has a local connection to the places the pilgrim passes through. The guide goes with us, providing context, information, and interpretation. Managing time, conditions, and circumstances, the guide curates the experience of others.

Whereas guides go with us, scouts go before us, preparing the way, calling back with warnings, advice, and encouragement. They set up camp, gather provisions, and welcome our arrival. We are not always blessed to have a mentor nor does every experience warrant a guide. Yet, on almost every journey, we benefit from those who have traveled before us.

HOSTS

Pilgrimage depends on people who offer safety, shelter, and sustenance. The host is a steward of pilgrimage, welcoming the stranger as Christ. Pilgrimage is epitomized by hosts and travelers gathered around the table of God.

THOSE ON THE SIDE OF THE ROAD

Pilgrims pass people along the way, including local residents who are rooted to the land as well as waylaid pilgrims on the side of the road: the hurt and injured, the poor and needy, the abused, confused, oppressed, and forsaken. If pilgrimage is more about the journey than the destination, then the pilgrim life is the Samaritan response to help those on the verge of the road.

THE GIFTS THAT OTHERS OFFER

To be a pilgrim is to embrace the gifts that others offer. Pilgrimage is not transactional. When we have little to offer, asymmetrical reciprocity governs the exchange. Pilgrimage is a spirituality of indebtment, first to God, then to strangers, hosts, guides, and mentors, which makes pilgrimage a journey of undeserved blessings.

---

1. On the role of the mentor, see Vogler, *Writer's Journey*, 39–47, which is discussed in Campbell, *Hero*, 106–17 as supernatural aid. Also see Lev Vygotsky's concept of the more knowledge other, which is summarized in McLeod, *Lev Vygotsky*.

PEOPLE-FOCUSED PILGRIMAGE

Since at least the days of Saint Anthony (d. 356), people have been the destinational focus of Christian pilgrimage.[2] Pilgrims visit living saints, monasteries, and Christian communities. Participating in the program of an ecumenical community, going on a short-term mission trip, taking a cultural immersion course, and meeting with ministry partners are expressions of people-focused pilgrimage, which emphasize living in community, learning from others, and serving those in need.

2. See Athanasius, *Life of St Anthony.*

PART 5

The Pilgrim Experience

BUILDING UPON OUR DEFINITIONAL framework of pilgrimage, we turn to the pilgrim experience itself, exploring its motives, experiences, and practices.

16

Pilgrim Motives

PILGRIMS PEREGRINATE FOR A host of reasons. There is a restlessness deep within the human soul that desires to journey, to explore the unknown, to encounter the sacred, to make sense of the world. We long to experience unfamiliar places, to peer through the cracks of creation, to reach for the kite tails of suspended mystery.

PROBLEMS AND MISSING PIECES

Something Missing

Pilgrimage is a response to something that is missing in our lives or lacking in society at large. From personal quests to the public march, pilgrimage is a physical admission that life is incomplete.

The More Out There

Asking if this is all there is, pilgrimage is the search for something more.

Restlessness

Pilgrims step away from structures, restraints, and routines, if only temporarily. Pilgrimage is the exhalation of a tired and restless soul.

Longing

Pilgrims are people of unfulfilled desire. Pilgrimage is a hunger for beauty, a yearning for truth, a thirst for justice. It's longing and waiting with purpose.[1]

Finding Ourselves

Pilgrimage allows us to become the person that otherwise alludes us, the person we were meant to be. It's a quest for identity, purpose, and self-discovery. To be a pilgrim is to search for the missing self.

Escaping from Ourselves

Pilgrimage is an elusive attempt to escape from ourselves.

Life Problems

Pilgrimage attends to life's pressing problems. Pilgrims seek wisdom, discernment, and solutions to the difficulties and dilemmas of life.

Questions of Faith

Pilgrimage is a physical response to questions of faith.

Brokenness

Pilgrimage is a response to brokenness, fragmentation, and emptiness.

Healing and Wholeness

Pilgrims seek healing and wholeness.

1. See Heuertz, *Pilgrimage*, 57–78.

Penance and Repentance

People go on pilgrimage to turn their lives around, to atone for their past, to reorient their lives in the direction of God.

Purification

Pilgrimage is a pathway of purification. It's washing in the river, expunging spiritual impurities. Pilgrims seek cleanliness and clarity. Exposed to the solicitousness of God, scarlet sins become white as snow (Isa 1:18).

LIFE CYCLES

Pilgrimage is a response to the transitions, disturbances, and interruptions of life.

Life Transitions

Life transitions are a common impetus of pilgrimage, which provides time and space to process the past, to experience change, and to prepare for what's ahead. Helping make sense of a changing world, pilgrimage moves us forward in transitional ways.

Life Interrupted

Pilgrimage emerges from the interruptions of life, such as illness, job loss, and pandemic. Some disruptions, like pregnancy, are ones of life-giving change.

New Life

People relocate in search of a better life. To start again in a new location is to experience the world as a pilgrim.[2]

---

2. The title of Puzo, *The Fortunate Pilgrim*, which is a fictional account of Italian immigrants in New York City, appeals to pilgrimage as a new life in a new location.

Mortality

Pilgrimage is a response to our own mortality, to aging as well as death. Patrick, a Santiago pilgrim from Ireland, walked the Camino when he was fifty to see if he was still alive: "Fifty years does something to a person."

THE WORLD IN WHICH WE LIVE

Pilgrimage is a response to the world in which we live.

Seeking Community

Pilgrims seek a sense of belonging, to be a part of something bigger. They seek community, connections, and interpersonal relationships.

For the Sake of Others

Pilgrimage is a physical expression of intercessory prayer. We dedicate journeys to others; we go on pilgrimage to memorialize loved ones. Standing in for others, we share our experience of the road with vicarious pilgrims.

To Change the World

Pilgrims journey, march, and protest to make the world a better place. They are servants of the road, heralds of the kingdom of God, committed to Christ's vision of heaven on earth.

A Counter-Cultural Journey

Pilgrimage offers an alternative vision to the fragmentation of modern society, providing a pathway for a world that has lost its way.

THE QUEST FOR ADVENTURE

Pilgrimage captures the human spirit of curiosity and adventure.

The Root of It All

Pilgrims want to go to where it actually happened, to the root of where it all began, to see the place with their very eyes.

The Spirit of Adventure

Pilgrims embrace the spirit of adventure. They explore unchartered territory, take pathways less traveled, and wander off the map.

Curiosity

Curiosity is an underrated virtue of the spiritual life.

Physical Accomplishment

From mountain climbing to long-distance walking, pilgrims are motivated by physical challenges. Pilgrims probe what's possible; they test their limits. Pilgrimage is an exercise in perseverance.

A HIGHER PURPOSE

Pilgrims pursue a higher purpose. They strive for something beyond themselves.

Enlightenment

From the comprehension of mystery to the illumination of God, pilgrims seek enlightenment, knowledge, and insight.

Simplicity

Thomas Merton speaks of the "grace of simplicity," which reveals the greater things of life.[3]

---

3. Mentioned in Least Heat-Moon, *Blue Highways*, 87.

Authenticity

Pilgrimage is a quest for what's real, for authentic experience, for the thing itself.[4]

Truth, Goodness, and Beauty

Pilgrims aspire to the highest ideals of truth, goodness, and beauty.[5] Some claim that we can only discover what we already have: "Though we travel the world over to find the beautiful, we must carry it with us or we find it not."[6]

Purity

Pilgrims seek purity of soul, mind, and body: "Blessed are the pure in heart, for they will see God" (Matt 5:8).

Renewal

Pilgrimage is the practice of spiritual renewal and regeneration.

Transcendence

Pilgrims seek transcendent journeys, tissue-thin thresholds, and spiritual conveyance between heaven and earth. Pilgrimage is transformational, life-changing experience.

A Search for Salvation

Pilgrimage is the search for salvation; it's a lost-to-found journey of amazing grace.

---

4. See Todd, *Thing Itself.*
5. See Scarry, *On Beauty*; Scruton, *Beauty.*
6. Quote attributed to Ralph Waldo Emerson.

Becoming Closer to God

Pilgrims are constantly growing in their love for God. Pilgrimage is a life-long journey of sanctification.

FOLLOWING THROUGH

Pilgrimage puts promise to pavement. It is the embodiment of follow through.

Oaths and Promises

Pilgrimage is a response to a promise that we made to God. It honors our commitment to Christ.

Expressions of Gratitude

Pilgrimage is an expression of gratitude for God's deliverance. It may be a public response to the end of a war, drought, or pandemic or an act of personal thanksgiving, such as for the recovery from an illness or the birth of a child.

HOMECOMINGS

Pilgrimage is reconnecting with people, places, and memories of the past. It's returning to familial centers of the soul.

ADDITIONAL CATEGORIES

The Reluctant Pilgrim

There are would-be pilgrims who refuse the call. By contrast, reluctant pilgrims are those who have been persuaded to venture forth but remain hesitant, unconfident, or unconvinced, at least, at the start. Reluctant pilgrims may stumble, fail, or abandon the journey. More commonly, the hesitant traveler is transformed by the journey.[7]

---

7. See Aist, *Jerusalem Bound*, 62.

An Open Agenda

The goal of pilgrimage is not always apparent. Pilgrims venture forth because God has called them, and the what, where, and why may only be revealed as the journey progresses. Those in the dark, without specified goals, are often more responsive to the directions of the s/Spirit.[8]

The Accidental Pilgrim

We sometimes stumble upon a holy place or casually traverse the sacred landscapes of others, like the late November morning I spent in Lourdes years ago on my way to Spain. People's access to place is often unfair. The longed-for destinations of some are incidental stopovers for others. The accidental pilgrim blurs the distinction between pilgrimage and tourism: one visits a holy place on vacation; a site of conscience is discovered on holiday. Pilgrimage occurs unexpectedly. Faith awaits the accidental pilgrim.

QUESTIONING MOTIVES

No aspect of the pilgrim life is more personal than motive. God calls us by name, and our calling is uniquely our own. Nonetheless, our motives may be challenged by others. Self-focused journeys, counter-cultural practices, and one's use of resources may be questioned for various reasons. While the criticisms of pilgrimage should likewise be critiqued, some motives are better than others.

Pilgrims wrestle with the what and why of the Christian journey. How can we ensure that pilgrimage does no harm to ourselves, to others, to the planet? How does a commitment to Christian stewardship inform and challenge pilgrim practices? When does the pursuit of religious experience become a form of spiritual gluttony? Pilgrims pray, listen, and discern. They test their thoughts, actions, and behaviors against biblical precedents, personal conviction, the wisdom of tradition, and the counsel of others.

8. See Aist, *Jerusalem Bound*, 60–62.

17

The Pilgrim Experience

LIVED EXPERIENCE, OR THE "what actually happens" of our lives, is the raw material of pilgrimage. Experience is thought plus feeling and implies the ability to learn from what has occurred.[1] Our discussion returns to the work of Victor Turner, examining liminoid experience in more detail, before exploring Joseph Campbell's theory of the hero's journey. The heart of the chapter is a general survey of categories of pilgrim experience.

LIMINOID EXPERIENCE

Van Gennep's Rites of Passage

As discussed with respect to communitas, understanding liminality's relationship to pilgrimage begins with Arnold van Gennep (1873–1957), whose 1909 book, *The Rites of Passage*, looks at life-cycle rituals in traditional societies. Rites of passage are ceremonies associated with a change of a person's social status. Through cultural puberty rites, for instance, boys become men and girls become women. What van Gennep detected was a universal pattern to rites of passage consisting of separation, margins, and aggregation.

A ritual begins with an act of separation in which participants are separated from their previous status or context; they leave their former world. In the second stage, the margins, participants are no longer in their former stage but have neither arrived nor advanced to their new status. The third

---

1. See Tuan, *Space and Place*, 9.

stage is aggregation, or reintegration, in which the person is reintroduced into society and assumes a new role.

Van Gennep also used the metaphor of a threshold, or a limen, to describe the process. Separation is pre-liminal; the margins, or the middle stage, is liminal, and reintegration, or the new normal, is post-liminal. Liminality refers to the middle stage of the ritual, which occurs between separation from the old world and reintegration into the new one. While the bulk of the ritual generally takes place in the liminal stage, all three phrases are marked by transition.[2]

Turner's Betwixt and Between

In the 1960s, anthropologist Victor Turner (1920–83) began using van Gennep's concepts in his own work on rites of passage, focusing on the middle liminal stage, which he describes as "betwixt and between" and "neither here nor there."[3] Those in a state of liminality have lost their previous roles, status, and authority. Norms are ambiguous. Life is in limbo. They have departed but haven't arrived. They are separated from the past but haven't attained their new status in society.[4]

In the 1970s, Turner turned his attention to historical Christianity, looking for similarities between traditional rites of passage and Christian practices. Christian rites of passage—i.e., rituals that change a person's status—include baptism, confirmation, and ordination, but Turner did not find a significant liminal, or mid-transitional, stage in these rites. He then turned to pilgrimage, which has well-defined phases of departure (separation), journey (margins), and arrival/return (aggregation).

Turner notes two primary differences between traditional rites of passage and Christian pilgrimage: (1) the former is obligatory and (2) its outcome is determined. Traditional rites of passage are required; pilgrimage is a voluntary practice. Whereas the outcome of a rite of passage is *determined* (e.g., boys become men; girls become women; a layperson becomes a priest), the results, or effects, of pilgrimage are flexible, ambiguous, and *open-ended*. Since the dynamics of liminality do not fully apply (pilgrimage

---

2. The 1960 English translation of the book incorrectly translates the middle section as "transition" instead of "margins."

3. See Turner, "Betwixt and Between."

4. Christians refer to the "already and not yet," to living in the age of the Holy Spirit between Christ's resurrection and the consummation of God's kingdom. While it denotes a sense of the "betwixt and between," there is no "already" in the margins. In the liminal state of "neither-nor," one has neither their former nor future status.

is *not* a classic rite of passage), Turner refers instead to the *liminoid,* or liminal-like, qualities of pilgrimage. Pilgrims are betwixt and between. Suspended between departure and arrival, they are neither here nor there. Yet, while transformation is a mark of pilgrimage, the pilgrim does not experience a change in societal status to the degree that occurs in a traditional rite of passage. Liminality projects *what will be*; liminoid experience, on the other hand, posits *what can be.* The liminoid, which is less determined, is marked by *potentiality.*

THE SPECIAL WORLD

The Hero's Journey

To be a pilgrim is to journey to a special world. In his 1949 book, *The Hero with a Thousand Faces,* Joseph Campbell (1904–87) identifies three universal phases in narrative myths, which he refers to as the monomyth, or the hero's journey. The protagonist (1) leaves his or her *ordinary world,* (2) crosses a threshold into a *special world* full of ordeals, allies, conflicts, and treasures, and (3) *returns home* a different person, sharing the rewards of the adventure with others.[5] His threefold structure consists of seventeen stages.[6]

Campbell's work has been adapted and revised, mostly notably by Christopher Vogler, a Hollywood screenwriter, whose *Writer's Journey*, first published in 1992, presents the journey as a twelve-stage process:

1. *The Ordinary World.* The hero begins in his or her ordinary, everyday world.

2. *The Call to Adventure.* Either internal or external forces shake up the hero and his and her world. The hero's life is about to change.

3. *Refusal of the Call.* The hero initially turns down the adventure.

4. *Meeting with the Mentor.* The hero meets a mentor who gives the hero training, tools, wisdom, and encouragement.

5. *Crossing the Threshold.* The hero enters the special world.

---

5. Campbell cites the work of van Gennep. See Campbell, *Hero*, 342.

6. Campbell's original seventeen stages are: (1) the call to adventure, (2) refusal of the call, (3) supernatural aid, (4) the crossing of the first threshold, (5) the belly of the whale, (6) the road of trials, (7) the meeting with the goddess, (8) woman as temptress, (9) atonement with the father, (10) apotheosis, (11) the ultimate boon, (12) refusal of the return, (13) the magic flight, (14) rescue from without, (15) the crossing of the return threshold, (16) master of two worlds, and (17) freedom to live.

6. *Tests, Allies, and Enemies.* The hero is tested, forms allies, and identifies the enemy, or the shadow.

7. *Approach.* The hero prepares for his or her challenge.

8. *The Ordeal.* Facing death and danger, the hero confronts and overcomes the shadow.

9. *The Reward.* The hero takes possession of a treasure gained through the ordeal.

10. *The Road Back.* The hero begins the journey back home. A remnant of the shadow pursues the hero. The journey remains precarious.

11. *The Resurrection.* Facing a final test, the hero undergoes his or her ultimate transformation.

12. *Return with the Elixir.* The hero returns home with the treasure, which he or she shares with others.

Heroes, who include ordinary people, are summoned on a journey, face challenges and ordeals, sacrifice and suffer, and emerge as wiser, more virtuous figures. For Vogler, the hero's journey is "a set of principles for living," "a handbook for life," and a "manual in the art of being human."[7] The hero's journey offers language, patterns, and archetypes for interpreting personal narratives, communal journeys, and stories of faith.[8]

Outside the Ordinary

The special world, or places beyond our everyday context, is fundamental to pilgrimage. Pilgrimage is breaking routine, crossing thresholds, changing our scenery. It's the spirituality of special places: elevated landscapes, settings of prayer, places of personal retreat.

The essential quality of a special world is its otherness, or contrast to our own. While it lies outside our everyday world, its operative feature may be its *neutrality* as much as its *exceptionality*. Foreign destinations can be remarkably indifferent to travelers. Nature does its best to ignore us. Yet, anonymity, neutrality, and indifference can provide room for personal transformation. Outside the ordinary, space lacks the gravity that otherwise holds us down. The neutrality of special-world places severs us from everyday entanglements, becoming landscapes of freedom, venues of possibility,

7. Vogler, *Writer's Journey*, xiii.

8. On the archetypes, or character functions, associated with the theory (i.e., hero, mentors, heralds, threshold guardians, allies, shadows, tricksters, and shapeshifters), see Vogler, *Writer's Journey*, 23–80.

incubators of growth.[9] Away from home, special-world places, such as camps and retreat settings, foster personal development and self-esteem.

THE THREE MARKS OF PILGRIMAGE

Pilgrimage is marked by one-off encounters, the voices of others, and personal self-reflection.[10]

One-Off Encounters

The pilgrim experience is characterized by singular events and one-off encounters, including passing interactions with others. Pilgrimage is a serial journey of irreducible moments, any one of which can change our lives.

The Voices of Others

Pilgrimage is steeped in stories, and the voices of others are the traveler's muse. God speaks through stories, and pilgrims allow themselves to be touched by what others have to say. The quotes of fellow travelers line the pathways of their mind. Pilgrims, in turn, are vehicles of other people's voices, carrying messages, helping others to be heard.

Self-Reflection

Pilgrimage is marked by self-reflection, personal examination, and life review.[11] Pilgrimage is a spiritual check-up, a time of honest assessment. Who am I? Where am I, and how am I doing? What can I affirm about myself and my relationship with God and others? Do I have cause for contentment, thanksgiving, and gratitude? What, on the other hand, is missing or incomplete? What should I change, and how should I live going forward? Is

9. Often the importance of the special world is its relatively neutral settings for reflecting upon our lives in the ordinary world.

10. See Joyce, *Unlikely Pilgrimage*. A fictional account of an improvised pilgrimage, the novel includes prominent examples of each of these marks.

11. Life review involves the evaluation of personal memories, which is especially prominent in older age. See Butler, "Life Review"; Westerhof, "Life Review"; Achenbaum, "Life Review." Also see Erikson, *Life Cycle*, esp. 64–66. Narrative therapy involves re-authoring our personal stories; it views problems as separate from people and recognizes the possibility of co-existing narratives. See White, *Narrative Practice*; Denborough, *Retelling the Stories*.

there a need to forgive or to be forgiven? While taking notice of ourselves doesn't mean that we necessarily need to change, pilgrimage is the practice of corrective living.

Examining one's life may be anything but reassuring, and pilgrimage can expose brokenness and despair.[12] The pilgrim life, however, is a journey of second chances. God uses self-reflection as a springboard for personal transformation: pain, regret, and alienation become departure points towards hope, wholeness, and reconciliation.

PILGRIM EXPERIENCE

Calling

Through signs, dreams, conversations, and prayer, God calls people on pilgrimage with or without revealing its purpose or destination. After a prominent career as a Catholic activist, Carlo Carretto was summoned by a voice: "Leave everything and come with me into the desert."[13] A calling may call us to go alone or to join or follow others. It may also require a leap of faith. We may be beckoned by extraordinary circumstances or jolted when things fall apart. Some callings invite us to sacrifice; others permit us to pursue the desires of our heart. Regardless, a calling turns pilgrimage into the business of God. Callings come with obligations: to journey faithfully, attending carefully to what God reveals along the way.

Good-Byes

Good-byes mark beginnings as well as endings. Pilgrims anticipate the journey; yet, tugging on their heartstrings is what they leave behind: people and places, situations, and relationships.

Sensuous Experience

Pilgrimage is a sensuous experience, full of sights, sounds, smells, tastes, and touches. It is a dialogue of the senses.

---

12. See Aist, *Jerusalem Bound*, 56–57.

13. Carretto, *Letters*, xi, xvii.

Perceptions and Observations

Pilgrimage is the art of observation. To be a pilgrim is to see the world differently, possessing a third-eye that discerns God's presence in the world, perceives spiritual dimensions in material expressions, and attends to the needs of fellow pilgrims.[14] Pilgrims see the familiar as new and the new as familiar, which is key to compassion, empathy, and reconciliation.

Events

Events are the frames of unfolding mystery. They are the actualized units of experience, imaginations birthed into existence, concrete actions that we cannot comprehend until they occur. Pilgrimage is a litany of instant moments and serial events, distinctly unique yet interconnected.

Incidents and Accidents

Pilgrimage is comprised of incidents and accidents, coincidence and happenstance, spontaneous surprises and unforeseen situations, both positive and negative, significant and inconsequential. The stuff that happens becomes the fabric of our lives.

Assurance and Uncertainty

Apart from God's presence, pilgrimage has few guarantees. Faith is a risky endeavor. It's uncertainty that's assured. We can never know beforehand what awaits along the way.

Challenges and Obstacles

Pilgrims walk through shadowed valleys and experience dark nights of the soul. The pilgrim way can be long and arduous, full of challenges, obstacles, and difficulties, potholes, molehills, and mountains, steep climbs, and sudden descents.

14. On the third-eye of the pilgrim, see Aist, *Jerusalem Bound*, 111, 140, 176.

Play and Pleasure

Pilgrimage is a joyful journey, and the intentionality of pilgrimage includes pleasure as well as prayer. Celebration, play, and enjoyment are important aspects of pilgrimage.

Temptations and Enticements

The pilgrim experience is full of sparkle, but all that glitters isn't gold. Pilgrimage is replete with temptations and enticements. Lairs have been laid along the way. The tree of knowledge is full of fruit.

Mistakes and Failures

Dead-ends, off-ramps, and aborted journeys are a concomitant part of the pilgrim journey, reminding us that failure is a norm of life. A realistic "where we are" spirituality, pilgrimage is the reckoning of our human imperfections. Pilgrims learn from mistakes and accept the disappointment and consequences they bring. The gospel of pilgrimage is that God can transform mistakes and failures into unexpected blessings: "Where you stumble and fall . . . there you discover gold."[15]

Second Chances

Pilgrimage is a grace-filled journey of second chances. Pilgrims turn around, retrace their steps, and try, try again.

Second Looks

Along with second chances, the pilgrim experience consists of second looks. Seeing people and places a second time clarifies questions, captures details, and crystallizes memories. Places change according to external conditions. We perceive differently based upon our temper, mood, and frame of mind. Second looks add texture, dimension, and comprehension to what we saw— and missed—the first time.[16] Giving someone a second look is the essence of compassion.

15. Campbell, *Thou Art That*, xiii. According to Campbell, "It is by going down into the abyss that we recover the treasures of life. Where you stumble, there lies your treasure." Campbell, *Joseph Campbell*, 24.

16. Jerusalem pilgrims traditionally visit the tomb of Christ more than once. See

...

Forgiveness, Reconciliation, and Wholeness

To be a pilgrim is to experience forgiveness. It's to know that wholeness enfolds us.

Noise and Distractions

Pilgrimage is full of noise, peripheral sounds, and minor irritants. Pilgrim noise is not the impediments that threaten to unravel a trip but the distractions and sideshows that compete with our focus. How does one distinguish between noise and substance? What is the difference between content and context? What lessons can be found in the extraneous details of the pilgrim life? While we're often wise to ignore the chatter, attending to the noise of pilgrimage can turn peripheral context into meaningful content.[17]

Silence

Silence has texture. It makes us fretful, lonely, and distraught; it can also calm and comfort us. Silence conveys the whisper of God.

The Small Stuff

Pilgrimage is a spirituality of the small stuff. God attends to the details, and meaning is found in the minutiae of life.

The Mundane

Much of the pilgrim life is simply mundane: dull, boring, and nondescript. It's life on hold. Pilgrims stand around, sit on buses, and wait in line. Pilgrim spirituality speaks to living well in the lulls, to dealing with the doldrums, to readjusting expectations of a yellow-brick journey. Will delays and disruptions be filled with beneficial choices, or will they be spent in restless ways? How we fill the gaps determines the tenor of our lives.

Nouwen, *Return*, 5–10, who describes seeing Rembrandt's painting, *The Return of the Prodigal Son*, two days in a row.

17. See Aist, *Jerusalem Bound*, 134–36, 171.

Meantime Moments

Pilgrimage is a spirituality of meantime moments. Between beginnings and endings, pilgrimage is what we do in the meantime.

Waiting

While a pilgrim's progress may be measured by movement, it's often a waiting game. Pilgrims are religious patients.

Rushing

As life intensified, pilgrimage contains moments that are rushed, harried, and hurried. Calm collapses; contingencies converge, and life becomes frantic. We run against time, hurrying our pace. Rushing from one commitment to another, we hasten to finish tasks, completing last-minute preparations. We anxiously travel with tight connections, desperately hoping to be in and on time. Distinguishing between urgency and importance, pilgrimage is the prayerful practice of slowing things down.[18]

Being

Pilgrims learn to *be* in the midst of doing. They learn to be *instead* of doing.

Mystery and Surprise

Pilgrimage is an appointment with mystery and surprise. Pilgrims stand on the verge of the unknown, gazing into the chasm of sacred mystery. Shadowed by the God of surprises, pilgrims live on the cusp of continuous revelation.

Awe and Wonderment

To be awed is to admire without understanding, to humbly accompany the unexplained. It is accepting grace in disbelief. To wonder is to indulge in amazement, to marvel at mystery, to stand before God in holy fear.

18. On managing the urgent, the non-urgent, the important, and the not important, see Covey, *7 Habits*, 159–69.

Scenes of Revelation

Apocalypse denotes something that is revealed or unveiled. Pilgrimage is an apocalyptic journey.

The Serendipitous

Pilgrimage is serendipitous, and pilgrims love to be surprised.[19] The art of pilgrimage is reclaiming the ability to be taken by surprise.[20]

The Spontaneous

Spontaneity is the urge to abandon routine, to awaken from slumbered patterns of life. Spontaneity rebels against unchanging scenery, meaningless repetition, and empty forms of habitual practice. The spontaneous is a momentary hiatus from everyday habit, seizing refreshment in short-lived exemptions. Spontaneity is living off-script in creative, life-affirming ways.

Spontaneity is best served with discernment and sensitivity to others. While it celebrates life in the Spirit, spontaneity may denote a distraction of purpose: it can open up new horizons or hinder spiritual progress. Impulsive behavior within a group context, especially on the road, can cause stress and dissension and jeopardize the well-being of others.

The Now

Embracing the sacrament of the present moment, pilgrimage is the practice of perception, awareness, presence, and attentiveness.[21]

The Moment

The "moment" refers to a life-changing, transcendent experience. It's that point of a journey when we say: "It is for this I have come."[22] Pilgrimage does not shun mountaintop moments, but neither are they occasions to pitch our

19. See Hjalmarson, *No Home*, 45, who states that tourists hate to be surprised, while pilgrims love to be surprised.

20. Foster, *Sacred Journey*, 78.

21. See Jean Pierre de Caussade, *Sacrament of the Present Moment*, first published in 1741, also known as *Abandonment to Divine Providence*.

22. Least Heat-Moon, *Blue Highways*, 33.

tent (Matt 17:1–8). Christian formation is the accumulative effect of lived experience, Christian practice, and spiritual disciplines.

Fatigue

Religious travel is exhausting, and fatigue is a certain companion.[23] Weariness is part and parcel of our earthly journey. Pilgrims rest and recover; they persevere and press on. Pilgrimage is the nexus of faith and fatigue.

Supplemental Material

A painting in a museum, a scene in a supermarket, billboards and road signs, a child flying a kite. Pilgrimage is full of supplemental material, or the stuff that completes the whole: the random snapshots, trivial moments, and extraneous substance that fill in the gaps. What appears at first to be isolated and unrelated forms the connective tissue of our lives.

EMOTIONS

Pilgrimage encompasses the spectrum of human emotions, including joy, elation, surprise, and relief, disappointment, frustration, guilt, and grief.[24] And "what is grief, if not love persevering?"[25] Emotions can be animating and life-affirming or destructive and debilitating. Personalizing the pilgrim experience, emotions ground us in our human condition, reminding us of both the limitations and possibilities of our earthly journey.

---

23. See Aist, *Jerusalem Bound*, 136–38.
24. On lament, see Blaine-Wallace, *When Tears Sing*.
25. *WandaVision*, episode 8, February 26, 2021.

18

Pilgrim Practices

WHAT DO PILGRIMS DO? What are the intentional practices and everyday approaches of the pilgrim life?

PERSPECTIVES AND ATTITUDES

Perceiving the World

To be a pilgrim is to see the world differently. Pilgrims have a heightened sense of awareness; they see possibilities and detect opportunities. On pilgrimage, we see the familiar with new eyes, perceive mysteries that are otherwise hidden to us, and assume a more expansive perspective of the earthly journey. Attentive to God's workings in the world, the pilgrim's third eye spots divine grace in the happenstance of life. Acute observers of the human condition, pilgrims discern the needs of others and respond with compassion.

Sacramental Possibilities

Pilgrims perceive signs of God's sacramental presence in the world. A sacrament is a partial physical expression of a larger invisible reality. They are places, events, and objects in which God's engagement with the world is manifest.

Anticipation

Pilgrims reflect upon the difference between anticipation and expectation. Whereas expectations can diminish an experience, anticipation fosters questions that lead to enlightenment.[1]

Gratitude

Pilgrims assume an attitude of gratitude; they are seasoned at saying "thank you."

APPROACHES AND PAUSES

Patience and Perseverance

Fueled by faith, hope, and anticipation, pilgrims proceed with patience and perseverance.

Ask, Knock, Seek, and Find

Pilgrims take an ask and knock, seek and find approach to the world (Matt 7:7). They are curious and inquisitive, bold and adventurous, assertive and resourceful. Pilgrims pursue dreams and desires, solutions, and remedies. They claim God's offer to ask and receive.

Questions and Queries

Questions are a portal to transformation. Pilgrims ask questions of others and query the world. Investigation keys discovery. Scrutiny fosters spiritual growth. Progress is the fruit of examination. The search for truth leads to more questions, and faith, in the end, is the accumulative recognition of our lack of understanding.

---

1. Campbell states, "One way to deprive yourself of an experience is indeed to expect it. Another is to have a name for it before you have the experience." Campbell, *Thou Art That,* 13. Also see Abbott, *Cambridge,* 60.

Pausing

From double-checking directions to appreciating special moments, pilgrims practice the art of pausing. Pilgrims pause to take a breather, to consider their progress, and to reassess their options. Pausing allows us to catch up with ourselves, to engage our inner voice, to encounter the presence of God. Pilgrims pause when they are in doubt, upset, or angry, preventing rash words and ill-advised decisions. Pilgrims pause when they pray, and they pray when they pause.

AGENCY, DISCERNMENT, AND RESPONSIBILITY

Free Will and Human Agency

Undergirded by grace, free will is a sacred gift. The Bible's injunction against fortune telling occurs for good reason: to know the future is to relinquish our faculties and, with it, the helm of our earthly journey. Surrendering to destiny dulls our resistance to sinful temptations. Resigning to fate, abdicating our moral agency, is to abandon God's image within us.

Discernment

Discernment is the ability to judge situations, making prayerful decisions, often in the absence of sufficient information. Seeking God's counsel, discernment is patient deliberation on matters that matter. While pilgrims seek specific answers, the fruit of discernment is often just the faith to move forward.

Saying No

Pilgrimage, at times, is a spirituality of saying no: discerning when something is *not* the timing of God, holding firm against temptation, asserting personal boundaries.

Responsibility

Personal responsibility is a mantra of pilgrimage. Responsibility concerns our ability to respond to others, our readiness to offer compassion, our willingness to have our course altered by human contact. Pilgrims make mistakes. Their choices are fallible; yet, they never give over control of their soul. Regardless of our situation—however challenging the context—our actions and reactions are always our own. Accountability is a measure of the journey.

INTENTIONAL DECISION-MAKING

At the heart of pilgrim spirituality is the practice of intentional decision-making. Intentionality speaks to our way of being in the world, our attentiveness to our surroundings, and the quality of our presence with others. Intentional decision-making is the practice of scrutinizing our rote reactions and habitual responses. Complacency, not spontaneity, is the opposite of intentionality.

Pilgrimage is an exercise in free will, an unceasing litany of choices, a celebration of human volition. Pilgrims are attentive to the aims, reasons, and motives behind the choices they make, including moral dilemmas, life choices, and arbitrary preferences. Since the same decision can be made for different reasons, motive gives meaning to behavior, framing the action with a particular, interpretive lens. *What* is chosen is often less important than *why* a choice is made. More generally, pilgrims kindle an awareness of the act of making decisions. While good intentions do not absolve us from the consequences of our behavior, international decision-making means that options are well-considered and one is conscious, at least, to some extent, that *this* has been chosen instead of *that*.

Moral Choices

Intentional decision-making involves choices that matter: our worship of God, personal behavior, our treatment of others, and our use of resources. The pilgrim life is full of moral choices between right and wrong, good and evil, between life-affirming and destructive behaviors.

Living in an Interdependent World

Intentional decision-making recognizes that our choices affect others. The resources we use, the products we buy, and the byproducts we create impact the world, locally and globally, in both positive and negative ways. Pilgrims are stewards of the environment; they conserve, preserve, reuse, and recycle. They support local markets, living wages, and fair-trade products.

Situational Choices

Intentional decision-making includes basic situational choices. The tenor of our lives is largely established by the choices we make. How do we respond to waits and delays or the change of plans? Do we exacerbate the situation or make positive, adaptive decisions? How do we decide between multiple choices? On a group pilgrimage, do we rest, journal, and go to bed early, or stay up late and visit with others? Each choice, no matter how small or mundane, has its own rewards, implications, and consequences.

Simple Choices

Simple choices, such as food and drink, exemplify how framing our decisions shapes the pilgrim life. The meaning of eating a dessert changes based upon whether it's savored and enjoyed or experienced as succumbing to a craving. An act of self-denial differs whether it's due to cost, calories, or spiritual fasting. Eating at McDonald's in a foreign country (or any restaurant serving food "from home") may be experienced as giving in to a cultural dependency or relished as a spiritual celebration, depending upon how it's framed. Not only does motive inform meaning, simple acts convey spiritual significance to the larger context in which they occur. Pilgrims navigate familiarity and foreignness, feasting and fasting, celebration and restraint through small acts of intentional decision-making.[2]

To summarize the practice of intentional decision-making with respect to simple situational choices:

- The same decision can be made for different reasons.
- Intent shapes the experience and meaning of an act, regardless how small or mundane.
- Each and every decision is a distinct and separate act with its own motives and meaning.
- The reason for doing something does not need to be important, lofty, or spiritual; intentional decision-making can be as basic as acknowledging our personal preference.
- The consistency of simple choices is not important. Rather, intentional decision-making concerns our creative participation in open-ended choices, which includes those with limited moral significance. The practice of making the same choice for different reasons (as well as

2. See Aist, *Jerusalem Bound*, 41–46.

making different choices for the same reason) allows us to explore various textures, meanings, and perspectives of life.

- Motive—or how we frame a decision—can transform an otherwise ordinary act into one of spiritual blessing (e.g., an indulgence becomes a celebration).

By taking a considered approach to decision-making, including relatively benign choices, otherwise ordinary actions become opportunities of self-reflection, spiritual encounter, and personal growth.

RITUALS, RHYTHMS, AND ROUTINES

The rituals and routines of the pilgrim life are broad, personal, and idiosyncratic.

Rituals

Even harder to define than pilgrimage, rituals include formal and informal practices that infuse meaning into individual and communal experience. Ritual diverges from ceremonial practices insomuch as ceremony confirms while ritual transforms. Ritual honors the past, but it speaks most profoundly to a vision of life that awaits realization. Ritual changes the way we see the world while changing our role within it.[3] Rituals mark time and place, beginnings and endings. They constitute communities, renew commitment, and create connections between God, ourselves, and others.

Everyday Routines

Routines are our familiarized patterns of living. They are the things we do, and how we do them, which involves the repetition of time, place, and sequence. Infusing our lives with structure, routines create space to experience God's presence in the everyday rhythms of life.

Embodied Prayer

Prayer is the currency of pilgrimage, the language of the road. In the nineteenth-century spiritual classic *The Way of a Pilgrim*, the anonymous

---

3. See Stephenson, *Ritual.*

author embarks on a quest to pray without ceasing (1 Thess 5:16).[4] Prayer is our earthen appeal for divine protection, guidance, comfort, and shelter for ourselves and others. It's asking God to share the mysteries of life and the secrets of faith. Prayer steeps the pilgrim life, soaking experience with Spirit, saturating pathways with the presence of God. Prayer helps us see that God has been with us all along.

Pilgrimage is a sensuous spirituality in which touch, taste, sight, smell, and sound shape our experience and apprehension of God, self, and the Other. Pilgrimage is an open-eyed spirituality, a dialogue of the senses. It's partial to kinetic rituals and forms of embodied prayer. Pilgrims pray with their bodies through their breath, steps, movements, and actions. They inhale God and emanate blessings. They sense God's spirit in the rhythms of their heart.

Contemplation and Meditation

Pilgrims rest in the presence of God, seeking peace, wholeness, and renewal. Contemplation, meditation, and mindfulness should properly engage the embodied contexts of our lives.

Feasting and Fasting

Pilgrims feast and fast, taking their cues from Christ, who associates the acts with the comings and goings of the bridegroom, which he likens to himself. Fasting happens in his absence; feasting occurs in his presence (Mark 2:19). Fasting recognizes that something or someone is missing: the presence of God, the well-being of ourselves or others, the wholeness of creation. Invoking the virtue of perseverance, fasting uses the material negation of something, such as food and drink, as an expression of spiritual longing.

To fast is to acknowledge that the bridegroom is still on his way.[5] Fasting and its related expressions are embodied witnesses that all is not right with the world. We fast by lighting a candle when someone is in surgery and march in the streets to protest injustice.

Fasting models pilgrimage in a number of ways. First of all, fasting employs the language of movement. One *goes* on a fast, which conveys a sense of *journey*. Second, fasting is a period of *time*. Both pilgrimage and

4. See French, *Way of a Pilgrim*.

5. Among the themes of fasting are readiness, preparation, and anticipation. Fasting reminds us of our human limitations and vulnerabilities, strengthening our dependency upon God. The Bible critiques ostentatious displays and fasting as a meritorious act.

fasting denote a time set apart from ordinary circumstances; in doing so, they remind us of what matters. Evoking memories of the past (e.g., the life of Christ), they are practices of Christian remembrance. Anticipating the kingdom of God, they lean us into the future. A framework of feasting and fasting is imposed upon the liturgical calendar, structuring our Christian journey with additional meanings, perspectives, and connections. Third, waiting for the bridegroom is a temporal status that translates into *spatial terms* as being displaced, out of place, and far from home.[6] Feasting marks arrival and return. Finally, both practices express the Christian *virtues* of perseverance and fortitude. Fasting fosters resolve through the practice of learning to say "no," which prepares us for real world situations.

Reading

Reading has the power to transform our lives. It allows us to be vicarious pilgrims, encountering people whose lives are different from our own.[7] Akin to listening to the voices of others, reading supplements—and becomes—our own experience. Reading provides additional images, quotes, narratives, and concepts that inform, layer, and interpret our lives. While reading lends itself to virtual travel, religious and secular writings, literature, non-fiction, and books of local interest significantly enrich physical journeys.[8]

Special Occasions

Marking anniversaries, achievements, and milestones, pilgrimage is a spirituality of special occasions. Pilgrims mark things as they happen, including beginnings and endings, crossing thresholds, reaching landmarks, and obtaining goals and benchmarks. They ritualize memories, commemorating meaningful events from the past. Celebrating life and honoring others, special occasions are created by the convergence of time, place, and people.

---

6. On the application of Lenten practices to foreign travel, see Aist, *Jerusalem Bound*, 41–46.

7. See Teuton, *Native American Literature*, xix–xx.

8. I read approximately forty books during my ten-month around-the-world pilgrimage. When I unpacked my backpack upon arriving in Australia from Africa, I had seventeen books in my bag!

THE PRACTICE OF UNCOMFORTABLE EXPERIENCE

Pilgrimage is the intentional practice of uncomfortable experience. Pilgrims seek ways to stretch themselves, to leave the comforts of home, to traverse the unfamiliar, and to live vulnerably with others. Pilgrims recognize that character, discipline, and willpower are forged through trying situations. The practice of uncomfortable experience supplies us with a reservoir of resiliency that we can call upon in difficult times. Engaging the Other can be an uncomfortable experience; yet, we grow in empathy and solidarity towards others when we step outside our comfort zone. Pilgrimage is a spirituality of discomfort, which produces strength, character, perseverance, and compassion.

CHANGES, ADDITIONS, AND ADJUSTMENTS

Revisions and Readjustments

Pilgrims are lifelong learners, unafraid to revise their course. Pilgrimage is a journey of readjustments, revisions, tweaks, and alterations. The pilgrim life is a modified journey.

Leaving Things Behind

Pilgrimage is a spirituality of letting things go and leaving things behind, which occurs throughout the journey.[9]

Collecting Things Along the Way

While leaving things behind, pilgrims collect blessings along the way. They acquire knowledge, wisdom, and perspectives as well as physical objects. Souvenirs keep memories alive. They are material reminders of spiritual experience. They allow holiness to travel with us, providing a means of sharing the sacred with others.[10]

9. See Granberg–Michaelson, *Without Oars.*

10. On the material objects of pilgrimage, including souvenirs, see Aist, *Jerusalem Bound*, 115–25. Also see Ousterhout, *Blessings*; Warton, *Selling Jerusalem.*

BEYOND OURSELVES

Engaging the Other

Pilgrims welcome, encourage, and accompany others. They build bridges, cross boundaries, and break down barriers.

Cultural Humility

Pilgrims proceed with cultural humility, which consists of a threefold commitment to (1) critical self-reflection and lifelong learning, (2) the identification and mitigation of power and privilege, and (3) institutional accountability.[11] Cultural humility offers a corrective to an overemphasis on cultural competence, or cultural intelligence, which focuses upon our knowledge of other cultures. Although knowledge is needed, attaining competency of the cultural Other is, at best, a long-term task, and that just pertains to *one* other culture.[12] False confidence in one's understanding fosters generalizations and stereotypes, and presumed or partial knowledge can be deceptive, and even harmful, especially when decisions are made affecting those of other cultures.[13] While pilgrims are committed to learning about the Other (cultural knowledge is still a goal), cultural humility is the philosophy that governs the approach.

Stewardship and Advocacy

Pilgrims considers how their daily choices and habits of consumption impact the environment and affect local and global economies. Pilgrims are responsible stewards and fair-trade advocates. They promote justice, equality, and human rights.

---

11. See Tervalon and Murray-García, "Cultural Humility."

12. See Middleton, *Cultural Intelligence*, who states throughout that cultural intelligence can only be acquired through extensive, long-term experience working with other cultures.

13. Tervalon and Murray-García describe a situation in a multicultural medical center in which cultural stereotypes of pain tolerance negatively affected diagnostic care. See Tervalon and Murray-García, "Cultural Humility."

EXPERIENCE, MEANING, AND MEMORY

Experience and Meaning

Pilgrimage is the religious insistence that experience has meaning. Interpretation occurs in real time, and we are constantly making sense of things as they happen. Yet, home is where we ultimately go to consider the sacred. Mark Twain wrote concerning his experience of Jerusalem: "We do not think in the holy places; we think in bed, afterwards, when the glare and the noise and the confusion are gone."[14] Our everyday world is where the lessons of the journey take hold.

To say the journey is never over is to affirm that experience lives with us long after the events have occurred, that we are constantly learning from the past. As John, a young Dutch doctor, told me during a week at Taizé: "I am still learning from a year I spent eight years ago in a leprosy colony in India." Reflection is the thoughtful interrogation of experience, situations, and events. What former things have meaning, and what from our past will we continue to carry with us?

Memory and Commemoration

According to Walter Brueggemann, "Without memory we become imprisoned in an absolute present, unaware of the direction we have come from, and therefore what direction we are heading in. Without memory there can be no momentum, no discernible passage of time, and therefore no movement or velocity."[15] Pilgrimage is the practice of remembering what matters. As a journey back in time, pilgrimage is the recognition, commemoration, and revivification of biblical stories, the life of Christ, and the faith of our ancestors. Expressing transgenerational memory, pilgrimage doesn't necessarily teach us new lessons; it reminds us of old ones. As for our own lived experience, pilgrimage produces memories that become touchstones of faith. It can also dislodge unsettling recollections of our past. How do we curate burdensome memories and reconcile unresolved stories? What and how should we remember and forget?

Memory is a public debate. Public commemoration and memorialization, including statues, place names, and heritage festivals, express what societies consider to be important. They reveal who "we" are, our values and virtues, while exposing imbalances of power between dominant and

14. Twain, *Innocents Abroad*, chapter 55.
15. Brueggemann, *Hopeful Imagination*, 56.

non-dominant groups. What happened, and who controls the narrative? How and when do groups decommemorate the past? Memorialization is not confined to watershed events and generational heroes. Pilgrimage includes the physical expression of everyday memories, or the practice of vernacular memorialization.

PART 6

Applications of Pilgrim Spirituality

BEFORE TURNING TO RELIGIOUS travel, everyday Christianity, social outreach, and congregational formation, we will review the principles of pilgrim spirituality.[1]

---

1. Chapters 20–23 present cursory discussions of the respective sectors, each of which warrant book-length elaborations of their own.

19

Principles of Application

REVIEWING THE FRAMEWORK

ACKNOWLEDGING THE BREADTH OF pilgrimage, the book has presented a *comprehensive* definition. Pilgrimage is the *experience* of God, self, and the Other through time, place, journey, and people and the thoughts, images, and reflections thereof. Its ultimate objective is the *union* of God, self, and the Other.

Our approach employs the *family resemblance theory*. Appealing to a series of overlapping similarities rather than a common denominator, the theory states that traits associated with a phenomenon need not be present in every expression. While it holds pilgrimage together, things may be frayed at the edges.

Christian pilgrimage does not describe every journey or just any destination but pertains to those that adhere in some way to the biblical *prototype*, or *metatemplate*. An amalgamation of scriptural images, the prototype casts our earthly existence as a salvific or redemptive journey from the garden of Eden to New Jerusalem via incarnational intervention. The prototype maps the roads to God while accounting for our human condition. Pilgrim experience is not always—or necessarily—sacred. Just as all situations have spiritual potential, pilgrim spirituality transcends simple dichotomies between the *sacred* and the *profane*.

Our comprehensive definition functions as a warehouse of possibilities, indicating what pilgrimage *can be* as much as what it already is. The point underscores the various ways definitions are used. We are less interested in capturing pilgrimage in a phrase than we are in using definitions as tools for enhancing the Christian life. Our specific objective is Christian formation. To that end, we need additional definitions to facilitate our quest.

The quotable quotes of pilgrim wisdom, *aphorisms* help us see, explore, and interpret experience in focused, though limited, ways. Aphoristic assertions, which may at times be contradictory (pilgrimage is tensional), are indispensable tools of spiritual investigation, and the *transformative* reach of pilgrim spirituality is most effective when aphoristic definitions complement a comprehensive approach.

Therefore, our framework creates a symbiotic relationship between a comprehensive definition, which identifies the spectrum of possibilities, and an unlimited number of additional definitions that probe and interpret lived experience. To change the metaphor, our comprehensive definition is the palette of colors, while paint is applied with aphoristic brushes.

In sum, our framework focuses on the experience—and union—of God, self, and the Other. Pilgrim spirituality gives definitional status to the Other, attends to the self, and seeks the presence of God in the facts in which we find ourselves. Pilgrim spirituality probes the dimensions of time, place, journey, and people, while recognizing the personal, corporate, incarnational, metaphorical, and tensional character of the pilgrim life. Exploring the motives, experiences, and practices of pilgrimage, the book has provisioned the Christian journey, which consists of perceiving spiritual encounters, engaging situational context, enhancing lived experience, and pursuing the objectives of the Christian faith.

PRINCIPLES OF APPLICATION

Having reviewed the framework, we turn to the principles of application.

- Pilgrim spirituality is the spirituality of being *on pilgrimage*, a self-determined status that includes physical journeys, set aside experiences, and the overall trajectory of our lives.

- More fully, pilgrim spirituality is *the application of pilgrimage themes* to any and all areas of our lives. It applies to the *parts* as well as the whole. Pilgrim spirituality is not principally concerned with the iteration of complete expressions. Rather, it's the application of its constituent parts to the lived experience of our lives (e.g., its themes, images, concepts, and virtues).

- Pilgrim spirituality is governed by the principle of *overlapping similarities*. We are interested in connections, commonalities, and convergence between pilgrimage and other fields, theories, and phenomena, including scholarly, secular, and interfaith sources.

- *Assuming a pilgrim identity* is transformative. It changes our perception, imbuing experience with enhanced meaning. At the same time, we do not have to use the terms *pilgrim* and *pilgrimage* to employ pilgrim spirituality.

- As *a spiritual frame*, pilgrim spirituality provides a lens for seeing, perceiving, and interpreting experience. As an introspective mirror, it detects brokenness as well as beauty. Offering a kaleidoscopic gaze into the world, the religious imagination of pilgrimage delights in the diversity of God's children and the splendor of God's creation.

- Pilgrimage is a theology of *journeys, stations, and status, locations, pathways, and narrative patterns*, including one-way journeys, liminoid transitions, displacement, and returning home.

- Pilgrimage is *a spirituality of embodied virtues*. Pilgrim spirituality is the practice of the fruits of the Spirit, such as faith, hope, and anticipation, patience and resiliency, humility, generosity, and gentleness, love, mercy, and compassion. As the imitation of Christ, pilgrimage is as much about *character* as it is about movement.

- Pilgrimage, in many ways, is *what we are already doing*. Pilgrim spirituality helps us identify ongoing practices in pilgrimage terms.

- Pilgrimage is a *spirituality of potentiality*. It discerns possibilities of spiritual encounter, enhancing our Christian journey.

- Pilgrimage is a *retroactive spirituality*. It provides a meaningful frame for interpreting past experience.

- Pilgrimage is *a collaborative spirituality*. Acknowledging that we're stronger together, pilgrimage espouses an interdependent approach to Christian practice. Recognizing that no one way has all the answers, pilgrimage depends upon the input of others. Attending to those who are suffering, pilgrimage is a theology of accompaniment, committed to safeguarding the dignity of fellow pilgrims. Espousing virtues, such as crossing boundaries, welcoming strangers, and engaging the Other, pilgrimage supports interpersonal expressions of mission, evangelism, and social justice, including peace and reconciliation, mediation and conflict resolution, human rights, economic justice, and racial and gender equality. Offering perspectives on vulnerability, grace, and redemption, pilgrimage is a second-chance spirituality that walks alongside other ways of seeking God.

20

Religious Travel

PILGRIM SPIRITUALITY OFFERS A roadmap for enhancing physical journeys. Religious travel is transformative; pilgrim spirituality makes it more so. Conveying the wisdom of biblical, historical, and contemporary pilgrims, pilgrim spirituality is the *conscious* perception, *intentional* engagement, and *considered* response to religious travel.

Testimonies abound. "If you're Christian and you have lost your first Love, a pilgrimage can help you fall in love again."[1] Pilgrim memoirs capture the magic of religious travel—life-changing personal narratives, the voices of others, local culture, history, and landscapes.[2] While encouraging vicarious participation in other people's stories, pilgrim spirituality offers theological tools for deepening the experience and meaning of physical journeys.

Reflection is needed on the privileged nature of travel. While God is constantly calling people on pilgrimage, religious travel, especially to foreign destinations, requires financial resources, travel documents, adequate health, and disposable time that leaves behind a sizeable portion of Christians around the world. The tension is endemic to the Christian life at large. What is the proper use and distribution of wealth and resources? How do we walk together as fellow pilgrims, mitigating the imbalance of power? How can we best ensure a table of equals? While the issues are complex, God may call us, at times, to stay at home, to focus on local concerns, to send funds to global partners instead of going ourselves. As we consider our

1. Foster, *Sacred Journey*, 146.

2. See, for instance, Lash, *Pilgrimage*; Boers, *Way*; Martin, *Jesus*; Egan, *Pilgrimage*. Also see Cousineau, *Art*.

place in the world, pilgrimage asserts itself as a journey of social, economic, and environmental justice.

21

Everyday Christianity

ALONG WITH THE PRINCIPLES of application (see chapter 19), pilgrim spirituality resources day-to-day faith through (1) the lessons of physical travel and (2) the life-as-journey metaphor that views *all* experience in pilgrimage terms. Pilgrim spirituality applies to everyday Christianity precisely because *everyday life is a pilgrimage.*

PHYSICAL TRAVEL AND EVERYDAY LIFE

There are notable differences between physical travel and everyday life. Whereas day-to-day life is familiar, patterned, and habitual, travel is a serial encounter with the new, the unknown, and the unfamiliar. Travel exchanges the predictability of routine for the flux and flow of novelty, change, and the unexpected. It's characterized by the constant alteration of scenery, context, and perspective. Sometimes, we travel simply to distance ourselves from home, to experience the freedom of space, to reach the point when our only worries are the immediate concerns of the road.[1] While everyday life is immersed in God, the grass looks greener away from home.

LINKS WITH PHYSICAL TRAVEL

Even so, there are numerous links between physical travel and everyday life. First of all, pilgrimage has been described *as a microcosm of life*, or as *life*

1. See Least Heat-Moon, *Blue Highways*, 9.

intensified, suggesting that the difference between travel and everyday life is more quantitative than qualitative. Travel is a "compressed, more vivid version of life: the highs and lows [come] quickly upon each other."[2] While travel may be more intense, it resembles everyday life all the same.

Secondly, religious travel *as time set aside* to address important issues—such as health, relationships, commitments, and transitions—is generally *focused on everyday issues*. The motives of pilgrimage travel are often concerned with the realities, demands, and prayerful possibilities of day-to-day life.

Third, through first-hand knowledge and the wisdom of others, everyday spirituality incorporates *the experience and lessons of physical travel*. The life-as-journey metaphor assumes that we know more about physical journeys than we do about the abstract nature of the earthly life. Knowledge about physical traveling renders insights into our everyday journey of faith.

Fourth, the lessons of travel are *transferable*. The point of wisdom is that it applies to life at large. How one faces challenges and obstacles, deals with needs, problems, and desires, interacts with others, and perceives the sacred *on the road* shapes one's character back home. Long after physical journeys have come to an end, their impact continues in our day-to-day lives.

Finally, elements of travel are *present in everyday life*. The quotidian Christian journey contains beginnings and endings, departures and arrivals, changes and transitions. We don't have to travel to the far side of the world to experience liminoid conditions. Thresholds are literally at our door, and we can find ourselves between and betwixt, for better or worse, without ever leaving home.

In short, everyday pilgrimage draws upon the lessons of physical travel, the metaphor of journey, and the application of pilgrimage themes. We do not need to be *on pilgrimage* to be pilgrims nor is pilgrim spirituality limited to the sphere of religious travel. Pilgrim spirituality integrates the goals, themes, and virtues of traditional forms of pilgrimage into everyday Christian practice.

EVERYDAY THEMES OF PILGRIMAGE

Everyday life is full of pilgrimage themes. We live embodied lives, bound by time and place. Life consists of the personal, the corporate, the physical, and the metaphorical. Tensions abound. Our encounters of God, self, and the Other are the essence of everyday life, while the categories of pilgrim

2. Kaplan, *In Europe's Shadow*, 201.

experience relate to the here and now of home. One-off encounters, the voices of others, and self-reflection occur in everyday settings. Day-to-day life consists of sensuous experience, events, incidents, and accidents, challenges and obstacles, doubts and uncertainties, noise and distractions, mistakes, failures, and second chances. Our quotidian journey includes waiting, pausing, and lingering, the spontaneous and the serendipitous, awe and wonder, mystery, and surprise.

The pilgrim practices her craft in the ordinary world of everyday life. Pilgrim spirituality is about daily nourishment, self-care, personal identity, intentional decision-making, and our interactions with others. Pilgrimage as everyday spirituality speaks to how we see ourselves and others, how we navigate vulnerability and alienation, embody perseverance and resiliency, and engage the stranger. Healing and wholeness, reconciliation, and justice speak to the everyday journey of Christian pilgrims.[3]

PERSONAL DIRECTIONS

The spirituality of everyday life concerns our spiritual location and, concomitantly, our spiritual direction. Our personal journeys are nurtured through everyday disciplines and means of grace. Pilgrim spirituality includes monastic prayers and mystical writings as well as contemplation, meditation, and mindfulness. It occurs through intentional spiritual direction from *The Spiritual Exercises* of Ignatius of Loyola to the guidance of a personal spiritual director. It includes forms of personal and group therapy as well as twelve-step programs.

---

3. On the sacred practices of everyday life, see Warren, *Liturgy* and Martin, *Ministry*.

22

The Social Applications
of Pilgrimage

EXPLORING DEFINITIONAL FRAMES OF social pilgrimage, this chapter focuses on how we *think* about pilgrimage as an expression of Christian outreach, service, and social justice, including concepts of mission and evangelism. The discussion addresses two tendencies in our conceptualization of the pilgrim life. First of all, Protestant pilgrimage has been dominated by an emphasis on personal spirituality, characterized by the expression that it's "really about the inner journey." While pilgrimage encompasses the inner life, it rejects the bifurcation of the body and the soul. The Christian life is *embodied experience*; it's a sensuous, incarnational journey, particularized in time and place, which includes our social interactions. Secondly, pilgrimage has often lacked a conceptual basis that frames it in social terms. Our task is to define social pilgrimage as *directly* as we can, asserting, for instance, that engaging the Other and crossing boundaries are definitional standards rather than secondary affirmations.

WAR AND PEACE

I asked Sister Giovanna if she had ever been to Medjugorje, a small village in Bosnia-Herzegovina, where, in 1981, six young people began seeing daily visions of the Madonna. "We went through Medjugorje and spent a night outside the church sleeping on the ground," she replied. "We were actually on our way to Sarajevo—2,700 of us on a peace march during the war. We walked carrying flags with rainbows on them. For ten straight nights, we slept under the stars. Many of us were over seventy years old!

"We were eventually rerouted away from Sarajevo because of the heavy fighting. Still, our destination city was in the middle of the war. As we entered the city, we were walking single file, carrying our rainbow flags. We could see soldiers in the streets and snipers on the rooftops. The day was very hot, and we were all very tired. All of a sudden, a huge thunderstorm came up, soaking every one of us.

"Then the rain stopped. As the clouds rolled away, the sun came out, and there, in the middle of this war-torn city, was the biggest, most beautiful rainbow any of us had ever seen! We all cheered, throwing our hats and flags into the air. Enemy soldiers stood looking at us—and the sky—in amazement. The peace that prevailed for those few hours was beautiful. For a moment, God had stopped the war."

From pedestrian marches to the writings of social reformers, pilgrimage has fundamental associations with peace, justice, and reconciliation. Prominent examples include The Great Pilgrimage of 1913, organized by the National Union of Women's Suffrage Societies, which involved women marching to London from all over England and Wales, culminating in a rally in Hyde Park attended by over 50,000 people.[1] Addressing desegregation and voting rights in the United States, the civil rights movement held the Prayer Pilgrimage for Freedom in Washington, DC on May 17, 1957. Mildred Norman (1908–81), better known as the Peace Pilgrim, walked more than 25,000 miles between 1953 and 1981 in support of international peace and nuclear disarmament.[2] The diaries of Catholic social activist Dorothy Day (1897–1980) were published in 1948 under the title, *On Pilgrimage*, while Martin Luther King Jr. penned "My Pilgrimage to Non-Violence" in 1958.[3]

More recently, the World Council of Churches launched an initiative named *An Invitation to the Pilgrimage of Justice and Peace* in 2019, while denominational efforts include a three-month program on racism and racial equality, "Pilgrimage to the Land of Love," offered by the Mountain Sky Conference of the United Methodist Church.

1. See Robinson, *Hearts*.

2. See Peace Pilgrim, *Peace Pilgrim*. The witness of the Peace Pilgrim is that the goal of pilgrimage can be a *thing* or a *cause* instead of a place.

3. See Day, *On Pilgrimage*; King, "My Pilgrimage."

THE ABRAHAMIC STRANGER

Moving from explicit precedents to definitional frames, we begin with Abraham, who left home and family to follow God in a foreign land. While the story reminds us that we are strangers in the world, the hermeneutical pivot calls us to see Abraham in the face of others. In other words, our application of the story should move from *being* Abraham to how we *respond* to Abraham. The Abrahamic imperative entreats us to welcome strangers with compassion, generosity, and hospitality—to see Abraham as the Other and the Other as God.[4] The virtue of hospitality espoused in the narrative informs our Christian response to foreigners, to immigrants, migrants, and refugees, to the wayfaring traveler as well as the local stranger.

The Abraham story revolves around place—leaving home and following God to the land that God would show him—and we can speak of Abraham's experience of displacement and his identity as a second-place person. Yet, the concept of the stranger is ultimately tied to one's relationship to others.

Citing Abraham, early Irish and Anglo-Saxon Christians left home to become pilgrims for life (*peregrini pro Christi*). Some moved permanently to Rome; others went as monks and missionaries to Germany. Still others went famously out to sea, searching for a desert in the ocean.[5] Not all expressions were considered equal. The seventh-century *Life of Columbanus* states that the superior way was neither living on cliffs nor going out to sea; rather, it was living among a foreign nation, even if one lived as a hermit. After Columbanus (who died in Bobbio, Italy in 615) "had been many years in the cloister [in Ireland] he longed to go into strange lands, in obedience to the command which the Lord gave Abraham."[6] What the text means by strange lands is clarified in a conversation between Columbanus and a holy woman who was living in the Irish countryside. Two degrees of pilgrimage are discussed. The lesser pilgrimage involved forsaking one's family while still living in one's homeland. The greater form of pilgrimage meant living among *strangers* in a foreign, *inhabited* land. In the words of the holy woman: "Twelve years have passed by, since I have been far from my home and have sought out this place of pilgrimage. . . . And if [my weakness] had not prevented me, I would have crossed the sea and chosen a better place among strangers as my home."[7]

---

4. See Gen 18; Heb 13:2.

5. See Aist, "Pilgrim Traditions," 14–15; Adomnán, *Life*, 1.16.

6. Jonas, *Life*, chapter 9.

7. Jonas, *Life*, chapter 8.

The text makes two important points. First of all, Abraham's calling as a stranger was interpreted in terms of one's relationship with *other people* rather than merely in terms of one's geographical location. Secondly, while the degree to which the Irish were missionaries is debatable, they valued the foreign context of social pilgrimage over domestic forms of the Christian life.

The etymology of pilgrimage likewise pertains to the stranger. The English word *pilgrim* is ultimately derived from the Latin, *peregrinus* (*per* + *ager*, or "through the field"), which denotes a foreigner living outside the laws of one's homeland. Lacking legal protection, a *peregrinus* is a person of vulnerable status.[8] In short, there are biblical, historical, and etymological frames for defining pilgrimage in terms of the stranger.

BEYOND ABRAHAM

Along with the Abrahamic stranger, there are additional ways to conceptualize pilgrimage in social terms. Emulating others, or walking in their footsteps, is a recognized concept of pilgrimage, epitomized by the imitation of Christ (1 Pet 2:21). As followers of Jesus, pilgrims embody his words and deeds: reaching out to the poor, welcoming the outcast, engaging the religious and ethnic Other, and espousing the values of God.[9] Pilgrimage as the imitation of Christ means being people of compassion, loving our enemies, and living by the Golden Rule.[10]

Jesus sent his disciples on mission journeys to preach the gospel, proclaiming that the kingdom of God was at hand. The New Testament depicts evangelistic pilgrimage as healing the sick, raising the dead, cleansing lepers, and casting out demons (Matt 10:5–8). The missionary pilgrim declares the year of the Lord and announces good news to the poor: the release of captives, the recovery of sight to the blind, and freedom for the oppressed (Luke 4:16–19).

Pilgrimage can also be framed by companionship. Companions are co-travelers, literally, those with whom we have bread. To be a pilgrim is to walk alongside another, to manifest God's presence, to participate in the grace of accompaniment. Pilgrims find ways to be present with others, to be in solidarity with the needs, dreams, and aspirations of fellow travelers. Recognizing that we're on a common journey, pilgrim spirituality challenges us

---

8. On the definition and legal protections of pilgrims (*peregrini*), see Adolf, "Peregrinus," 626–27; Larson, "From Protections"; Burns, *Las Siete Partidas*, title 24, 264–66.

9. See Robinson, *Jesus.*

10. Matt 5:42–44; Luke 6:31.

to discover similarities—and a shared sense of purpose—with those who are ostensibly different from us. Seeing both the proximate and distant Other as companions, pilgrims act in ways that promote economic justice, human rights, and the dignity of all.

Sister Giovanna taught me the concept of pilgrimage as "the street":

> For many years, I worked with the mentally ill. I also gave hos-
> pitality to traveling pilgrims. Then I asked God to allow me to
> be a pilgrim. I have been a pilgrim ever since. I used to go on
> pilgrimage throughout Italy, hitchhiking without any money,
> though never alone. Now hitchhiking is illegal so I carry enough
> money with me for a bus ticket. There are a lot of poor people
> in Italy, a lot of refugees. People living on the streets. By being a
> pilgrim, my heart learns to hear the cries of those who have no
> choice but to be pilgrims.

Sister Giovanna is referring to two types of pilgrims: those suffering in the streets and the servants of the road who hear their cries and respond with compassion.[11] Pilgrimage is not always an intentional, let alone a privileged, journey.

Pilgrimage as "the street" frames the human condition in pilgrim terms. Streets are the highways and byways of life, its alleyways and underpasses, street corners and curbsides, bus stops and way stations. Pilgrimage as the street refers to the homeless, the poor and impoverished, the vulnerable and displaced, the abused, the addicted, and the mentally-ill. It speaks to those working the streets, whether for profit or survival, as well as those without a roof, including migrants and refugees.[12]

We've previously discussed Sister Giovanna's description of the three-fold moments of life—hermitage, pilgrimage, and community—in which she defines the pilgrim as one who goes out into the streets, learning about the world, hearing the cries of others, and helping those in need. Pilgrimage is a call to accompany the human condition, which takes us to "less-than-sacred" locations in search of the "least of these" in whom we see the face of Christ.

Finally, it is worth reiterating that the life-as-journey metaphor encompasses the entirety of life. As a comprehensive expression of the Christian faith, pilgrimage consists of the imperative to love and serve the world.

11. Those who suffer are also servants.
12. On the Holy Family as refugees, see Matt 2:13–23.

THE SOCIAL FRAMES OF PILGRIMAGE

The social dimensions of pilgrimage can thus be framed in the following ways:

- through the Abrahamic emphasis on the stranger;
- through the Latin word for pilgrim, *peregrinus*, which refers to the vulnerability of foreigners;
- through medieval understandings of pilgrimage as living among a foreign people;
- through associations of the pilgrim life with hospitality;

- through the concept of pilgrimage as the imitation of Christ;
- through biblical concepts of mission and evangelism;

- through historical precedents that associate pilgrimage with peace, justice, and social change;
- through metaphors of progress (e.g., King's pilgrimage to non-violence);
- through the idea of a shared journey towards a common goal (e.g., a pilgrimage of justice);

- through quotable quotes, such as Sister Giovanna's statement "that by being a pilgrim my heart learns to hear the cries of those who have no choice but to be pilgrims";
- through the concept of pilgrimage as "the street";
- through the pilgrim concept of companionship and walking alongside others;
- through overlapping similarities with forms of physical walking, namely, marches and public protests;[13]

- through the intersection of place and memory, including sites of conscience and various forms of memorialization;
- through stories of remembrance, resiliency, and resistance; and

---

13. According to Solnit, the "collective walk brings together the iconography of the pilgrimage with that of the military march and the labor strike and demonstration." Solnit, *Wanderlust*, 57. Not all marches demand social change; some support the status quo.

- through the life-as-journey metaphor, which encompasses *all* areas of life, including social relations.

The above frames underscore the direct relationship between pilgrimage and the social dimensions of the Christian life. Social pilgrimage is as old as Abraham, and social issues are pilgrim concerns. In short, the transformative reach of social pilgrimage is enhanced when we employ definitions that are directly couched in social terms, such as engaging the Other, the imitation of Christ, and pilgrimage as the street.

PILGRIMAGE AS ECO-SPIRITUALITY

Pilgrimage extends beyond our interactions with other people to our stewardship of creation. Pilgrimage concerns our place in the world and our care for the planet, which includes the following concepts, values, and practices:

- Nature has a numinous quality. Specific locations, landscapes, and physical formations (such as mountains, forests, and deserts) have associations with the sacred and have been approached—and avoided—as human destinations. More generally, the majesty of God is experienced through the wonders of creation. As the footstool of God, the earth is a sanctuary of divine presence. Caring for creation is an act of worship.

- Pilgrims trust in God and God's creation for sustenance. Praying for daily bread becomes, in turn, a pilgrim's prayer for the sustainability of the planet. The pilgrim image of gleaning conjoins the concepts of sustenance, stewardship, and care for others.[14]

- Interdependency is a Christian virtue. Not only are we dependent upon the planet, our actions and behaviors have a long-term effect upon the world. The interdependent life directs our attention to people as well as the planet.

- The pilgrim's commitment to the Other includes our stewardship of the physical world, which God has given to us as a sacred trust. Rejecting a "passing through" mentality that devalues creation, pilgrim spirituality acknowledges that certain practices of pilgrimage have contributed to humanity's abuse and exploitation of the world. Pilgrims are trustees as much as transients. Pilgrimage as eco-spirituality espouses the virtues of humility, care, and responsibility.

14. See, for instance, the Society of St. Andrew (www.endhunger.org). Also see the 2000 film by Agnès Varda, *The Gleaners & I.*

- By contrast, mistreatment, cruelty, and the exploitation of the world result in personal and spiritual alienation, which is starkly expressed in *The Rime of the Ancient Mariner*. Killing the albatross is an act of *self*-destruction as well as a sin against creation.[15]

- Pilgrims exercise sustainable practices for future pilgrims. We sanctify life when we plant trees knowing that we will never be able to sit in their shade.[16]

While care for creation is an integral value, the eco-spirituality of pilgrimage warrants significantly more attention.

STRENGTHENING THE SOCIAL APPLICATIONS OF PILGRIMAGE

Moving forward, our attention to the social dimensions of pilgrimage can be strengthened in the following ways. First of all, we need to give *definitional status to the stranger, or the Other*. The strand of pilgrimage that focuses on the stranger and includes concepts of hospitality, engaging the Other, crossing boundaries, and tearing down borders transcends the traditional conceptualization of pilgrimage as physical and metaphorical journeys.

Secondly, we must recognize that *appealing to pilgrimage as an inward journey undermines its social applications*. The "spiritualization" of the pilgrim life has been a principal obstacle to realizing the social transformations that pilgrimage fosters. The assertion that pilgrimage is "really about the inner journey" is, at best, a half-truth; at worst, it distorts the Christian life. Pilgrimage should not be divorced from its physical dimensions nor relegated to an interior practice. Pilgrimage is an embodied, incarnational spirituality that give primacy to human concerns in time and place.

Third, the social applications of pilgrimage can be strengthened through *an emphasis on virtues*. Pilgrimage is the quest of Christian virtues, including love, mercy and compassion, forgiveness, and reconciliation.

Fourth, *the prophetic strand of pilgrimage should be further developed*. Pilgrimage offers embodied opposition to the status quo. It favors place over space—the particular, localized, and heterogenous over the homogenizing forces of the modern world. The contemporary resurgence of pilgrimage is, in part, a grassroots response to the dehumanizing dominance of space, technology, and globalization. The prophetic strand of pilgrimage includes

15. On *The Rime of the Ancient Mariner*, published by Samuel Taylor Coleridge in 1798, see Gardner, *Annotated* and Guite, *Mariner*.

16. There are various attributions to the saying.

sites of conscience, the decolonization of memorialization, and attention to the stories of others. Remembrance itself is a form of resistance.

Fifth, *Christian pilgrimage should reconsider its eschatological vision*, which has traditionally maintained an otherworld spirituality that views the earthly life as a transient journey to heaven.[17] As we've previously emphasized, it is not the world and its people that rise to heaven; rather, New Jerusalem *descends to earth*, complementing Jesus' insistence that the kingdom of God is among us.[18] Just as Jesus' ministry addressed the needs of the world, our Christian journey should take us *into* the world, not out of it. By recasting the *direction* of our eschatology, we're better positioned to be agents of social change.

Finally, we need to reconsider *the relationship between stranger, place, and journey*. They are related insomuch as a foreigner is one who has left home and has traveled elsewhere. A foreigner may permanently settle somewhere, establishing roots and raising children, yet remains a foreigner, like Abraham, due to his or her relationship to *place*. In other words, a person retains a foreign identity due to a *past* journey rather than ongoing movement.

The consequence of associating strangers with their place of origin is the implication that they don't belong where they are. This is expressed in the tendency of dominant cultures to treat the ethnic Other as someone who is "not from here" or to ask "where are you *really* from?" The proximate Other includes the recently arrived; yet, the vast majority of everyday strangers, including the ethnic, cultural, and religious Other, are *not* those who have recently traveled, while second-generation families are native to the land. Associating the proximate Other with distant places denies, disempowers, and delegitimizes their presence, voice, and status in both subtle and coercive ways. Pilgrim spirituality espouses an ethic of welcoming the stranger that doesn't presume where the Other belongs.

In sum, pilgrimage is the Christian faith in action. Pilgrim spirituality speaks to the most pressing and intractable social issues. Pilgrimage promotes human rights, peace and reconciliation, mediation and conflict resolution, interfaith and ecumenical relations, international, multicultural, and secular engagement, and gender, racial, and economic equality. Pilgrimage is both *the experience of being* and *our response to* immigrants, migrants, and refugees, the homeless and the mentally-ill, the vulnerable and destitute. It walks in solidarity with the downtrodden and stops for those on the side of the road. Pilgrimage embraces the Other, embodies hospitality, and charts

---

17. See John 17:1–19; 1 Pet 2:11; Heb 11:13.

18. See Rev 21:2, 10; Luke 17:21.

the course of compassion. Seeking the union of God, self, and the Other, pilgrims are harbingers of social justice, and once we pause to survey the journey, its social applications are clear from the start.

23

Congregational Formation

CONGREGATIONAL PILGRIMAGE RANGES FROM organizing the entirety of congregational life around the twinned virtues of pilgrimage and hospitality to employing pilgrimage expressions to sustain, nourish, and even jump-start a congregation.[1] Congregational applications include (1) recognizing pilgrimage-related concepts, themes, and practices already in use, (2) enhancing existing expressions through language and awareness, and (3) implementing new ideas, programs, and practices.

THE CONGREGATIONAL STORY

Pilgrimage is the narrative history of the people of God, and congregational pilgrimage begins with a shared awareness of its past and present journey: the visionary faith of former leaders, changes, transitions, low points, and landmarks, current obstacles and opportunities as well as future goals and anticipated challenges. Pilgrimage is the story of our corporate identity—the who we are, where we've been, and the people we want to be. Pilgrimage theology provides tools for discerning the past history, present identity, and future direction of a congregation, including resources for the merger and closure of congregations, organizations, and institutions.

Congregational memory, which can be both a blessing and a burden, is central to the story. How do congregations celebrate their history without getting stuck in the past? How do they reckon with past events, seeking

1. On Christian hospitality, see Pohl, *Making Room*; Newman, *Untamed Hospitality*; Sykes, "Making Room"; Westerhoff, *Good Fences*.

healing, forgiveness, and reconciliation? Pilgrim congregations confront their past in ways that allow them to move forward in grace-filled ways. They discern how the past offers wisdom for being God's people today. They face tomorrow's challenges by standing on the shoulders of others.

Organizational language shapes the congregational story. Mission, value, and vision statements can be strengthened through the use of pilgrim language, which fosters congregational identity, instills a shared commitment to common goals, and guides behaviors and practices through a transformative vision of the world.

Conveying the congregational story as a pilgrimage narrative reminds, guides, and empowers God's people in the particularities of time and place. As communities of remembrance, pilgrim congregations are attentive to anniversaries, commemorations, and special occasions. As contemporary congregations in time and place, they adjust their journeys to the needs of the world.

PHYSICAL PREMISES

While a congregation's presence extends beyond its walls, pilgrimage reminds us that places matter. Pilgrim congregations attend to their physical settings, which, as set-aside centers of human activity, should be sanctuaries of hope, shelters of protection, hospices of healing. How do churches use their spaces? What messages and meanings do our buildings impart? John Inge applies the concept of shrines to local churches. Shrines convey a threefold witness to the world: past event, present experience, and future hope.[2] Whereas many churches no longer have a sense of a sacred place, a shrine offers an alternative geography to the landscape around it. Expressing the function of a shrine, pilgrim churches communicate God's past, present, and future presence.

WORSHIP

Beyond themes contained in readings, prayers, hymns, and sermons, pilgrim worship incorporates pilgrimage concepts. Worship is an act of commemoration, involving the retelling of sacred stories and the reenactment of rituals that invoke God's presence in time and space. Worship conveys the *in progress* nature of our earthly journey. Baptism and confirmation are rites of passage. Communion, among other things, is a means of spiritual provision.

2. See Inge, *Christian Theology*, 103–22.

Worship is the manna of our wilderness journey, a time for nourishing our souls.

Pilgrim expressions of worship are virtually unlimited. Appealing to both our personal and corporate sense of God, pilgrim worship conjoins incarnational experience with metaphorical exploration. It proclaims the pathways of God while fostering the mysteries of faith. As a sensuous encounter, participants touch, taste, see, hear, and smell. Pilgrim worship contains visual imagery, physical movement, interactive participation, and interpersonal dialogue. In step with pilgrimage, worship extends beyond the benediction to everyday life.

CONGREGATIONAL LIFE

From informal fellowship to regular events and special occasions, pilgrim spirituality speaks to the common life of congregations, to the everyday journey of the people of God, and to the Holy Spirit's presence in both large and small group settings. Christian community offers spiritual comfort, guidance, and accountability, people to laugh with and cry with, guides, mentors, and fellow companions. Christians gather in community to share with one another their experiences of the street (pilgrimage) and their time alone with God (hermitage).

AGE-LEVEL MINISTRIES

From the image of the earthly life as a journey to God to rites of passage and theories of human development, pilgrimage offers a dynamic framework for age-level ministry. The developmental journey of children, youth, and young adults, the transitions of life, the life-review practices of older adults, and the Christian commitment to lifelong learning merge pilgrim concepts with age-level interests. Attentive to the end-of-life journey, pilgrim congregations provide compassionate care for the dead and the dying, while proclaiming the post-life promises of God through resurrection celebrations.

CONGREGATIONAL OUTREACH

Pilgrim congregations embody hospitality: welcoming visitors, seeking out the lost and lonely, proclaiming and practicing reconciliation. Pilgrim congregations open their doors and make room at the table. While hospitality is a wall-to-wall virtue, church occurs in the streets: engaging strangers, listening to others, serving people in need. Discipleship—following Jesus and helping others, growing in God and loving the Other—is at the heart of the pilgrim church. A spirituality of accompaniment, pilgrim theology offers congregations an interpersonal approach to mission, evangelism, and social outreach.

THE PASTOR AS PILGRIM

While all congregants are pilgrims, pastors are pilgrims in ways that literally set them apart. Ordination is one of Christianity's rites of passage (i.e., a layperson becomes a priest). Pastors, priests, and ministers assume the roles of mentor, guide, and companion to fellow pilgrims; yet, they often belong and *don't belong* to the communities they serve, living in the liminal tension of the betwixt and between. This stems, in part, from their set-aside status and the authority they hold as a spiritual leader, in which they are often seen as a representative, or vicar, of Christ. The pilgrimage nature of ministry is further expressed when clergy are appointed by an external authority rather than chosen by the congregation. In itinerant systems, like Methodism, pastors are moved around on a regular basis. Pastors are religious travelers called to serve God's people away from home in territories that are not their own. Embodying the tension of Abraham, the pastor is an outsider who is simultaneously leader, guest, host, partner, and friend.

ADMINISTRATION, GOVERNANCE, AND STEWARDSHIP

Pilgrim congregations give prayerful consideration to policies and best practices regarding leadership, authority, and church governance, the protection of the vulnerable, and human resources. What are our employment practices? How do we treat and train volunteers, engage stakeholders, and honor individuals? How does leadership address interpersonal and intragroup conflict? Pilgrimage is a spirituality of accountable life-giving relationships, and administrative best practices are nothing less than an institution's way of treating people.

Structuring church life around the twinned themes of pilgrimage and hospitality extends to congregational stewardship, to the use and management of resources, care for the planet, and practices of economic justice. The stewardship of church resources includes remembering the gifts, offerings, and sacrifices of others. How are dedications, memorials, and bequests acknowledged, remembered, and, at times, retired?

CONGREGATIONAL TRAVEL

Pilgrim congregations embrace responsible expressions of religious travel, including traditional forms of pilgrimage, local journeys, mission trips, camps, retreats and conferences, and the visitation of domestic and global partners. Physical journeys—and time spent together away from home—can renew, strengthen, and inspire congregations.

PART 7

Moving Forward

24

The Theological Contributions
of Pilgrimage

THEOLOGICAL CONTRIBUTIONS

PILGRIMAGE HAS OFTEN BEEN seen as a marginal expression of the Christian life, and its association with sacred places, personal piety, and the inner journey has marked it as a non-intellectual endeavor. On the contrary, pilgrim spirituality is robustly theological, engaging how we *think* about God and the earthly life, offering contributions and correctives to theology at large. Pilgrim spirituality is the interrogation of lived experience, specifically as it relates to God, self, and the Other, and what's refined in the process are the tools of the Christian faith. Pilgrim spirituality sharpens how we think; it makes us better theologians.

As an intentional approach to the Christian life, pilgrim spirituality understands that language shapes identity, images frame experience, and concepts fuel spiritual practice. How we think, the questions we ask, and the language we employ forge the direction of our faith.

Pilgrim spirituality stresses the importance of definitions and how they function for examining the religious life. Definitions are not static statements that delineate phenomena but are frames for exploring the world. Definitions illuminate phenomena; multiple lenses help us to see in 3D. While comprehensive definitions identify the spectrum of possibilities, individual frames focus, examine, and interpret experience.

Offering an expansive model of the Christian life, pilgrim spirituality appropriates related domains to perceive and explore the world. By ultimately adhering to a biblical template, it frees itself to probe secular sources, gleaning insights from non-Christian fields. Seeing ourselves through other people's eyes enhances our understanding of who we are, our self-identity, and our religious and cultural traditions. Recognizing how we are both similar and different from others fosters curiosity, reflection, growth, and compassion.

Pilgrimage brings metaphor to the forefront of spiritual exploration. Pilgrim spirituality calls Christians to a deeper understanding of the exploratory function of metaphor, which is fundamental to religious language.

Pilgrim spirituality underscores the importance of proverbial wisdom. Exemplifying the exploratory task of theology, aphorisms capture the insights of lived experience, while functioning, in turn, as interpretative tools for engaging the world.

Pilgrims recognize the role of questions as an instrument of faith. The Christian life is an inquisitive journey, and transformation is fueled by interrogation. Pilgrims ask questions about the nature of God, the meaning of life, and the world in which they live. They seek divine assistance, question power and authority, and query the cause of injustice. Theological pathways are marked with questions.

Pilgrimage asserts the tensional nature of theology. While questions are the cornerstone of theology, faith is the absence of clear-cut answers. Pilgrimage reminds us that life is unfinished, incomplete, and unresolved. Embracing contradictions, tensions, and paradoxes, pilgrimage offers a counterpoint to theologies that mislead with absolute answers.

In the absence of answers, faith is advanced through a commitment to pilgrim virtues, including perseverance, hope, and reconciliation. Pilgrim spirituality offers a virtue-based approach to Christian practice.

Pilgrimage reminds us that the spiritual life is an embodied journey. Recognizing that the twinning of spirit and matter patterns God's way in the world, pilgrim spirituality offers a corrective to theologies that cleave the body from the soul. Theology, moreover, should be contextualized in time and place. As an incarnational theology, pilgrimage embodies the universals of God through the particularities of human experience. It favors place over space, the particular, localized, and heterogenous over the homogenizing— and dehumanizing—forces of globalization, assimilation, and acculturation.

Always on the move towards God, pilgrimage is the lifelong process of sanctification. Pilgrim spirituality reminds us that the Christian life is a process not an event. Pilgrim theology engages the entirety of who we are over the totality of our earthly lives.

Pilgrim spirituality values the relational experience of God, self, and the Other over catechetical approaches to the Christian life. Finding meaning through the actuality of lived experience, it favors story, memory, and narrative over doctrine, precepts, and dogma. Giving an ear to others, pilgrimage is a theology of dialogue.

Concerned for the welfare of their earthly companions, pilgrims take an interpersonal approach to mission and evangelism. Pilgrimage re-envisions Christian service and our collective struggle for social justice.

A theology of interdependence and stewardship, pilgrimage concerns both people and planet.

Pilgrim spirituality reminds us that effective theology has breadth and balance. A comprehensive expression of the Christian life, pilgrimage integrates personal and social holiness, acts of piety and mercy, community, the street, and time alone with God.

Finally, pilgrimage speaks in versatile ways to individuals, communities, and institutions. Inclusive of seekers, searchers, and the unchurched, agnostics and atheists, and those of other religions, pilgrim spirituality employs simple language and non-specialist terminology that appeal to our common human journey in relatable ways. Pilgrimage provides a vernacular for ecumenical, interfaith, and secular discourse.

THE FIELD OF PILGRIM SPIRITUALITY

Having examined definitions, concepts, tools, and theories, the field of pilgrim spirituality begins to take shape.[1] What is the curriculum, in part or whole, for seminary courses, ordinand training, and congregational programs? What are the themes, topics, and related domains that need further attention? By no means complete, the study of pilgrimage includes the following:

- *Definitional approaches.* Whether we begin by surveying the biblical and historical sources, considering etymologies, or reflecting upon contemporary expressions, pilgrimage studies must consider the role and function of definitions. At some point, a working definition is needed. Giving definitional recognition to the Other, our comprehensive definition identifies time, place, journey, and people as the means by which we encounter God, self, and the Other. Aphoristic definitions allow us, in turn, to explore the pilgrim life with differing frames of focus.

- *The characteristics of pilgrimage.* We have characterized pilgrimage as personal, corporate, incarnational, metaphorical, and tensional, each of which are units of study.

1. For a "textbook" that takes a traditional approach, see Harman, *Sociology.*

- *Anthropological theories.* The anthropological theories of pilgrimage, which address the relationship between pilgrimage and society, are basic to pilgrimage studies. Does pilgrimage support the status quo (Durkheim), oppose the structures of society (Turner and Turner), or consist of various contested narratives (Eade and Sallnow)?

- *Patterns of pilgrimage.* Pilgrim theology includes the various patterns, or templates, of pilgrimage. One-way patterns include Abrahamic pilgrimage, the earthly life, and sanctification as well as development theories, such as Maslow's hierarchy of needs and Erickson's theory of psycho-social development. Attention should be given to rites of passage, especially to the theory of liminality and the distinguishing features of liminoid experience. Return patterns include concepts of homecoming, restoration, and reconciliation (e.g., a return to the garden) and the framework of the hero's journey. Progressive spirals, paradigm shifts, and regressive progress are additional patterns of life.

- *Theological tools.* The theological tools of pilgrimage include metaphors, aphorisms and proverbial wisdom, liminality (liminoid experience), the hero's journey, the family resemblance theory, and mental maps as well as other concepts discussed in the book. The tools of pilgrimage are what we use to frame, explore, and question the world.

- *Theological categories.* The sacred and the profane, time and place, the transcendence and immanence of God, sin and salvation, our responsibility to others, and the eschatology of pilgrimage are prominent theological categories.

- *A theology of place.* Central to pilgrim spirituality is the theology of place, which consists of a nuanced approach to sacred places, the distinction between space and place, and the question of differentiated places.[2] What are the topographical elements, juxtapositions of place, and place-related concepts, including those from the field of human geography, that inform our sense of place?

- *Time and memory studies.* Memory concepts and practices include shared and collective memory, commemoration, and memorialization. Pilgrim spirituality reflects on the Christian experience of time.

- *Narrative studies.* First-person stories and the voices of others are integral to pilgrimage. The fields of narratology, autobiography,

---

2. On a Christian theology of place, see Inge, *Christian Theology*; Sheldrake, *Spaces*; Bartholomew, *Where Mortals Dwell*; Brown, *God*; Hjalmarson, *No Home*.

autoethnography, life review, and narrative therapy are related domains of pilgrimage.[3]

- *Corporate experience.* The study of corporate pilgrimage includes
  Turner's theory of communitas, the concept of short-term Christian
  community, pilgrimage as group identity, congregational applications,
  and the image of the pilgrim church.

- *Embodied experience.* Incarnational theology, embodied experience,
  and the interrelatedness of body and spirit are emphasized in contemporary pilgrimage writings. Pilgrim spirituality examines the embodied context of our earthly lives.

- *Personal spirituality.* Embracing biblical, historical, and contemporary
  traditions, pilgrim spirituality includes personal spirituality and faith
  formation, contemplation and mysticism, and spiritual direction.

- *Christian disciplines.* Pilgrim spirituality is a companion to Christian
  disciplines: Bible study, prayer, journaling, fasting, tithing, worship,
  and Holy Communion. Kinetic rituals and embodied forms of prayer
  include labyrinth walks and the Stations of the Cross.

- *Historical and literary sources.* From Jerusalem to the ends of the
  worlds, the field of pilgrim spirituality consists of a wide array of
  historical, mystical, and literary sources.[4] Texts range from *The City
  of God* and *The Interior Castle* to *Pilgrim's Progress* and *The Way of a
  Pilgrim.* Spiritual writings include *The Imitation of Christ, The Spiritual
  Exercises,* and *The Sacrament of the Present Moment.*

- *Social applications.* Pilgrim spirituality addresses the social mandates
  of the Christian faith. Social frames include Abrahamic pilgrimage,
  an emphasis on the Other, the imitation of Christ, and the pilgrim
  of the street. Pilgrims cross borders, dissolves boundaries, and break
  down barriers; they seek ways of accompanying others through times
  of conflict, mediation, and problem solving. Pilgrimage takes an

---

3. See, for instance, Abbott, *Cambridge*; Bal, *Narratology*; Adams et al., *Autoethnography*; Butler, "Life Review"; Westerhof, "Life Review"; Achenbaum, "Life Review";
White, *Narrative Practice*; Denborough, *Retelling the Stories.* For narratives of illness,
see Frank, *Wounded Storyteller.*

4. For editions of Jerusalem pilgrimage texts, see Wilkinson, *Egeria's Travels*;
Wilkinson, *Jerusalem Pilgrims*; Wilkinson, *Jerusalem Pilgrimage*; McGowan and Brad-
shaw, *Pilgrimage.* On pilgrimage in Celtic Christianity, see Aist, "Pilgrim Traditions";
Bradley, *Following*, 125–33; Sheldrake, *Living Between Worlds.*

interpersonal approach to social outreach, while recasting our notion of short-term mission.[5]

- *Cultural humility.* Pilgrim spirituality espouses the theory of cultural humility and its threefold commitment to (1) critical self-reflection and lifelong learning, (2) recognizing and mitigating imbalances of power and privilege, and (3) institutional accountability.[6]

- *Eco-spirituality.* Pilgrim spirituality emphasizes responsible stewardship and care for the planet.

- *Comparative pilgrimage.* Gleaning from others, Christians benefit from the study of interreligious, secular, and cultural pilgrimage. Comparative pilgrimage includes dark tourism and sites of conscience.[7]

In short, the field of pilgrim spirituality is the thought and practice of Christian formation, which is the lifelong process of becoming like Christ. It consists of a body of identifiable material that can be learned, taught, and practiced.

5. Most discussions on short-term mission use traditional concepts of pilgrimage (e.g., Turnerian theories), including pilgrimage as personal spirituality, while neglecting its social applications (e.g., engaging the Other). Framed this way, pilgrimage is what happens when short-term mission fails to meet its own goals and standards. See Haynes, *Consuming Mission*; Howell, *Short-Term Mission.* From short-term Christian community to the social applications of pilgrimage, our framework critiques, resources, and reshapes short-term mission, recasting it as a transformative template of pilgrimage.

6. See Tervalon and Murray-García, "Cultural Humility."

7. See Olsen and Korstanje, *Dark Tourism.*

25

The Challenges
of Pilgrim Spirituality

THE BREADTH OF PILGRIMAGE

MOVING FORWARD, WHAT ARE the challenges of pilgrim spirituality? We return to where we started, recognizing the breadth of pilgrimage, which includes the life-as-journey metaphor that renders the entirety of our lives as pilgrim content. Doubling down on the point, we've promulgated an expansive definition, while claiming that pilgrimage is a comprehensive expression of the Christian life. Yet, if pilgrimage is *everything*, does it have any meaning?

The issue is not whether the concept of pilgrimage is too broad but whether our definitional framework is robust enough to engage its breadth in effective ways. Insomuch as it resources a broad, balanced, and meaningful approach to the Christian life, our framework is dynamic enough to engage the spectrum of lived experience.

It does so by employing multiple types of definitions, expounding the characteristics of pilgrimage, breaking pilgrimage down into its component parts, appealing to a biblical prototype, and explicating principles of application. Our approach is facilitated by the family resemblance theory, which, in appealing to a series of overlapping similarities, holds the phenomenon together while allowing for the absence of any one element in any given expression.

THE BIBLICAL PROTOTYPE

We've argued that Christian pilgrimage is based on a biblical prototype, an amalgamation of Scripture that depicts the earthly life as a journey to God. There are variants of the prototype, and its differing interpretations are reflected in the diversity of Christian traditions, past and present. Questions remain. To what extent does a biblical prototype exist in sufficient, if equivocal, detail to govern the thought and practice of Christian pilgrimage? To what degree does its amalgamated nature, alternative patterns, and variant interpretations undermine the concept?

THE PARTICULAR AND THE UNIVERSAL

Pilgrim spirituality shares the theological challenge of reconciling the particular and the universal. Christianity embraces the particularism of the incarnation while espousing a universal vision of the body of Christ. Theological praxis must counter the dehumanizing forces of globalization at the same time it addresses the factionalism of local identities.

METAPHORS AND APHORISMS

Pilgrim spirituality probes eternal truths with linguistic tools. While metaphors and aphorism saturate the Bible, they present certain challenges in how they are used, interpreted, and (mis)construed. Our use of metaphorical language implicitly recognizes that theological pursuit is an exploratory journey more than a discipline of established beliefs. Transcendent realities cannot be fully known, and in the absence of empirical knowledge, the indirect nature of metaphor is our best and only method.

Perhaps, the biggest challenge to employing linguistic tropes is understanding them in the first place. What are they, and how do they function? How do we recognize and interpret them? Metaphors and aphorisms are assertive statements containing a "yes and no" tension that turns them into effective investigative tools. Metaphors are not *literally* true, while proverbial wisdom is seldom *universally* true in *each and every* situation.

We need to distinguish between theological precepts that we hold to be *always* true (e.g., God is love) and aphoristic statements that interpret experience but do so as half-truth assertions. It's better to travel than arrive. Pilgrimage is life intensified. Life is a journey of losing things along the way. Pilgrim theology asks if the opposite holds true as well.

THE CHALLENGE OF TENSIONAL THEOLOGY

Metaphors and aphorisms are just two expressions of the tensional nature of pilgrimage, which includes (1) the difficult, (2) the in-between, and (3) the paradoxical. First, tension is what strains and stretches our lives. Enduring tension requires patience and perseverance, stamina, and resiliency. Secondly, something is in tension when its locational position is betwixt and between, or neither here nor there, which characterizes liminoid experience. Third, tensional theology includes paradoxes, contradictions, and antithetical notions, or things that are mutually exclusive yet simultaneously true. Tensional theology speaks to the unknown, unfinished, and unresolved nature of human experience.

Pilgrim spirituality proceeds, at times, in opposite directions. One author runs with the notion that we're born to be creatures of movement, that our innate instinct is to be on the move, that God is unequivocally on the side of the nomad.[1] Others identify a sense of place as our fundamental aspiration.[2] Are purpose and identity forged through placemaking or are they contingent upon peripatetic experience? What, again, is the relationship between the sacred and the profane, between centers and edges, between this world and the world to come?

Tensional pathways create a dynamic journey, but when do they obstruct rather than instruct, confuse rather than inform? When do we concede that a contradiction cannot be held together or that something is simply wrong or doesn't belong? A problem with tensional theology is that it can serve as a catch-all category that fosters sloppy and imprecise thinking.

PILGRIMAGE, PLAGUES, AND THEODICY

Spanning the human condition, pilgrim spirituality speaks to (1) extraordinary encounters, (2) quotidian experience, and (3) life at its worst. Death, suffering, evil, and tragedy call all theologies into account. Addressing suffering, perseverance, and death, pilgrimage confronts the questions, emotions, and meaning of life. The mettle of pilgrim spirituality lies in how well it accompanies people through valleys of death and despair.

1. See Foster, *Sacred Journey*, xiv.

2. According to Hjalmarson, "Pilgrimage is an important part of the Christian life, but it was not what we were made for. . . . We were made for place." Hjalmarson, *No Home*, 18. Brueggemann states, "The essential restlessness of our world is the voice of the disposed demanding a share of the land." Brueggemann, *Land*, 205. Also see Lane, "Landscape."

DEMOGRAPHIC DIFFERENCES

Pilgrim spirituality places a premium on God's blessing of embodied existence and the uniqueness of each individual, which raises provocations. Some people like their bodies; others do not. Some are healthier than others. Our place of birth is a lottery, and some lives are particularly hard. Life is unfair.

A challenge of pilgrim theology is reconciling the inequalities of our earthly journeys. Pilgrim spirituality may work just fine for those who like their lives, but what about those who don't? Is there a survival of the fittest element to pilgrim spirituality that needs to be acknowledged? Does pilgrimage support or contest the injustices of the status quo?

Pilgrimage calls us to consider our individual differences, beginning with wealth and want. We need to be careful of Christian expressions that divide the world along economic lines, which applies to the privileged nature of religious travel. At the same time, pilgrim piety has particular associations with the poor. How does economic standing and financial position effect our Christian journeys?

The thought and practice of pilgrim spirituality must be continually evaluated to ensure the agency and equality of all, regardless of age, race, class, and gender. Female travelers face gender-based stereotypes and issues of health and safety unlike and often caused by their male counterparts. At home, do the everyday themes of pilgrim spirituality speak differently to men and women? To what extent does pilgrim spirituality support human rights, including the lived experience of LGBTQ+ people?[3] Our theological challenge is to create space for cooperation, collaboration, and companionship, while safeguarding the respect, dignity, and well-being of one another. In doing so, pilgrimage becomes a countercultural journey.

THE PROMISE OF TRANSFORMATION

Another challenge to pilgrim spirituality is the promise of personal and social transformation. Life, however, has few guarantees. The spiritual journey is a risk and a painful one at times. Pilgrimage involves suffering and sacrifice. Transformation, moreover, is not a walk in the park. Talk is easy; change is hard. Transition is few people's forte. Everyone wants progress, but fewer embrace the work that's involved. Complete transformation—the

---

3. For a memoir that speaks consciously from a woman's perspective, see Heuertz, *Pilgrimage*. For a gay Christian's pilgrimage in search of God in America, see Chu, *Does Jesus?*

miracle of metamorphosis—is a life-to-death-to-life-again process. To be a pilgrim is to count the cost. To drown in baptism waters. To plow without turning back. To walk in darkness. To journey to the cross. To die to self. The baptized emerges with renewed breath. The crucified is resurrected. While certain things die for good, other things die to be raised again. A similar process of transformation holds for communities and organizations as well as individuals.

THE DECLINE OF THE WESTERN CHURCH

Christianity faces *the precipitous decline of the Western church*, which, for pilgrimage, is both a challenge and an opportunity. What is the relationship between the decline of the church and the contemporary appeal of pilgrimage? Does a re-envisioned approach to pilgrimage offer hope for Christian believers, communities, and institutions, particularly in the West?

The reasons for the decline of the church in Western societies are complex, transcending simple solutions, and a return to the past is not what we're after. Evoking the liminoid experience of pilgrimage, how does the church journey forward when it doesn't know where it's going?[4]

The discourse lends itself to the popularized distinction between the *religious* and the *spiritual*: the church epitomizes religion, whereas the recent awakening of pilgrimage represents "authentic" spirituality. Pilgrim spirituality certainly critiques tradition while expressing countercultural qualities. Pilgrimage, however, is a historical expression of the body of Christ. As an ancient spiritual practice, pilgrimage is a creative means of regeneration not a contemporary alternative to the church.

At the same time, Christianity is bigger than the sum of its institutions. As the Holy Spirit renews the church, pilgrimage offers pathways of hope for a sustained Christian presence in the world. In the meantime, pilgrimage is not a Sisyphean attempt to scale the tower of Babel; rather, it's God's gift of the Bethlehem cradle, where, alongside the Magi, we encounter the vulnerability of the incarnation. In facing the challenges of the earthly journey, we are reminded that the pilgrim life is the unfinished work of God.

---

4. Confronting an uncertain future, the Western church is adopting the language of liminality to describe its status, identity, challenges, and potential. See Beaumont, *How to Lead*; Carson et al., *Crossing Thresholds*.

CONTINUING THE CONVERSATION

Our definitional framework is a work in progress. There are gaps to fill and points to expound. We've claimed, for instance, that pilgrims perceive the world differently, but what does that mean? Can pilgrims simply flip on a switch, or is awareness enhanced over time? How can we see the world differently, let alone clearly, when our vision is conditioned and clouded by culture, society, and personal experience?

There are tensions that need explication. How is pilgrimage simultaneously a journey of surrender, agency, and collaboration? How do we avoid being pilgrims of "good intentions," ensuring that we heal the world with love and service rather than harm it through paternalistic attitudes and misdirected acts of charity? How do we engage the Other when our knowledge of the Other is incomplete? There is more to be said about the individual journey, about identity and destiny, risks and responsibilities, simplicity and sacrifice, dreams and adventures. There are stories to tell of love and longing, suffering and sadness, elation and laughter, emotions, passion, and sacred moments, and, as always, the meaning of life.

There's more to explore, but that's always the case with pilgrimage. It's unfinished, incomplete, and requires the input of others. *Pilgrim Spirituality* invites readers on a conversational journey to discuss "the things that have happened" and what's "burning within us." Our earthly sojourn continually plays out on the road to Emmaus, where pilgrimage ends—and begins—with our shared encounter of the risen Christ (Luke 24).

26

Towards a Pilgrim-Themed Spirituality

PILGRIMAGE IS A LIFE-GIVING, life-changing experience, and even our understanding of it is a journey. Our grace-based pursuit of God instills a longing within us to understand pilgrimage better, to enhance the meaning of lived experience, and to approach the pilgrim life as a means of Christian formation. A critical step in conceptualizing pilgrimage and actualizing its potential is the establishment of a definitional framework that considers the phenomenon as a whole. The book has established broad yet recognizable parameters that inform what pilgrimage is, or more importantly, *what it can be.*

While pilgrimage is an experiential spirituality, it is theologically robust: how we *think* about pilgrimage matters. Pilgrim spirituality emphasizes the power of language and the importance of theological tools in shaping our Christian identity, engaging lived experience, and interpreting its subsequent meaning. The book invites readers to adorn the mantle of pilgrimage, to see God, self, and the Other through the eyes of a pilgrim, and to embody the virtues of the pilgrim life.

Offering a transformative framework for the Christian life, *Pilgrim Spirituality* provides a roadmap for everyday Christians. However, just as map is not the territory, the book is not the journey. Pilgrimage takes place *out there* in the real world beyond the pages of the book. The final chapter sends the reader out to encounter God, self, and the Other in more intentional, life-giving ways.

THE ALLURE OF LONG-DISTANCE WALKING

Long-distance walking and the spirituality it fosters epitomizes pilgrimage, and the contemporary revival of the ancient practice features the pedestrian journey. Lacing our boots, reducing provisions to a knapsack, and setting off for the distant horizon appeal, in irreducible ways, to the human spirit, its urge for movement, and its quest for meaning. The foot journey clarifies, simplifies, and authenticates, reveals, exposes, and challenges, connects, heals, and harmonizes our life, faith, and relations with others.[1]

Exemplified by the Camino de Santiago and regional pathways around the world, long-distance walking cultivates a dependency upon God's grace and the succor of others, while exacting a spirituality of personal management, situational discernment, healing, wholeness, and reconciliation. Engaging the body, mind, and soul, the foot trek is marked by physical challenges, personal introspection, the voices of others, expanding perspectives, and the blessings of one-off encounters. Physical pathways facilitate interpersonal connections in profound and intimate ways. Walking helps us think, helps us pray, helps us love, and helps us play, and as many have testified, "I've never felt more alive than when I was walking the Camino."

The points ring true of my own Camino journeys, and long-distance walking informs my understanding of contemporary pilgrimage. Freedom, joy, and wonder are palpable on the road, and contenders for my next adventure, though unlikely for the moment, compete in my mind. Since I currently reside in Italy, the Via Francigena beckons, an interest that Italian television occasionally indulges with features on the route. Interviewing pilgrims and showcasing local residents, villages, and landscapes, they present the Via Francigena as a living culture, one that is rooted to the land yet attuned to the human journey and the spiritual symbiosis between host and traveler. While pilgrimage appeals to universal values, it's a celebration of the particular: the irreducibility of personal experience in unique, localized places.

I would also like to visit the Presbyterian Church of the Mountain in Delaware Water Gap, Pennsylvania, which runs the oldest hiker hostel on the Appalachian Trail. The church understands its ministry in pilgrim terms, offering the hospitality of shelter, showers, and nourishment, providing space for the sharing of stories, and embracing the transformative nature of physical journeys.

---

1. The point extends to all means of long-distance physical journeys, including walking, biking, horseback riding, and transport by wheelchair. See Gray and Skeesuck, *I'll Push You.*

Pilgrim Spirituality encourages the pursuit of pedestrian journeys; yet, once we ponder the Holy Land experience or reflect upon the Abrahamic stranger, we're reminded that long-distance walking is but one template of a larger phenomenon.

JOURNEYS, STATIONS, AND STATUS

All expressions of pilgrimage include an element of journey, or movement. Yet, in certain instances, it's finished, dormant, or less prominent than other dimensions, such as time, place, or a sense of the foreign. Consequently, we've collectively focused on time, place, journey, and people, together with an emphasis on the Other. In doing so, we've recast pilgrimage as a spirituality of journeys, stations, and status.

Our position derives from an examination of biblical, historical, and contemporary expressions. We've appealed throughout the book to Abrahamic pilgrimage. Abraham journeyed to Canaan, but once he was there, regardless of his subsequent movements, he's a pilgrim due to his identity as a stranger and his displacement from home. Abrahamic pilgrimage is a function of place, station, and status. It's the experience of being—and our reaction to—the Other. It's the status of being a second-place person. A sense of movement is no longer a defining factor.

What do we make of Anglo-Saxon Christians in the eighth century who, in the spirit of Abraham, moved to Rome to live near Peter's tomb, living a life of stability while calling themselves pilgrims for Christ? Since their journey from England was over, movement was reduced to a latent sense of their future resurrection. Their pilgrimage became one of place, station, and status.

While these examples encompass foreign destinations, the predominate expression of medieval pilgrimage was local pilgrimage to nearby shrines in which the element of journey had little bearing. Local pilgrimage conjoins place and prayer.

Along with place-based expressions, we've emphasized the idea of pilgrimage as time set aside (or imposed) for a particular purpose, including times for healing or discernment, challenging periods, and the transitions of life. Whether or not a physical journey is involved, pilgrimage as a phase of life appeals to the metaphor of journey, but its operative dimension is a period of time that is effectively experienced as a station, stage, or status. Attending a camp or a retreat does not require movement beyond the journey to get there. It remains a pilgrimage in the sense of a sojourn in a special world that temporarily breaks the continuum of life.

Pilgrimage should not be defined by where it started but by *what it's become* and *where it can take us*. A metaphor, though rooted in movement, may come to mean something else. Our understanding of a phenomenon— and the definitional frames that we use—change over time, and our modest shift has been the definitional recognition of time, place, and the stranger. Pilgrimage, in turn, is a spirituality of journeys, stations, and status.[2]

A COMPREHENSIVE MODEL OF THE CHRISTIAN LIFE

We close the volume by underscoring the comprehensive, practical, and transformative nature of pilgrimage. Pilgrimage is a balanced, holistic, and comprehensive spirituality that embraces spontaneity, routine, rhythm, and harmony. As a celebration of embodied existence, pilgrimage takes an incarnational approach to the Christian life. Pilgrims encounter God in the materiality of creation. The body matters and, with it, the particularity of time and place.

While certain expressions focus on the self, understanding pilgrimage primarily in terms of an inner journey is incomplete. Social issues are pilgrim concerns. As imitators of Christ, pilgrims engage the cultural, ethnic, and religious Other. Conveying a gospel of peace and reconciliation, they cross borders and boundaries, finding commonalities with others. Pilgrimage focuses our attention on the street, where we are called to serve those who have no choice but to be pilgrims: the homeless, the abused, and the mentally-ill as well as immigrants, migrants, and refugees. Following in Christ's footsteps, pilgrimage is God's mandate to serve and accompany others.

In short, pilgrimage casts a comprehensive vision of the Christian life. Embracing God, self, and the Other, pilgrimage is the integrated practice of spending time with God, participating in community, and engaging the world. Pilgrim spirituality uses concepts of time, place, journey, and people to shape identity, create community, and inform human relations. It's a spirituality of personal discipleship, congregational formation, and social outreach. Pilgrim spirituality provides a lens for re-envisioning the Christian life, allowing us to discover what we have not previously seen, taking us to

---

2. See Greenia, "What Is Pilgrimage?" 13, who represents the traditional position that travel is essential. To maintain the position that all expressions of pilgrimage have an element of journey is to look through the long end of the telescope. The position is correct, but it lacks, at times, a clarifying or meaningful focus. Time, place, station, and status often provide more operative lenses.

places otherwise out of reach. Even so, pilgrimage is not a new way of being Christian nor a novel way of doing church. It is an ancient practice, rooted in Scripture, that has holistic applications for modern-day Christians.

PILGRIMAGE AS PRACTICAL THEOLOGY

Accessible, relevant, and applicable, pilgrimage epitomizes practical theology. Sourced in Scripture and grounded in personal experience, pilgrim spirituality offers an everyday approach to the Christian faith that bridges traditional expressions of Christianity with a contemporary sensibility that speaks to our way of being in the world. It's as simple as a Bible study on Ruth, a walk through the neighborhood, or a celebration of a birthday. It's told through stories, expressed through poetry, and evoked through prayer and worship.[3]

Pilgrimage, in short, is the Christian life in action. Pilgrim spirituality reads Scripture through the hermeneutic of inclusion: embracing Jesus' definition of neighbor, searching the streets for the lost and wounded, creating space at the table, fostering communities of unlikely companions. Placing emphasis on people rather than precepts, pilgrimage is a spirituality of personal and social transformation, grounded in Christ's vision of the kingdom of heaven.

Theology, in a word, is the thoughtful approach to God. It's using our minds in reasoned and critical ways. While focused on practical applications, pilgrim spirituality is profoundly theological. It digests Scripture, grapples with tradition, and engages historical Christianity. At the same time, pilgrim spirituality eschews the idea that the pilgrim life can be authenticated by a theological litmus test. Pilgrim theology is not a set of defined beliefs nor a particular way of being religious. Rather, pilgrimage is a spirituality of prayer and worship, Christian virtue, and everyday faith. It is the navigation of lived experience and the attentive care of the soul. It involves acts of piety and devotion as well as justice and compassion. Taking a pragmatic approach to the spiritual life, the pilgrim journey is one of agency, intentionality, and personal responsibility. It's the praxis of right living, immersed in grace, guided but unbound to doctrinal traditions. A journey of practical holiness, pilgrimage is a grace-empowered life shorn of mere forms of religious practice (2 Tim 3:5).

---

3. For an example of contemporary pilgrim poetry, see Whyte, *Pilgrim*.

A TRANSFORMATIVE SPIRITUALITY

While pilgrimage is holistic, practical, and accessible, its transformative nature is, in many ways, its primary appeal. Pilgrimage is a spirituality of change, growth, and progress.

Life Changes

There are few guarantees in life, though change, welcomed or not, tops the list. Life contains instant and immediate changes: birth, conversion, and life-changing experiences, the momentous event that wakes us up, the sudden change of circumstances, the unexpected twist in the plot. Fortune appears; tragedy strikes. Life changes without warning or transition. We blink our eyes, and the world is different.

Other transformations are slow, gradual, and incremental. Pilgrimage is change over time, and transformation is often an accumulative outcome rather than the effect of a singular event. Slow change isn't easy to perceive. Yet, life is seldom static, at least, not for long. It creeps and crawls; it flows and slowly slips away. Pilgrimage patiently fosters spiritual growth during the ostensibly stagnant periods of our lives.

While facilitating the individual journey, pilgrimage is a spirituality of corporate movement and systemic change. Transcending the self, Christian transformation is a community affair. We grow as families, congregations, neighborhoods, and societies.

Our approach to transformation often overlooks the dolor of change. Change hurts, and even positive outcomes have a cutting edge. Growth, progress, and transformation include a sense of loss, and pain, grief, and sorrow often accompany successful journeys. Even so, transformation is a cause of joy. There's an inexplicable wonder when we become people we've never been before and profound gratitude when change is redemptive: restoring Christ's image within us, rectifying our relationship with God, reconciling ourselves with others.

Transcending Our Human Condition

In *Bosnia Chronicle*, Noble prize winner Ivo Andrić (1892–1975) describes how life overwhelms our individual existence: "Life now revealed itself as an endless line tapering to infinity, with nothing permanent or secure about it, a spiteful recession of mirrors that opened and doubled back on themselves, stretching ever deeper and farther, to an illusory vanishing point."[4] Human life is tenuous and illusionary. We are people of impermanence. Life is swifter than a weaver's shuttle (Job 7:6); it withers away like grass (Ps 102:11).

Pilgrimage is the counterpoint to passive resignation. Pilgrimage is what we do when we wonder why we're here. It's staring at infinity and seeing a chasm, then pressing on for a closer look. It's stepping back in wonder, awed by a God who hung the stars. Pilgrimage is the dance we do when nothing else makes sense. It's being touched by a creative grace that bends the universe, transforming us once again into who we were—and are destined to be—an embodied and beloved image of God.

Kindling the fire of the Holy Spirit, pilgrimage is a transformational spirituality. God uses pilgrimage to change us; it does so in eternal ways. The transient becomes permanent, the changeable immutable. Pilgrim progress is our metamorphosis into everlasting people.

In the meantime, the pilgrim journey transforms our will and desires, our goals, vision, and values, our thoughts, actions, and behaviors. It changes how we live and how we love. Pilgrimage frees us to rest in God's grace while empowering us to accompany others with a fearless and heartfelt love.

GOD'S UNFINISHED JOURNEY

While pilgrimage follows a sequential process of preparation, journey, and arrival, pilgrims participate in all three phases at once. We anticipate, experience, and interpret different things at the same time. Life is simultaneous, layered, and overlapping. It is, above all, unfinished and incomplete.

The adage asserts that the journey is never over, and as lifelong learners, pilgrims are constantly gleaning from past experience. What pilgrims discover in the aftermath of lived experience is that the God of the journey is the God of reflection. As John, a Dutch doctor, told me at Taizé: "I am still learning from a year I spent in a leprosy colony in India." Life provides us with experiences to sift through for ages, and wisdom is the fruit of lifelong reflection.[5]

The idea that the journey never ends transcends lessons and learning. Memories can be sustaining in and of themselves. My wife and I continue to be nourished by memories of a Christmas spent together on the Arctic Circle, while spring brings recollections of the sun-soaked beaches of Crete. Sublime memories—the sacred, the beautiful, the intimate, the unique—are founts of life-giving blessings.

4. Andrić, *Bosnia Chronicle*, 117.
5. See Aist, *Jerusalem Bound*, 151–59.

Casting a comprehensive vision of the Christian life, a primary aim of the book has been to address imbalances—real or perceived—in the image and practice of pilgrimage while stretching our understandings of it in less traveled directions. In the meantime, pilgrims are a work in progress. We are seldom sanctified, to say the least. Perfect love proves elusive, and we tend to keep the Other at bay. *Experiences* of God, self, and the Other are common enough, but *union* and *unity* are well down the road. We're constantly learning along the way, but that doesn't mean that we'll ever arrive. The ultimate quandary of pilgrim spirituality is that it seeks unobtainable destinations.

Pilgrimage tends to be associated with images of personal agency: the pilgrim sets out on a journey, navigates obstacles, resists temptation, and patiently perseveres, steadfastly placing the next foot forward. Notwithstanding our emphasis on human responsibility, nothing commences, exists, or continues without the presence of God.

The book ends on precisely this point: pilgrimage is divine grace in progress. It is not only *our* journey that remains unfinished but *God's* as well. Human existence has been God's work all along, and the good news is that God's journey is far from over. God's pledge to God's people is to be a pilgrim God, and as a partner in perseverance, God is with us for the long haul. God has authored the pilgrim life as a means of grace. Instead of wandering when they're lost, pilgrims prayerfully sojourn in place knowing that help is on the way. Christ is the ladder, the bridge, and the lifeline, sent from heaven, placed on earth. Ever with us, beside us, and before us, God leads, guides, and carries us home. Pilgrims rest in God's arms knowing "that neither death, nor life, nor angels, nor rulers, nor things present, nor things to come, nor powers, nor height, nor depth, nor anything else in all creation, will be able to separate us from the love of God in Christ Jesus our Lord" (Rom 8:38–39). Pilgrimage is life with God by any other name.

Bibliography

Abbott, H. Porter. *The Cambridge Introduction to Narrative*. 2nd ed. Cambridge: Cambridge University Press, 2008.

Achenbaum, W. Andrew. "Life Review." In *Robert N. Butler, MD: Visionary of Healthy Aging*, 1–23. New York: Columbia University Press, 2013.

Adams, Tony E., et al. *Autoethnography*. Oxford: Oxford University Press, 2015.

Adichie, Chimamanda Ngozi. "The Danger of a Single Story." TED Talk, July 2009. https://www.ted.com/talks/chimamanda_ngozi_adichie_the_danger_of_a_ single_story.

Adomnán of Iona. *The Life of St Columba*. Translated by Richard Sharpe. London: Penguin, 1995.

Ahlgren, Gillian T. W. *Entering Teresa of Avila's Interior Castle: A Reader's Companion*. Mahwah, NJ: Paulist, 2005.

Aist, Rodney. *The Christian Topography of Early Islamic Jerusalem: The Evidence of Willibald of Eichstätt (700–787 CE)*. Turnhout: Brepols, 2009.

———. *From Topography to Text: The Image of Jerusalem in the Writings of Eucherius, Adomnán and Bede*. Turnhout: Brepols, 2018.

———. *Jerusalem Bound: How to Be a Pilgrim in the Holy Land*. Eugene, OR: Cascade, 2020.

———. *Journey of Faith*. Fayetteville, AR: Self-Published, 1997.

———. "Pilgrim Traditions in Celtic Christian Practice." *Perichoresis* 15.1 (2017) 3–19.

———. *Voices in the Wind: Stories, Thoughts and Reflections Along a Contemporary Christian Pilgrimage*. South Bend, IN: Cross Cultural, 2002.

Andrić, Ivo. *Bosnian Chronicle: A Novel*. Translated by Joseph Hitrec. New York: Arcade, 1993.

Appleton, George, ed. *The Oxford Book of Prayer*. 2nd ed. Oxford: Oxford University Press, 2009.

Aquinas, Thomas. *The Summa Contra Gentiles of Saint Thomas Aquinas*. Book 1. London: Burns, Oates & Washbourne, 1924.

Aristotle. *The Rhetoric and the Poetics of Aristotle*. Translated by W. Rhys Roberts and Ingram Bywater. New York: The Modern Library, 1984.

Athanasius. *The Life of St Anthony*. In *Early Christian Lives*, translated by Carolinne White, 1–70. London: Penguin, 1998.

Augustine. *The City of God*. Translated by William Babcock with notes by Boniface Ramsey. Hyde Park, NY: New City, 2012.

————. *Confessions.* Translated by Henry Chadwick. Oxford: Oxford University Press, 2008.

Bailey, Kenneth. *Jesus through Middle Eastern Eyes: Cultural Studies in the Gospels.* Downers Grove, IL: InterVarsity, 2008.

Bal, Mieke. *Narratology: Introduction to the Theory of Metaphor.* 4th ed. Toronto: University of Toronto Press, 2017.

Bartholomew, Craig G. *Where Mortals Dwell: A Christian View of Place Today.* Grand Rapids: Baker, 2011.

Beaumont, Susan. *How to Lead When You Don't Know Where You're Going: Leading in a Liminal Season.* Lanham, MD: Rowman & Littlefield, 2019.

Berger, Adolf. "Peregrinus." In *Encyclopedic Dictionary of Roman Law,* 626–27. Philadelphia: The American Philosophical Society, 1953.

Berry, Wendell. *A Timbered Choir: The Sabbath Poems 1979–1997.* Washington, DC: Counterpoint, 1999.

Black, Max. *Models and Metaphors.* Ithaca, NY: Cornell University Press, 1962.

Blaine-Wallace, William. *When Tears Sing: The Art of Lament in Christian Community.* Maryknoll, NY: Orbis, 2020.

Block, Peter. *Community: The Structure of Belonging.* San Francisco: Berrett-Koehler, 2008.

Boers, Arthur Paul. *The Way Is Made by Walking: A Pilgrimage Along the Camino de Santiago.* Downers Grove, IL: InterVarsity, 2007.

Bolsinger, Tod. *Canoeing the Mountains: Christian Leadership in Uncharted Territory.* Downers Grove, IL: InterVarsity, 2015.

Bradley, Ian. *Following the Celtic Way: A New Assessment of Celtic Christianity.* London: Darton, Longman & Todd, 2018.

————. *Pilgrimage: A Spiritual and Cultural Journey.* Oxford: Lion, 2009.

Brown, David. *God and Enchantment of Place.* Oxford: Oxford University Press, 2004.

Brueggemann, Walter. *Hopeful Imagination: Prophetic Voices in Exile.* Philadelphia: Fortress, 2004.

————. *The Land.* Philadelphia: Fortress, 1977.

————. *The Message of the Psalms: A Theological Commentary.* Minneapolis: Augsburg, 1984.

Buber, Martin. *I and Thou.* Translated by Walter Kaufmann. New York: Scribner's Sons, 1970.

Bunyan, John. *The Pilgrim's Progress.* Oxford World's Classics. Edited by W. R. Owens. New ed. Oxford: Oxford University Press, 2008.

Burdick, Alan. *Why Time Flies: A Mostly Scientific Investigation.* New York: Simon & Schuster, 2017.

Burns, Robert I., ed. *Las Siete Partidas,* vol. 1: *The Medieval Church: The World of Clerics and Layman.* Philadelphia, University of Pennsylvania Press, 2000.

Butler, R. N. "The Life Review: An Interpretation of Reminiscence in the Aged." *Psychiatry* 26 (1963) 65–76.

Caird, George. *The Language and Imagery of the Bible.* London: Duckworth, 1980.

Cambiaso, Giovanna Negrotto. *I Sentieri Inesplorati: Autobiografia di una Pellegrina Dietro l'Invisibile.* 3rd ed. Padua, Italy: Edizioni Messaggero Padova, 2013.

Campbell, Joseph. *Hero with a Thousand Faces.* 3rd ed. Novato, CA: New World Library, 2008.

———. *A Joseph Campbell Companion: Reflections on the Art of Living*. New York: HarperPerennial, 1991.

———. *The Power of Myth*. With Bill Moyers. New York: Anchor, 1991.

———. *Romance of the Grail: The Magic & Mystery of the Arthurian Myth*. Novato, CA: New World Library, 2015.

———. *Thou Art That: Transforming Religious Metaphor*. Novato, CA: New World Library, 2001.

Campo, Juan Eduardo. "American Pilgrimage Landscapes." *The Annals of the American Academy of Political and Social Science* 558 (July 1998) 40–56.

Carretto, Carlo. *Letters from the Desert*. Anniversary ed. Maryknoll, NY: Orbis, 2002.

Carson, Timothy, et al. *Crossing Thresholds: A Practical Theology of Liminality*. Cambridge: Lutterworth, 2021.

Chu, Jeff. *Does Jesus Really Love Me? A Gay Christian's Pilgrimage in Search of God in America*. New York: HarperPerennial, 2014.

Coelho, Paulo. *The Alchemist*. 25th Anniversary ed. Translated by Alan R. Clarke. New York: HarperOne, 2019.

———. *The Pilgrimage: A Contemporary Quest for Ancient Wisdom*. Translated by Alan R. Clarke. New York: HarperCollins, 1996.

Cohen, Eric. "Pilgrimage and Tourism: Convergence and Divergence." In *Sacred Journeys: The Anthropology of Pilgrimage*, edited by Alan Morinis, 47–61. Westport, CT: Greenwood, 1992.

———. "Who Is a Tourist? A Conceptual Clarification." *Sociological Review* 22.4 (1974) 527–55.

Cousineau, Phil. *The Art of Pilgrimage: The Seeker's Guide to Making Travel Sacred*. New ed. San Francisco: Red Wheel Weiser Conari, 2012.

Covey, Stephen R. *The 7 Habits of Highly Effective People: Powerful Lessons in Powerful Change*. 25th Anniversary ed. New York: Simon & Schuster, 2013.

Crampton, Georgia Ronan, ed. *The Shewings of Julian of Norwich*. Kalamazoo, MI: Medieval Institute, 1993.

Crossan, John Dominic, and Richard G. Watts. *Who Is Jesus? Answers to Your Questions about the Historical Jesus*. Louisville: Westminster John Knox, 1999.

Davies, J. G. *Pilgrimage Yesterday and Today*. London: SCM, 1988.

Davies, Oliver, and Denys Turner, eds. *Silence and the Word. Negative Theology and Incarnation*. Cambridge: Cambridge University Press, 2002.

Davies, Oliver, with Thomas O'Loughlin. *Celtic Spirituality*. Classics of Western Spirituality. Mahwah, NJ: Paulist, 1999.

Day, Dorothy. *On Pilgrimage*. Grand Rapids: Eerdmans, 1999.

de Caussade, Jean Pierre. *The Sacrament of the Present Moment*. Translated by Kitty Muggeridge. New York: HarperCollins, 1989.

Denborough, David. *Retelling the Stories of Our Lives: Everyday Narrative Therapy to Draw Inspiration and Transform Experience*. New York: Norton, 2014.

Dobson, Eric. "Buber in Ten Minutes." Youtube video. March 2014. https://www.youtube.com/watch?v=16Cr82mLhkw.

Dostoevsky. *Brothers Karamazov*. Translated by David Magarshack. Harmondsworth, UK: Penguin, 1958.

Durkheim, Émile. *The Elementary Forms of the Religious Life*. Translated by Joseph Ward Swain. London: George Allen & Unwin, 1915.

Eade, John, and Michael Sallnow, eds. *Contesting the Sacred: The Anthropology of Christian Pilgrimage*. Abingdon, UK: Routledge, 1991.

Edwards, Jonathan. "The Christian Pilgrim; or The True Christian Life, a Journey towards Heaven." In *The Works of Jonathan Edwards*, vol. 2, 243–46. Edinburgh: Banner of Truth, 1974.

Egan, Timothy. *A Pilgrimage to Eternity: From Canterbury to Rome in Search of a Faith*. New York: Viking, 2019.

Eliade, Mircea. *The Sacred and The Profane: The Nature of Religion*. San Diego: Harcourt Brace Jovanovich, 1987.

Erikson, Eric H. *The Life Cycle Completed*. Expanded version with new chapters on the ninth stage of development by Joan M. Erikson. New York: Norton, 1998.

Foer, Joshua. *Moonwalking with Einstein: The Art and Science of Remembering Everything*. New York: Penguin, 2012.

Foster, Charles. *The Sacred Journey: The Ancient Practices*. Nashville: Thomas Nelson, 2010.

Frank, Arthur W. *The Wounded Storyteller: Body, Illness, and Ethics*. 2nd ed. Chicago: The University of Chicago Press, 2013.

French, R. M. *The Way of a Pilgrim: And the Pilgrim Continues His Way*. San Francisco: HarperSanFrancisco, 1991.

Freyne, Sean. "Jesus the Pilgrim." In *Pilgrimage* (*Concilium* 1996, vol. 4), edited by Virgil Elizondo and Sean Freyne, 25–34. London: SCM, 1996.

Gardner, Martin. *The Annotated Ancient Mariner*. New York: Bramhall, 1965.

Geary, James. *I Is an Other: The Secret Life of Metaphor and How It Shapes the Way We See the World*. New York: HarperCollins, 2011.

———. *The World in a Phrase: A Brief History of the Aphorism*. London: Bloomsbury, 2011.

Gitin, Seymour. *The Road Taken: An Archaeologist's Journey to the Land of the Bible*. University Park, PA: Eisenbrauns, 2021.

Granberg-Michaelson, Wesley. *Without Oars: Casting Off into a Life of Pilgrimage*. Minneapolis: Broadleaf, 2020.

Gray, Patrick, and Justin Skeesuck. *I'll Push You: A Journey of 500 Miles, Two Best Friends, and One Wheelchair*. Carol Stream, IL: Tyndale House, 2017.

Greenia, George. "What Is Pilgrimage?" *International Journal of Religious Tourism and Pilgrimage* 6.2 (2018) 7–15.

Guite, Malcolm. *Mariner: A Theological Voyage with Samuel Taylor Coleridge*. Downers Grove, IL: InterVarsity, 2018.

Hammond, Claudia. *Time Warped: Unlocking the Secrets of Time Perception*. Edinburgh, Canongate, 2012.

Harman, Lesley D., ed. *A Sociology of Pilgrimage: Embodiment, Identity, Transformation*. London, Ontario: Ursus, 2014.

Hastings, Ross. *Missional God, Missional Church: Hope for Re-evangelizing the West*. Downers Grove, IL: InterVarsity, 2012.

Haynes, Robert Ellis. *Consuming Mission: Towards a Theology of Short-Term Mission and Pilgrimage*. Eugene, OR: Pickwick, 2019.

Hershel, Abraham Joshua. *The Sabbath*. New York: Farrar, Straus and Giroux, 2005.

Heuertz, Phileena. *Pilgrimage of a Soul: Contemplative Spirituality for the Active Life*. 2nd ed. Downers Grove, IL: InterVarsity, 2017.

Howell, Brian M. *Short-Term Mission: An Ethnography of Christian Travel Narrative and Experience*. Downers Grove, IL: InterVarsity, 2012.

Hughes, Gerard. W. *God of Surprises*. London: Darton, Longman & Todd, 1985.

———. *In Search of a Way: Two Journeys of Spiritual Discovery*. London: Darton, Longman & Todd, 1986.

———. *Walk to Jerusalem: In Search of Peace*. London: Darton, Longman & Todd, 1991.

Hjalmarson, Leonard. *No Home Like Place: A Christian Theology of Place*. 2nd ed. Portland, OR: Urban Loft, 2015.

Ignatius of Loyola. *The Spiritual Exercises of Saint Ignatius*. Translated by George E. Ganss, S.J. Chicago: Loyola, 1992.

Inge, John. *A Christian Theology of Place*. Aldershot, UK: Ashgate, 2003.

James, William. *Principles of Psychology*, vol. 1. New York: Henry Holt, 1890.

Jansson, Laura S., and Clare Freeman. *Fertile Ground: A Pilgrimage through Pregnancy*. Chesterton, IN: Ancient Faith, 2019.

Jonas. *The Life of Columban*. Translations and Reprints from the Original Sources of European history, vol. II, no 7, edited by Dana Carleton Munro. Philadelphia: University of Pennsylvania Press, 1895.

Joyce, Rachel. *The Unlikely Pilgrimage of Harold Fry*. New York: Random House, 2012.

Kaplan. Robert D. *In Europe's Shadow: Two Cold Wars and a Thirty-Year Journey through Romania and Beyond*. New York: Random House, 2016.

King, Martin Luther, Jr. "My Pilgrimage to Nonviolence." *Fellowship* 24 (1 September 1958) 4–9.

Lakoff, George, and Mark Johnson. *Metaphors We Live By*. With a new afterword. Chicago: University of Chicago Press, 2003.

———. *Philosophy in the Flesh: The Embodied Mind and its Challenge to Western Thought*. New York: Basic, 1999.

Lane, Belden C. "Landscape and Spirituality: A Tension between Place and Placelessness in Christian Thought." *The Way*. Supplement (1992) 4–13.

———. *The Solace of Fierce Landscapes: Exploring Desert and Mountain Spirituality*. Oxford: Oxford University Press, 1998.

Larson, Atria A. "From Protections from *miserabiles personae* to Legal Privileges for International Travellers: The Historical Development of the Medieval Canon Law Regarding Pilgrims." *GLOSSEA: European Journal of Legal History* 19 (2019) 167–86.

Lash, Jennifer. *On Pilgrimage: A Time to Seek*. London: Bloomsbury, 1999.

Least Heat-Moon, William. *Blue Highways: A Journey into America*. New York: Fawcett Crest, 1982.

Levine, Amy-Jill. *Short Stories by Jesus: The Enigmatic Parables of a Controversial Rabbi*. New York: HarperOne, 2014.

Levine, Robert. *A Geography of Time: The Temporal Misadventures of a Social Psychologist*. New York: Basic, 1997.

Lynch, Kevin. *The Image of the City*. Cambridge: MIT Press, 1960.

Mann, Thomas. *The Magic Mountain*. Translated by John E. Woods. New York: Knopf, 1996.

Mannion, Gerard. "The Pilgrim Church: An Ongoing Journey of Ecclesial Renewal and Reform." In *The Cambridge Companion to Vatican II*, edited by Richard R. Gaillardetz, 115–35. Cambridge: Cambridge University Press, 2020.

Margalit, Avishai. *The Ethics of Memory*. Cambridge: Harvard University Press, 2002.

Margry, Peter Jan. *Shrines and Pilgrimage in the Modern World: New Itineraries into the Sacred*. Amsterdam: Amsterdam University Press, 2008.

Martin, James, SJ. *Jesus: A Pilgrimage*. New York: HarperOne, 2014.

Martin, Shannan. *The Ministry of Ordinary Places: Waking Up to God's Goodness around You*. Nashville: Thomas Nelson, 2018.

Matter, E. Ann, "Mystical Marriage." In *Women and Faith: Catholic Religious Life in Italy from Late Antiquity to the Present*, edited by Lucetta Scaraffia and Gabriella Zarri, 31–41. Cambridge: Harvard University Press, 1999.

Mayes, Thompson M. *Why Old Places Matter: How Historic Places Affect Our Identity and Well-Being*. Lanham, MD: Rowman & Littlefield, 2018.

McFague, Sallie. *Metaphorical Theology: Models of God in Religious Language*. Philadelphia: Fortress, 1982.

———. *Models of God: Theology for an Ecological, Nuclear Age*. Philadelphia: Fortress 1987.

———. *Speaking in Parables: A Study in Metaphor and Theology*. Philadelphia: Fortress, 1975.

McGowan, Anne, and Paul F. Bradshaw. *The Pilgrimage of Egeria: A New Translation of the Itinerarium Egeriae with Introduction and Commentary*. Collegeville, MN: Liturgical, 2018.

McLeod, S. A. "Lev Vygotsky." *Simply Psychology*. (August 2018). https://www.simplypsychology.org/vygotsky.html.

———. "Maslow's Hierarchy of Needs." *Simply Psychology* (March 2020). https://www.simplypsychology.org/maslow.html.

Middleton, Julia. *Cultural Intelligence: The Competitive Edge for Leaders Crossing Boundaries*. London: Bloomsbury, 2014.

Morinis, Alan. *Sacred Journeys: The Anthropology of Pilgrimage*. Westport, CT: Greenwood, 1992.

Newbigin, Lesslie. *The Open Secret: Sketches for a Missional Theology: An Introduction to the Theology of Mission*. Grand Rapids: Eerdmans, 1978.

Newman, Elizabeth. *Untamed Hospitality: Welcoming God and Other Strangers*. Grand Rapids: Brazos, 2007.

Nguyen, Viet Thanh, ed. *The Displaced: Refugee Writers on Refugee Lives*. New York: Abrams, 2018.

Niebuhr, H. Richard. *Christ and Culture*. New York: Harper & Row, 1951.

Niebuhr, Richard R. "Pilgrims and Pioneers." *Parabola* 9.3 (1984) 6–13.

Nouwen, Henri J. M. *The Return of the Prodigal Son: A Story of Homecoming*. New York: Doubleday, 1992.

Olsen, Daniel H., and Maximiliano E. Korstanje, eds. *Dark Tourism and Pilgrimage*. Boston: CABI, 2020.

Otto, Rudolf. *The Idea of the Holy*. Oxford: Oxford University Press, 1924.

Ousterhout, Robert. *The Blessings of Pilgrimage*. Urbana, IL: University of Illinois Press, 1990.

Outler, Albert C. *Evangelism & Theology in the Wesleyan Spirit*. Nashville: Discipleship Resources, 1996.

Page, Max. *Why Preservation Matters*. New Haven, CT: Yale University Press, 2016.

Paulinus of Nola. *Letters*. In *Letters of St Paulinus of Nola*, vol. 2, translated by P. G. Walsh. Westminster, MD: Newman, 1967.

Peace Pilgrim. *Peace Pilgrim: Her Life and Work in Her Own Words.* Santa Fe: Ocean Tree, 1983.

Pink, Daniel H. *When: The Scientific Secrets of Perfect Time.* New York: Riverhead, 2018.

Pohl, Chistine D. *Making Room: Recovering Hospitality as a Christian Tradition.* Grand Rapids: Eerdmans, 1999.

The Protoevangelium of James. In *The Apocryphal New Testament,* translated by J. K. Elliot, 48–67. Oxford: The Oxford University Press, 1993.

Puzo, Mario. *The Fortunate Pilgrim: A Novel.* New York: Atheneum, 1964.

Ratzinger, Joseph. *Homily at Fr. Luigi Giussani's Funeral Mass.* February 24, 2005. https://www.communio-icr.com/articles/view/funeral-homily-for-msgr.-luigi-giussani.

Reader, Ian. *Pilgrimage: A Very Short Introduction.* Oxford: Oxford University Press, 2015.

Richards, I. A. *The Philosophy of Rhetoric.* New York: Oxford University Press, 1965.

Robinson, Bob. *Jesus and the Religions: Retrieving a Neglected Example for a Multi-Cultural World.* Eugene, OR: Cascade, 2012.

Robinson, Jane. *Hearts and Minds: The Untold Story of the Great Pilgrimage and How Women Won the Vote.* Ealing, UK: Transworld, 2018.

The Rule of Saint Benedict. Edited by Timothy Fry, O.S.B. New York: Vintage, 1998.

Scarry, Elaine. *On Beauty and Being Just.* Princeton: Princeton University Press, 1999.

Scruton, Robert. *Beauty: A Very Short Introduction.* Oxford: Oxford University Press, 2011.

Shakespeare. *As You Like It,* 1623.

———. *Hamlet,* 1603.

———. *Romeo and Juliet,* 1597.

Sheldrake, Philip. *Living Between Worlds: Place and Journey in Celtic Spirituality.* London: Darton, Longman & Todd, 1995.

———. *Spaces for the Sacred: Place, Memory, and Identity.* Baltimore: Johns Hopkins University Press, 2001.

———. *Spirituality: A Very Short Introduction.* Oxford: University of Oxford, 2012.

Smith, Jonathan Z. *To Take Place: Towards Theory in Ritual.* Chicago: University of Chicago Press, 1987.

Solnit, Rebecca. *Wanderlust: A History of Walking.* New York: Penguin, 2001.

Soskice, Janet Martin. *Metaphor and Religious Language.* Oxford: Clarendon, 1985.

Stephenson, Barry. *Ritual: A Very Short Introduction.* Oxford: Oxford University Press, 2015.

Sumption, Jonathan. *Pilgrimage: An Image of Mediaeval Religion.* London: Faber & Faber, 1975.

Sussman, Steve. *Substance and Behavioral Addictions: Concepts, Causes, and Cures.* Cambridge: Cambridge University Press, 2017.

Sykes, Stephen W. "Making Room for the Other: Hostility and Hospitality from a Christian Perspective." In *The Religious Other: Hostility, Hospitality, and the Hope of Human Flourishing,* edited by Alon Goshen-Gottstein, 53–68. Lanham, MD: Lexington, 2014.

Teresa of Avila. *The Interior Castle: Study Edition.* Translated by Kieran Kavanaugh, OCD. 2nd ed. Washington, DC: Institute of Carmelite Studies, 2020.

Tervalon, Melanie, and Jann Murray-García. "Cultural Humility Versus Cultural Competence: A Critical Distinction in Defining Physician Training Outcomes in

Multicultural Education." *Journal of Health Care for the Poor and Undeserved* 9.2 (1998) 117–25.

Teuton, Sean. *Native American Literature: A Very Short Introduction*. Oxford: Oxford University Press, 2018.

Thomas à Kempis. *The Imitation of Christ by Thomas a Kempis: A New Reading of the 1441 Latin Autograph Manuscript*. Edited and translated by William C. Creasy. Macon, GA: Mercer University Press, 2007.

Todd, Richard. *The Thing Itself: On the Search for Authenticity*. New York: Riverhead, 2008.

Tuan, Yi-Fu. *Space and Place: The Perspective of Experience*. Minneapolis: University of Minnesota Press, 1977.

———. *Topophilia: A Study of Environmental Perception, Attitudes, and Values*. Englewood Cliffs, NJ: Prentice-Hall, 1974.

Turner, Edith. *Communitas: The Anthropology of Collective Joy*. New York: Palgrave Macmillan, 2012.

———. "Communitas, Rites of." In *Encyclopedia of Religious Rites, Rituals and Festivals*, edited by Frank A. Salamone, 97–101. London: Routledge, 2004.

Turner, Victor. "Betwixt and Between: The Liminal Period in *Rites de Passage*." In *The Forest of Symbols: Aspects of Ndembu Ritual*, 93–111. Ithaca, NY: Cornell University Press, 1967.

Turner, Victor, and Edith Turner. *Image and Pilgrimage in Christian Culture*. New York: Columbia University Press, 1978.

Twain, Mark. *Innocents Abroad*. Hartford, CT: American, 1869.

van Gennep, Arnold. *The Rites of Passage*. 2nd ed. Chicago: University of Chicago Press, 2019.

Vogler, Christopher. *The Writer's Journey—25th Anniversary Edition: Mythic Structure for Writers*. 4th ed. Studio City, CA: Wiese, 2020.

Warren, Tish Harrison. *Liturgy of the Ordinary: Sacred Practices in Everyday Life*. Downers Grove, IL: InterVarsity, 2016.

Warton, Annabel Jane. *Selling Jerusalem: Relics, Replicas, Theme Parks*. Chicago: University of Chicago Press, 2006.

Webb, Diana. *Medieval European Pilgrimage*. Basingstoke: Palgrave, 2002.

———. *Pilgrims and Pilgrimage in the Medieval West*. London: I. B. Tauris, 1999.

Westerhof, Gerben J. "Life Review and Life-Story Work." In *The Encyclopedia of Adulthood and Aging*, 1st ed., edited by Susan Krauss Whitbourne, 1–5. Chichester, UK: Wiley & Sons, 2016.

Westerhoff, Caroline. *Good Fences: The Boundaries of Hospitality*. Boston: Cowley, 1999.

Wetzel, James. *Augustine's City of God: A Critical Guide*. Cambridge: Cambridge University Press, 2012.

White, Michael. *Narrative Practice: Continuing the Conversation*. New York: Norton, 2011.

Whyte, David. *Pilgrim: Poems by David Whyte*. Langley, WA: Many Rivers Press, 2012.

Wiederkehr, Macrina. *Seven Sacred Pauses: Living Mindfully through the Hours of the Day*. Notre Dame, IN: Sorin, 2008.

Wilkinson, John. *Egeria's Travels*. 3rd ed. Warminster, UK: Aris & Phillips, 1999.

———. *Jerusalem Pilgrimage, 1099–1185*. With Joyce Hill and W. F. Ryan. London: Hakluyt Society, 1988.

————. *Jerusalem Pilgrims before the Crusades*. 2nd ed. Warminsterm, UK: Aris & Phillips, 2002.

Williamson, Marianne. *A Return to Love: Reflections on the Principles of "A Course in Miracles."* New York: HarperPerennial, 1993.

Wirzba, Norman. *Living the Sabbath: Discovering the Rhythms of Rest and Delight.* Grand Rapids: Brazos, 2006.

Wittgenstein, Ludwig. *Philosophical Investigations.* Translated by G. E. M. Anscombe. Oxford: Blackwell, 1963.

World Council of Churches. *Come and See: A Theological Invitation to the Pilgrimage of Justice and Peace.* Faith and Order Paper Number 224. Geneva: World Council of Churches, 2019.

Wynn, Mark R. *Faith and Place: An Essay in Embodied Religious Epistemology.* Oxford: Oxford University Press, 2009.

Subject Index

Abraham, 6, 33, 82, 84, 95, 96–97, 98,
     100, 111, 149, 212–13, 216, 218,
     223, 241
Abrahamic pilgrimage, 6, 33, 34,
     96–97, 149, 152, 212–13, 215,
     230, 231, 241
accidental pilgrims, 174
agency (personal), 4, 51, 68, 79, 92,
     189, 236, 238, 243, 246
alienation, 2, 17, 33, 44, 66, 82, 91, 92,
     96, 115, 143, 150, 180, 209, 217
American pilgrimage, 35, 37, 63, 240
Anglo-Saxon Christians, monks, 149,
     212, 241
aphorisms, 43, 46, 87–88, 202, 228,
     229, 230, 234, 235
Appalachian Trail, 240
asceticism, ascetic pilgrims, 106
authenticity, 39, 41, 43, 80, 172, 237
autobiography, 15, 30, 51, 87, 230–31

bereavement, 83, 103, 137
betwixt and between, 45, 55, 78,
     176–77, 208, 223, 235
biblical prototype of pilgrimage, 83,
     85, 89, 91–95, 201, 233, 234
body of Christ, 52, 53, 64, 76, 80,
     123–24, 136

calling, as pilgrim experience, 1–3, 21,
     174, 177, 180, 205, 214
Camino de Santiago. See Santiago,
     Camino de.
Catholicism, 1, 7–8, 62, 80, 135, 180,
     211

Celtic Christianity, 3, 32, 99, 212, 231,
     also see Irish Christians, monks.
chronos and kairos time, 136
coerced, or forced, pilgrims, 7, 41, 84,
     85, 98, 105, 147, 154
Columbanus, 212
commemoration, 21, 22, 44, 64, 81,
     84, 86, 133, 134, 139, 197–98,
     221, 230
communitas, 38, 54–56, 58, 61–62,
     80, 175, 231
companionship, 7, 17, 20, 52, 54, 58,
     76, 80, 96, 103, 113, 121, 151,
     161, 186, 213–14, 215, 222, 223,
     229, 231, 236, 243
compassion, 27, 33, 59, 67, 79, 82, 83,
     88, 119, 121, 181, 182, 187, 195,
     203, 212, 213, 214, 217, 219, 228,
     243
conceptual metaphors, 5–6, 76
container theory of place, 141
contemplation, 67, 80, 193, 209, 231
convalescence, 83, 103, 137
corporate dimension of pilgrimage, 9,
     22, 37, 51, 52–65, 92, 95, 99, 113,
     123, 151, 159, 202, 208, 220, 222,
     229, 231, 244
cultural humility, 196, 232
curiosity, 170, 171, 228

dark tourism, 232
decline of the Western Church, 237
discernment, 5, 19, 74, 80, 83, 86, 88,
     100, 103, 134, 157, 168, 174, 185,
     187, 189, 220, 221, 240, 241

Disney Land, Disney World, 22–23, 37

eco-spirituality, 216–17, 232
ecumenical dimensions of pilgrimage, ecumenical communities, 1, 2, 9, 10, 57, 80, 82, 83, 85, 163, 218, 229
Egypt, Egyptians, 9, 52, 102, 105
embodied prayer, 7, 22, 43, 44, 83, 84, 192–93
emotions, 5, 15, 16, 17, 20, 23–25, 28, 30, 35, 43, 51, 59, 69, 82, 117, 131, 144, 148, 186, 235, 238
Erickson's theory of psycho-social development, 85
eschatology of pilgrimage, 52, 94, 139, 218, 230
exiles, 63, 91, 94, 98, 105

fair trade, 120, 190, 196
family resemblance theory, 7, 39–42, 85, 118, 201, 230, 233
fasting, 50, 106, 113, 191, 193–94, 231

gathering of the nations, 2, 53, 108, 124
genius loci, 147
Giovanna Negrotto, Sister, x, 33, 64, 210, 214
gleaning, 8, 34, 85, 97, 216, 228, 232, 245
globalization, 140, 146, 217, 228, 234
God is in the facts, 65, 67–69, 111, 202
Graceland, 37
Great Pilgrimage (of 1913), the, 211
group identity as pilgrimage, 62–63, 231

hermitage experience, 64, 79, 130, 212, 214, 222
hero's journey, 152, 175, 177–78, 230
Holy Land, 2, 4, 9, 31, 58, 59, 62, 68, 82–84, 102, 104, 136, 159, 241
hospitality, 7, 20, 21–22, 33, 41, 82, 87, 88, 97, 103, 113, 119, 212, 214, 215, 217, 218, 220–24, 240

human condition, 30, 47, 65, 92, 125, 186, 187, 201, 214, 235, 244

I–It, I–Thou relationships, 55, 124–25
imitation of Christ, 45, 93, 203, 213, 215, 216, 231, Jesus as pilgrim, 105–6
immanence, the immanent, 64, 78, 79, 112, 230
immigrants, 97, 149, 169, 212, 218, 242
incarnation, incarnational theology, 3, 8, 9, 51, 65–69, 77, 92, 94, 95, 103, 111, 112, 140, 201, 202, 210, 217, 222, 228, 229, 231, 234, 237, 242
intentional decision-making, 45, 87, 190–92, 209
interdependence, 53–54, 76, 79, 90, 116, 229
interfaith, interreligious dimensions of pilgrimage, 9, 10, 80, 82, 83, 85, 203, 218, 229, 232
International Coalition of Sites of Conscience, 63
Iona Community, 82
Irish Christians, monks, 149, 157, 212–13
Italy, 1, 2, 33, 143, 212, 214, 240

Jerusalem, including Jerusalem pilgrimage, Jerusalem pilgrims, ix, 2, 32, 63, 67, 91, 94, 95, 98, 99, 100, 101, 105–6, 108, 145, 182, 197, 231, New Jerusalem, 53, 91, 92, 94, 108, 135, 201, 218
Jewish pilgrim festivals, 99–102
justice (social), 10, 79, 83, 84, 102, 120, 159, 168, 196, 203, 206, 209, 210, 211, 214, 215, 219, 223, 229, 243

labyrinths, 32, 84, 231
life review, 85, 179, 222, 231
life transitions, 5, 6, 9, 24, 29, 30, 39, 41, 55, 68, 78, 82, 83, 86, 136, 158, 169, 176, 203, 208, 220, 222, 236, 241, 244

liminal, liminality, 3, 54, 55–56, 76, 79, 107, 175, 176–77, 223, 230, 237

liminoid (liminal-like), 38, 54–56, 78, 175–77, 203, 208, 230, 235, 237

liturgical calendar, time, 50, 132, 134–36, 193–94

local pilgrimage, 84, 153, 241

long-distance walking, 3, 21, 82, 84, 171, 240–41

long-term Christian community, 63–65, 220–24

Lourdes, 174

Marian theology, Marian shrines, 7–8, 37, 83

Maslow's hierarchy of needs, 85, 118, 152, 230

medieval pilgrimage, 2, 8, 32, 37, 123, 135, 153, 215, 241

meditation. See contemplation.

Medjugorje, 210–11

mementos, 16, 86, 195

memory, memories, ix, 15, 17, 19, 21, 22, 24, 30, 33, 44, 50, 63, 64, 67, 81, 82, 83, 85, 86, 87, 95, 98, 101, 103, 113, 114, 130, 131, 133, 144, 145, 148, 154, 173, 179, 182, 194, 195, 197–98, 215, 220, 228, 230

mental maps, 142, 143–44, 230

metaphor, metaphorical theory, 5, 6, 9, 33, 46, 52, 55, 69–77, 79, 80, 83–84, 91, 92, 93, 95, 97, 111, 112, 123, 141, 145, 151, 157, 158–60, 176, 202, 207, 208, 214, 215, 216, 217, 222, 228, 229, 230, 233, 234, 235, 241, 242

Methodism, 1, 7, 9, 16, 25, 211, 223

mission and evangelism, pilgrimage as, 97, 106, 107, 149, 203, 210, 213, 215, 222–23, 229, 212–13, also see short-term mission.

monumentalism, monuments, 64, 98, 133

mundane, the, 29, 35, 45, 48, 49, 50, 79, 95, 132, 183, 191

mysticism, the mystical, 44, 118, 123, 151, 209, 231

narrative therapy, 85, 179, 231

noise of pilgrimage, 49, 183, 197, 209

omnipresence of God, 8, 78, 138–39

one-off encounters, 22, 30, 32, 58, 59, 113, 179, 209, 240

ordinary time, 48, 50, 100, 132

ordinary world, 23, 37, 47–49, 50, 56, 61, 145, 177–79, 209

Orthodox Christianity, 135, 136

othering the Other, 120

pastor as pilgrim, 223

Peace Pilgrim, 211

people-focused pilgrimage, 83, 163

perceptual dimension of pilgrimage, 3, 9, 49, 50, 51, 67, 70, 131, 134, 137, 146, 181, 182, 185, 187, 203, 205, 227, 238

peregrinus, peregrini, 33, 212, 213, 215

perseverance, 45, 86, 87, 88, 93, 96, 98, 129, 134, 158, 171, 186, 188, 193–94, 195, 228, 235, 246

personal management, 82, 87, 45, 116–17, 240

pilgrim church, 52–53, 63, 65, 108, 221, 223, 231

pilgrimage theories, 38–39, 54–56, 230, 231

Pilgrim's Progress, 32, 93, 115, 157, 231

placemaking, 149, 235

practical theology, pilgrimage as, 9, 79, 117, 242–44

Prayer Pilgrimage for Freedom (1957), 211

process, pilgrimage as, 158–59

profane, the, 3, 35, 42, 46–50, 87, 132, 139, 140, 145, 150, 201, 230, 235

Project for Public Spaces, 149

progress, pilgrimage as, 159–60, 215

prophetic nature of pilgrimage, 102, 217–18

protest marches, 84, 167, 170, 193, 210–11, 215

Protestantism, 1, 3, 7–9, 62, 77, 80, 135, 138, 210

provisions and supplies, 76, 92, 117, 156–57, 162, 221, 240

reconciliation, 2, 9, 33, 44, 82, 83, 107,
    119, 180, 181, 183, 197, 203, 209,
    211, 217, 218, 221, 222, 228, 230,
    240, 242, 244
reenactment of sacred stories, 22, 99,
    102, 133, 221
refugees, 32, 85, 97, 149, 212, 214,
    218, 242
religious imagination, 3, 44, 203
reluctant pilgrims, 173
remembering, remembrance, 46, 57,
    63, 64, 98, 102, 131, 133, 134,
    194, 197, 215, 218, 221, 223,
resiliency, 45, 88, 195, 203, 209, 215,
    235
responsibility, 53–54, 59, 60, 79, 88,
    118, 189–90, 196, 216, 224, 230,
    232, 238, 243, 246
rites of passages, 54–55, 152, 175–77,
    221, 222, 223, 230
rituals, 34, 35, 37, 40, 48, 55, 61, 64,
    86, 101, 104, 113, 133, 139, 155,
    175–76, 192–93, 221
Rome, 2, 32, 149, 212, 241
routines, the routine, 45, 50, 113, 131,
    132, 146, 154, 167, 178, 185, 192,
    207, 242

Sabbath, 132, 134, 135
sacrament, sacramental theology, 22,
    59–60, 133, 185, 187, 231
sanctification, 160, 173, 228, 230
Santiago, Camino de, 2, 4, 8, 9, 19–22,
    27–30, 33, 56, 58, 82, 84, 116–17,
    136, 170, 240
secular, the, 3, 8, 9, 10, 47–48, 64, 80,
    84, 85, 154, 158, 194, 203, 218,
    227, 229, 232
self-actualization, 118
self-care, 45, 103, 116–17, 118, 152,
    209
self-discovery, 117, 118, 168
self-management. See personal
    management.
self-reflection, pilgrimage as, 82,
    179–80, 192, 196, 209
sensuous experience, 51, 67, 180, 193,
    209, 210, 222

serendipity, the serendipitous, 15, 17,
    113, 185, 209
short-term Christian community, 2,
    54, 56–63, 87, 231, 232
short-term mission, 3, 9, 11, 41, 57,
    58, 60, 82, 83, 85, 163, 224, 232
sites of conscience, 63, 83, 84, 139,
    148, 174, 215, 217–18, 232
souvenirs, 16, 86, 195
space and place, 138, 139, 140, 144,
    217, 228, 230
special world, the, 44, 145, 150,
    177–79, 241
spiritual inertia, 158
spiritual marriage, 123
spontaneity, the spontaneous, 54, 55,
    56, 88, 124, 181, 185, 190, 209,
    242
stability, 148, 241
Stations of the Cross, 19–22, 84, 231
stewardship, 106, 174, 190, 196, 216,
    223–24, 229, 232
street, pilgrimage as the, 7, 33, 34, 43,
    64, 79, 83, 106, 214–16, 222, 229,
    231, 242, 243
supplemental material (of pilgrim-
    age), 186
supplies. See provisions.
Synod of Whitby, 136

Taizé, 24, 58, 82, 197, 245
Temple, temples, 73, 100–101, 104,
    105, 139
tension, tensional theology, 4, 5, 36,
    37, 51, 70, 75, 78–79, 80, 92, 93,
    94, 112, 147, 202, 205, 233, 228,
    229, 234, 235, tension of the
    particular and the universal, 3,
    8, 65, 67, 80, 140, 144, 217, 288,
    234, 240
theodicy, 235
third-eye of a pilgrim, 181
time set aside, pilgrimage as, 6, 7, 33,
    44, 48, 83, 103, 132, 135, 136–37,
    208, 241
topophilia, 148
tour, tourism, tourist, 45–46, 57, 62,
    185

transcendence, the transcendent, 19, 35, 66, 71–73, 75, 77, 78, 79, 112, 115, 118, 124, 172, 185, 230, 234

Ulysses' ship, 65
utopias, 148

Via Francigena, 84, 240
virtues of pilgrimage, 5, 41, 82, 87, 88, 92, 121, 129, 134, 194, 197, 202, 203, 212, 216, 217, 220, 228, 239, 243

voices of others, 9, 23, 26, 27–30, 102, 107, 179, 180, 194, 205, 209, 218, 230, 235, 240
vulnerability, the vulnerable, 23, 33, 45, 88, 97, 102, 104, 105, 193, 195, 203, 209, 213–14, 215, 218, 223, 237
The Way of a Pilgrim, 192–93, 231

Wesley, John, 9, 62
World Council of Churches, 23, 45, 159, 211

Author Index

Adichie, Chimamanda Ngozi, 120
Andrić, Ivo, 44–45
Aquinas, Thomas, 72, 112
Aristotle, 69
Athanasius, 163
Augustine, 53, 72, 129

Bailey, Kenneth, 72
Benedict XVI, Pope, 80
Berry, Wendell, 138
Brueggemann, Walter, 139, 140, 158,
    197, 235
Buber, Martin, 55, 124–25
Bunyan, John, 93, 115, 157

Caird, George, 72
Campbell, Joseph, 72, 112, 117, 122,
    152, 162, 175, 177, 182, 188
Campo, Juan Eduardo, 34–35, 37, 38
Carretto, Carlo, 180
Coehlo, Paolo, 85
Coleridge, Samuel Taylor, 217
Covey, Stephen, 53–54, 184
Crossan, John Dominic, 73

Day, Dorothy, 211
Dostoevsky, 116
Durkheim, Émile, 48, 139, 230

Eade, John, 35, 37, 38–39, 56, 230
Eliade, Mircea, 48, 139, 143

Foster, Charles, 43, 77, 104, 143, 145,
    158, 185, 205, 235

Granberg-Michaelson, Wesley, 116,
    157, 195

Hastings, Ross, 52
Heschel, Abraham, 132, 135
Heuertz, Phileena, 116, 122, 152, 158,
    168, 236
Hjalmarson, Leonard, 37, 46, 77, 146,
    147, 152, 185, 230, 235
Hughes, Gerard W., 25, 68, 151

Ignatius of Loyola, 209
Inge, John, 8, 139, 140–41, 146, 221,
    230

James, William, 129
Johnson, Mark, 76
Julian of Norwich, 78

King, Martin Luther, Jr., 159, 211

Lakoff, George, 76
Least Heat-Moon, William, 85, 171,
    185, 207
Lewis, C. S., 77

Margry, Peter Jan, 11, 35
Maslow, Abraham, 85, 118, 152, 230
McFague, Sallie, 72–76, 80
Merton, Thomas, 171
Morinis, Alan, 36

Niebuhr, Richard R., 30, 45, 46, 113,
    147
Nouwen, Henri, 182–83

Otto, Rudolf, 48

de Paul, Vincent, 152
Paulinus of Nola, 67
Peace Pilgrim, 211

Reader, Ian, 11, 36, 37

Sallnow, Michael, 35, 37, 38–39, 56,
    230
Shakespeare, 19, 46, 70
Sheldrake, Philip, 3, 10, 147, 230, 231
Smith, Jonathan Z., 139, 143
Solnit, Rebecca, 215
Soskice, Janet, 69–70

Stephenson, Barry, 35, 37, 40, 192

Teresa of Avila, 123, 151
Tuan, Yi-Fu, 140, 148, 175
Turner, Victor or Edith, 35–39, 44, 46,
    54–56, 175–77, 230, 232
Twain, Mark, 197

van Gennep, Arnold, 54–55, 175–76,
    177
Vogler, Christopher, 162, 177–78

Williamson, Marianne, 88
Wittgenstein, Ludwig, 40

Scripture Index

Scriptural references in the text are not always cited.

GENESIS

12:1	33, 96, 100
12:6–7	98
15:13	96
17:8	96
18	212
21:23	96
22:2	100
23	33
23:4	96
28:10–22	98
32:22–32	139
47:9	91

EXODUS

2:1–10	9
3	99
6:4	91
12:1–28	102
12:35–36	9
23:14–17	99
34:18–23	99

DEUTERONOMY

16:3, 6	102
6:16–17	99, 100

JOSHUA

4:19–22	98

RUTH

1:16	97

2 CHRONICLES

3:1	100

JOB

7:6	245

PSALMS

23	107
23:3–4	102
24:3	101
25:4	101
26:3	102
32:7	108
37:23, 2	102
56:13	102
84	101
84:5	91
102:11	245
119:54	91
120–34	101

ISAIAH

1:18	169
2:4	124
11:6	124

ISAIAH (continued)

30:29	91
40:3	91
55:8–9	71
65:25	124

EZEKIEL

5:5	101
38:12	101

HOSEA

2:19	123

JOEL

3:10	124

AMOS

8:14	91

MICAH

4:3	124
6:8	102

MATTHEW

1:1–17	97
7:13	94, 107
8:19–22	106
9:14–15	106
9:15	123
10:1, 7–8	107
10:9–10	106
13:24–42	123
16:15	111
18:12–14	68
18:20	113
25:40	113

MARK

2:18–20	106
2:19	193

LUKE

2:21–38	104
2:41–51	105
2:41–49	100, 139
4:16–19	213
5:33–35	106
5:44	120
6:31	213
9:58–62	106
10:25–37	119
15:3–7	68
17:21	94, 107, 218
24	238

JOHN

2:13–25	105
3:1–21	105
5:1–18	105
7–10	105
8:12	107
10:2–4	107
10:9	107
10:22–39	105
14:6	107
17:1–19	82, 94, 218
17:14–15	107
17:20–26	123

ACTS

7:6	96, 107
8:27	91
24:11	91

ROMANS

5:12–21	94
8:38–39	246
12:4–5	123

1 CORINTHIANS

2:16	93
9:24	92
12:12–31	123
12:12–27	53
15:21–29	94

2 CORINTHIANS

5:17	160
11:2	123

GALATIANS

5:22–23	88, 93

EPHESIANS

2	107
2:12	68

PHILIPPIANS

2:5–7	93
3:14	92

COLOSSIANS

3:12	88, 93

1 THESSALONIANS

5:16	193

1 TIMOTHY

6:11	88, 93

2 TIMOTHY

3:5	243
4:7	92

HEBREWS

11:1	78
11:8–19	33
11:8–9	97
11:13–19	107
11:13	94, 218
12:1	92, 118
13:2	212
13:8	65

1 PETER

2:11	94, 218
2:21	93, 213

REVELATION

5	124
7:9	124
21–22	124
21:2	94, 218
21:4	124
21:10	94, 218

CPSIA information can be obtained
at www.ICGtesting.com
Printed in the USA
JSHW021655110822
29137JS00001B/32